Cosmos and Character in
Paradise Lost

Cosmos and Character in *Paradise Lost*

Malabika Sarkar

First published in 2012 by
PALGRAVE MACMILLAN®
in the United States—a division of St. Martin's Press LLC,
175 Fifth Avenue, New York, NY 10010.

Where this book is distributed in the UK, Europe and the rest of the world,
this is by Palgrave Macmillan, a division of Macmillan Publishers Limited,
registered in England, company number 785998, of Houndmills,
Basingstoke, Hampshire RG21 6XS.

Palgrave Macmillan is the global academic imprint of the above companies
and has companies and representatives throughout the world.

Palgrave® and Macmillan® are registered trademarks in the United States,
the United Kingdom, Europe and other countries.

ISBN: 978–1–137–00699–8

Library of Congress Cataloging-in-Publication Data

Sarkar, Malabika, 1948–
    Cosmos and character in Paradise Lost / Malabika Sarkar.
        p. cm.
    ISBN 978–1–137–00699–8 (alk. paper)
        1. Milton, John, 1608–1674. Paradise lost. I. Title.

PR3562.S313 2012
821.4—dc23   2011050313

A catalogue record of the book is available from the British Library.

Design by Newgen Imaging Systems (P) Ltd., Chennai, India.

First edition: June 2012

10 9 8 7 6 5 4 3 2 1

Printed in the United States of America.

For Sudipto

CONTENTS

ACKNOWLEDGMENTS

Grateful thanks are due to many whose encouragement and support have made it possible for me to write this book. I wish to express my gratitude to Alastair Fowler, with whom I had a brief exchange of letters on Milton's astronomy, for his generous reference to me in the preface to his second edition of *Paradise Lost*, which I found immensely encouraging. I am particularly grateful to Gordon Campbell for his friendship and support, to David Hawkes for help at a crucial juncture, to Christopher Ricks and Mary Ann Radzinowicz who were my supervisors when I was a young student, and to fellow Miltonists at the International Milton Symposiums at Vancouver, Bangor, York, and London for their lively interactions. I am particularly grateful to Nicholas Roe for his advice and encouragement.

Most of the research for this book was done at the Cambridge University Library. I wish to express my gratitude to the staff of the Library, in particular those in the Rare Books Room where I have spent many happy hours. On my visits to Cambridge while working on this book I have received immense support from Clare Hall as visiting fellow and later as life member. To many distinguished academics from various fields I have met over the years during my frequent visits to Cambridge University I am deeply grateful for providing an atmosphere of emotional security and intellectual sustenance.

I would like to thank my former colleagues and students at Jadavpur University and the lively group at the Centre for Studies in Romantic Literature (CSRL) for their warmth and constant encouragement.

An earlier version of chapter six was published as an essay in *Milton and the Ends of Time*, edited by Juliet Cummins (first published 2003, first paperback edition 2010) and published by Cambridge University Press, and is reprinted by permission of the publishers. Part of chapter five appeared in *Milton Quarterly* vol. 18, no. 5, March 1984, and is reprinted by permission of the editor.

I thank Brigitte Shull, commissioning editor of Palgrave Macmillan, for her interest in the book and Joanna Roberts and the production team for seeing the book through to press.

CHAPTER 1

Introduction

John Milton was born in 1608, eight years after Giordano Bruno had been burnt at the stake and two years before Galileo's first discoveries with the telescope were published in *Sidereus Nuncius*. John Dee, that remarkable figure of Renaissance England, died the year Milton was born, but when he was a small boy, Thomas Harriot and the Northumberland circle[1] were still conducting experiments in alchemy and magic while Harriot was also engaged in telescopic observations in England at the same time as Galileo. The year 1614, when Milton was six, was a critical one in which Isaac Casaubon's dating of the Hermetica was announced, an event described by Yates as "a watershed separating the Renaissance world from the modern world,"[2] and the controversial Rosicrucian texts first appeared. The impact of these incidents that happened during Milton's childhood continued to reverberate throughout Britain and Europe for a considerable period of time. The late 1620s, Milton's university years, witnessed growing debate about the admissibility of the new astronomy into the university curriculum. The 1630s, the period of his self-education at Horton and Hammersmith, was marked by intense speculation regarding the scientific and millennial implications of the new stars of 1572 and 1604. Interest in alchemy and magic continued. In 1631, Arthur Dee, son of John Dee, published the *Fasciculus chemicus*, one of the most important sources of the history of alchemy. Robert Fludd's posthumously published work on magic, alchemy, and the harmony of the universe, the *Mosaicall Philosophy*, appeared in 1638. This was the year in which Milton made his famous visit to Galileo. The English version of Fludd's work appeared later, in 1659, the same year that Meric Casaubon announced to the world his *exposé* of Dee, *A True and Faithful Relation of What Passed for Many Years between Dr. John Dee...and Some Spirits*. In 1652 Elias Ashmole published *Theatrum Chemicum Britannicum* to draw attention to English achievements in alchemy; and Robert Boyle's questioning of Aristotelian physics as well as Paracelsian alchemical views of matter, *The Sceptical Chymist*, appeared nearly ten years later, in 1661. The first edition of *Paradise Lost* was published in 1667, the year Newton was made a fellow of Trinity College, Cambridge. In the years that followed, Newton's remarkable achievements in science were accompanied by a sustained interest in alchemy. These landmarks in the intellectual history of the seventeenth century tell their own story about a dizzying world of excitement and controversy surrounding alchemy, magic, and the new astronomy during Milton's lifetime. The seventeenth century was marked, not by the effortless emergence of science from magic and alchemy, but by the unfolding of a far more complex drama involving both a clash of scientific and magical mentalities and a persistent interweaving and coexistence of these apparently opposite tendencies. Milton's great intellectual and imaginative achievement was to draw upon and assimilate these complex intellectual crosscurrents into *Paradise Lost*.

"Newton was not the first of the age of reason" but "the last of the age of magicians"[3]—this assessment by the distinguished Cambridge economist John Maynard Keynes points to the complex character of the century and the ways in which magic, alchemy, and the sciences were intertwined. Indeed, it was not as if there were two rival camps—men of science on the one hand and another set who dabbled in esoteric thought. Often, the same individual was deeply involved with the new science as well as alchemy and hermetic and cabbalistic magic. One might look, for instance, at the intellectual field of Milton's younger contemporary, Robert Boyle (1627–91), whose nephew was one of Milton's pupils. Now remembered as a natural philosopher, Boyle began his early career as a writer, with devotional works such as *Seraphic Love*. Michael Hunter notes that while Boyle moved toward science as late as 1649–50, he, too, like Newton, simultaneously developed a keen interest in alchemy and the Paracelsian tradition.[4] *The Sceptical Chymist*, written in the 1650s and published in 1661, questioned both the Aristotelian four-element theory as well as the Paracelsian *tria prima*, urging a more philosophical approach on the part of chemists, which might lead one to think that Boyle had a greater commitment to the new science than to alchemy. However, as Hunter demonstrates, Boyle believed in the philosopher's stone and in the possibility of transforming base metal into gold. He points out that Boyle also had faith in magic and in the existence of a spirit world. At the same time, he was at the forefront of the new science and closely associated with the Oxford group of scientists led by John Wilkins. This wide range of interests in a man generally regarded as a leading seventeenth-century scientist shows that the tradition of the "Renaissance polymath," a term William Sherman[5] applies to John Dee, survived well into the closing years of the seventeenth century.

The argument of this book relies on a recognition of the survival, indeed the vibrancy, of this tradition of an inclusive range of interests incorporating both the new science and alchemy and magic throughout the seventeenth century. Milton could draw upon, and expect contemporary readers to be familiar with, this discourse. My contention in this book is that, as an intensely dramatic poem, *Paradise Lost* engages with the construction of character in new and unusual ways, and the tools Milton uses for this are often ideas and images drawn from urgently debated fields of new astronomy, chemistry, and vitalism, as well as hermetic and cabalistic magic and alchemy. *Paradise Lost* is a dramatic epic with just two human characters—Adam and Eve. Milton peoples the void with angels, devils, and two sets of personifications, Chaos and Night, and Sin and Death. This supporting cast throws light on the human pair at the center. Our understanding of Adam and Eve becomes significantly greater once we understand the contrasts and parallels Milton sets up with the help of these characters. I argue that much that is compelling and unexpected about Milton's characters in *Paradise Lost* is conveyed through a discourse that draws upon words, images, and ideas that were generated from the vital intellectual ferment of the new science, magic, and alchemy. Understanding this context adds significantly to knowledge and understanding of Milton's achievement in *Paradise Lost*. It is essential, therefore, to map, however briefly, this intellectual domain in which alchemy, magic, and prognostications mattered as much as the exciting debates about the emerging new science.

Individual interests and points of view, such as those of Robert Boyle, serve as an invaluable key with which to access this complex and vibrant world. In an attempt to recover this context, one should also not forget the groundswell of public opinion on this range of subjects created by important publications such as encyclopedias and almanacs. John Swan's *The Speculum Mundi*[6] may be taken as an example of the kind of contribution made by encyclopedias of the time. The *Speculum Mundi* was printed in Cambridge in 1635, and then reprinted in 1643, 1665, and 1670, reaching out to a wide section of the popular reading public. While Swan enjoyed a wider readership than the learned Nathanael Carpenter, fellow of Exeter College, Oxford, author of *Geography Delineated Forth in Two*

Bookes (1625), the *Speculum Mundi*, like the astronomical section of Carpenter's *Geography*, advocated the Tychonic geoheliocentric system. Both Carpenter's textbook on the subject of geography and Swan's popular encyclopedia thus entered into the debate about the new astronomy[7] in an age when people had not yet made up their minds regarding the validity of the Aristotelio-Ptolemaic, Tychonic, or the Copernican systems. To Swan, Tycho was "Noble Tycho, the Phenix of Astronomers,"[8] and he followed Tycho in challenging the notion of solid orbs. The diagram of the universe that appeared in the *Speculum Mundi* was that of the Tychonic geoheliocentric system. As the full title of the work—*Speculum Mundi, Or, a Glasse Representing the Face of the World*—shows, Swan's range of interests was not confined to cosmology. The work is divided into nine chapters. The first two chapters dwell on the beginning and inevitable end of the world and speculate on the time of year when the world began, while the remaining seven chapters give an account of the six days of creation. Interwoven into this account of creation are a wide range of subjects—astronomy, astrology, medicine, and alchemy. Citing Moses who said that the stars were "made for signs," Swan uses this authority both to legitimize astrology and prognostications—reading of the signs or stars—and to assert further the influence of the stars on human action. As an opinion-building publication, the *Speculum Mundi* made an important contribution to the dissemination of knowledge about this exciting range of subjects.

Almanacs played a role somewhat similar to encyclopedias in creating public opinion. Bernard Capp has described the almanac as "the greatest triumph of journalism until modern times."[9] At the height of its popularity, the seventeenth-century almanac was an encyclopedic work in its own right, conveying information on astrology, astronomy, magic, medicine, alchemy, politics, and a motley collection of other subjects. Sometimes advocating belief in alchemy and magic, at other times questioning their right to exist in Christian civil society, often invoking the specter of witchcraft in such discussions, almanacs succeeded in fueling controversies that increased interest in these and allied subjects. Almanacs were immensely popular throughout the century, recording a sales figure of 400,000 copies annually in the 1660s.[10] Among the most popular almanacs of the seventeenth century were those of Thomas Bretnor (fl. 1607–18), whose almanacs appeared in 1607 and from 1609–18, Richard Allestree (*ca.* 1581–*ca.* 1643), who produced almanacs from 1617–43, and William Lilly (1602–81), who published almanacs annually from 1644. They were household names, so that allusions to them in literary works,[11] such as those of Ben Jonson, was not unusual, and, as Capp suggests,[12] with the introduction of the practice of including a portrait of the almanac maker, "the features of William Lilly, circulated annually in thousands of copies for forty years, were probably the best known of anyone in England after the king." The primary focus of almanacs was on astrology. But, additionally, the discussions included references to alchemy and magic, as well as astronomy, sometimes even the new astronomy. After all, at the basis of all prognostications made in the almanacs was the observation and interpretation of the position of stars and planets. The most remarkable document from this point of view is Thomas Digges's 1576 appendix to a new edition of his father Leonard Digges's almanac, *A Prognostication Everlasting*. In that appendix, entitled "A perfit description of the Caelestiall Orbes," supporting the Copernican theory, Digges produced his influential diagram of the infinite universe in which the concentric spheres of the Copernican system are presented with the final sphere of the fixed stars extended outward, spilling over the margins of the page. Thomas Digges, a pupil of John Dee, was one of the ablest mathematicians of his age.

While Digges's almanac promoted knowledge about the new astronomy, William Lilly's widely circulated almanacs relied on traditional pre-Copernican astronomy. Although in *Englands Propheticall Merline* (1644)[13] Lilly asks, "Was all learning buried with Aristotle, or Astrology with Ptolemy? How great is the difference between those Phisicians that follow Galen, and those that adhere to Paracelsus?" his almanacs, unlike the scientifically sophisticated appendix of Thomas Digges, relied on traditional cosmology. Indeed, many of his annual almanacs for the late 1640s, with the ambitious title *Merlini Anglici Ephemeris*, contained English versions of Ptolemy as additional material. Interest in Paracelsian medicine and alchemy was a feature of many seventeenth-century almanacs including those of Lilly. In addition, Lilly's almanacs reveal a strong belief in magic. He appears to have had considerable personal faith in magic and the Address to the Reader in *Englands Propheticall Merline* is a spirited defense of astrology and of magic as represented in the *Demonologie* of King James. There is also the extraordinary story of Lilly's attempt to find buried treasure beneath Westminster Abbey and, on being interrupted by demons who raised a fierce storm, of how he "gave Directions and Command to dismiss the Daemons."[14] The entire account portrays Lilly's construction of himself, not only as Merlin, but also as a latter-day Prospero or John Dee. Indeed, at one point, Lilly compares himself directly with John Dee. In the dedicatory letter to Master John Thompson, merchant of the City of London, that prefaces *The Starry Messenger* (1645), Lilly writes with an apology for the brevity of the work: "This little Treatise... I present unto you.... John Dee a most Learned man Dedicated his Aphorismes to Gerard Mercator a man famous, and they consisted of less than five sheets."[15] The life and work of John Lilly, almost an exact contemporary of Milton, demonstrates the continuity of belief in magic into the late seventeenth century. Of course, unlike Milton, Boyle, and Dee, Lilly was neither a university man nor distinguished for his learning. His byline for all his printed works was "John Lilly, student of Astrologie." If Lilly could not provide his readers with informed knowledge, he appealed to them instead through an enormous input of sensation and melodrama. So far removed is he from direct contact with the advancement of learning of his age that he can produce a prognostication entitled *The Starry Messenger* without any apparent consciousness of a famous publication by Galileo with the same title with which both Donne and Milton were familiar. Yet Lilly was a man of the world, his printed work full of references to the conflict between king and Parliament, and he balances himself carefully between the two sides, declaring in *Englands Propheticall Merline*:

> Betwixt his Majesty and the Parliament, I desire to carry my discourse, and in so equall a balance, as I may not offend either his Majesty, whom I do honour as my Prince; or the Parliament, under whose protection I now live, and whose just rights I am bound to maintaine by Protestation.[16]

A controversial man, with an immensely popular series of almanacs, Lilly is a fascinating example of the kind of contradictions that characterized the early modern period and the survival of magic, alchemy, and prognostications in the seventeenth century, indeed the popularity and conviction with which these were cultivated. Finally, there is another aspect of Lilly to which Ann Geneva has drawn attention, a subversive linguistic strategy that he often adopts. Analyzing the prevalence of encrypting and encoding in the seventeenth century, she notes that while the tradition goes back to hermeticism and cabalism, "astrology and encrypting seem to have developed simultaneously."[17] Lilly hazarded many political predictions through such modes of encrypting. Geneva also believes that "what riveted Lilly's readership and kept them in thrall were just those daring treasonous and chilling astrological proclamations."[18]

The careers of men as intellectually far apart as Boyle and Lilly show the extent to which interest in alchemy and magic survived into the late seventeenth century, and it would not be surprising for Milton to expect his readers to have a level of knowledge about these subjects that he could draw upon in fashioning his narrative. There can be little in common between Lilly and Milton, but Lilly's immense popularity ensured that Milton could not have been unaware of him. With Robert Boyle, there are strong connections. Boyle's sister, Katherine Jones, viscountess Ranelagh, appointed Milton tutor first to her nephew, then to her own son Richard. Sarah Hutton describes her as "the leading woman intellectual of her generation, actively involved in contemporary politics, and deeply interested in educational, ethical, religious, and scientific matters"[19]; and her home in Pall Mall became a refuge for members of her family, including Robert, and for those interested in the new science. It was probably the venue where the meetings of the so-called Invisible College took place. Directly, as well as indirectly, the careers of Boyle and Lilly support the contention that the atmosphere was right for Milton and his contemporaries to be familiar with these complex intellectual currents of the seventeenth century, the amalgamation of science with alchemy and magic.

While print culture, in the form of encyclopedias and almanacs, encouraged an integrative growth of interest in the new astronomy, alchemy, and magic, what was the status of institutional encouragement of knowledge in the field in which it might be expected, the new astronomy? The inclusion of the new astronomy into the university curriculum was considered, but ran into controversy. The two chief centers of learning, the universities of Oxford and Cambridge, the arbiters of acceptable knowledge, adopted a policy of conscious opposition to the new science. As Mark H. Curtis pointed out,

> Of the several functions which universities today perform, two perhaps can be considered their fundamental missions: first, to preserve knowledge inherited from the past, perpetuating and refining it through teaching and scholarship; and second, to add to the inherited store of knowledge and wisdom by providing facilities and leisure for research into the unknown. Of these two functions only the first was thought to be an essential one for Oxford and Cambridge in the Tudor and early Stuart periods.[20]

In 1619, six years before Milton went up to Cambridge, Sir Henry Savile founded two professorships at Oxford, one of astronomy and the other of geometry. The statutes of the Savilian professor-ship[21] stipulated that the professor of astronomy was required to teach Copernican and other modern astronomical theories as well as the traditional Almagaest. Also, he was required to use suitable instruments to "take astronomical observations" and to make archival records of his findings. In Cambridge, although teaching continued to be conservative, there was no dearth of individual interest and knowledge. Perhaps it was in the fitness of things that the first Savilian Professor of Astronomy at Oxford was a Cambridge scientist, John Bainbridge. Like Marxist theory in literature departments in the 1960s and 1970s, the new astronomy was a much debated subject at Oxbridge in the 1620s. In sharp contrast, nearly 20 years before the institution of the Savilian professorship, Gresham College in London had been actively engaged in designing lectures that incorporated the new findings in astronomy.[22] Interestingly, the statutes of Gresham College provided that lectures on astronomy and geometry should be given twice a day, once in Latin in the morning for the learned and for foreigners and once in English in the afternoon for all those who would not be able to follow the Latin lectures. Gresham College therefore played an important role in the dissemination of knowledge about the new astronomy.

While Gresham College provided an institutional forum for advanced scientific discussions, such activities were also carried out within informal groups and led, ultimately, to the formation of the Royal Society. A. R. Hall identifies at least two, a group that Boyle called the "Invisible College" in 1646, where the leading figure was Samuel Hartlib, and another that included John Wallis, the mathematician John Wilkins, Francis Glisson, Theodore Haak, and others.

> Thus, a circle close to the government included the poet Milton, Oldenburg, probably John Pell (mathematician), Lady Ranelagh (Boyle's sister). In touch with this was another group (Boyle's "Invisible College"?), which included Hartlib, Boyle, Drury, Oldenburg, Plattes, Dymock, Petty, and evidently others. Then Wallis's group at Gresham College, also deeply committed to the republican regime, was linked with the universities and the "Invisible College." Finally, the Royalists (Evelyn, Brouncker, Moray) seem to have maintained amicable relations with individuals (at least) in these groups.[23]

It is possible to suggest that Milton, through his connections with Hartlib, Boyle, Lady Ranelagh, and John Pell, would have been in touch with the activities of the "Invisible College" and other such nonformal groups. With his acknowledged interest in mathematics, Milton is likely to have taken an interest in discussions about the new science to a greater extent than one imagines.

The new astronomy established a somewhat precarious though inevitable foothold in academia with the institution of the Savilian professorship. But what was the fate of alchemy and magic? Were they confined to individual interests or did they function as discourses legitimized by organizational acceptability? These more controversial subjects found a not wholly unexpected champion in the Puritan movement. In an unpublished dissertation, P. A. Trout[24] investigated the occult milieu of Puritan England and argued that, during the years 1640–60, many Puritans, particularly those of the left-wing sects, sought to revive the occult sciences. Defining the occult milieu specifically as astrology, Behmenism and Rosicrucianism, Trout suggested that the occult sciences attracted Puritans because they provided beliefs and "myths" that validated the intense millenarianism of left-wing Puritan groups. Myths, doctrines, and prophecies of hermetic magic legitimized their expectations of a "radical" or "perfect" reformation of the world. A similar integration took place with regard to alchemy and revolutionary discourse, particularly in the work of Gerard Winstanley.[25] In an analogy drawn from alchemy to explain radical change, the spirit of God, said Winstanley, is a consuming fire that burns up all the dross in man to reveal the inner being. This divine alchemy, Winstanley believed, was the catalyst for radical social change. It is interesting to note in this context that John Webster, chaplain in the parliamentary army, proposed the introduction of hermetic and Paracelsian texts into the university curriculum. Inevitably, the proposal raised a storm of protest.

In the light of the intense contemporary debate about the admissibility of these subjects into the university curriculum, the contribution of nonformal groups and private centers in encouraging both enthusiastic research and communication of knowledge about the new astronomy, alchemy, and magic cannot be stressed enough. In the late sixteenth century, such a center had been John Dee's house in Mortlake with its famous library, which contained one of the richest collections of books and manuscripts and provided a locus for politicians, poets, and scholars. In the early seventeenth century, there was another at Sion House where Henry Percy, ninth Earl of Northumberland, the so-called wizard earl, collected around him a group of scholars including the astronomer Thomas Harriot, the mathematician Walter Warner, and the geographer Robert Hues. Associated with both the

Dee circle and the Northumberland circle was Sir Walter Raleigh. The 1640s, in fact, was a time when many such nonformal groups with interest in the emerging science and in alchemy and magic operated in London and at Oxford and Cambridge.[26] Many of them also had political connections. The mathematician John Pell, for example, a contemporary of Milton at Cambridge and a friend of Walter Warner, was highly regarded by Cromwell who appointed him his political agent in the Protestant cantons of Switzerland. Interestingly, Pell was only too conscious that the use of numbers and signs at various levels of magic, especially the use of numerical computations by occultists for the purpose of conjuring spirits, left the scientist's use of numbers and signs open to the gravest suspicions. In a letter to Sir Charles Cavendish on August 7, 1644, Pell wrote:

> In the meane time I am not a little afraid that all Mr. Warner's papers, and no small share of my labours therein, are seazed upon, and most unmathematically divided between the sequestrators and creditors, who (being not able to balance the account where there appeare so many numbers, and much troubled at the sight of so many crosses and circles in the superstitious Algebra and that blacke art of Geometry) will, no doubt, determine once in their lives to become figure-casters, and so vote them all to be thrown into the fire, if some good body doe not reprieve them for pye-bottoms, for which purposes you know analogicall numbers are incomparably apt, if they be accurately calculated.[27]

Opposition to these varied fields, in particular the new astronomy, generally took the form of extreme righteousness. It may be worth mentioning here the famous Ross-Wilkins controversy, at least for the language of Ross's rejoinder. The young scientist John Wilkins's defense of the new astronomy was countered by the schoolmaster Alexander Ross in a book, published in 1646, whose very title assumes the rhetoric of an offended scholar: *The New Planet no Planet: or, The Earth no wandring Star: Except in the wandring heads of Galileans. Here Out of the Principles of Divinity, Philosophy, Astronomy, Reason, and Sense, the Earth's immobility is asserted; the true sense of Scripture in this point, cleared; the Fathers and Philosophers vindicated; divers theological and philosophical points handled and Copernicus his Opinion, as erroneous, ridiculous, and impious, fully refuted.* Reading between the lines of this paragraph-long title one can sense the frustration and anxiety of the conservative opposition at the revolution in thinking brought about by the new astronomy.

In spite of this atmosphere of debate, uncertainty, and controversy in the seventeenth century, there was an inescapable realization that the Renaissance world had been decisively altered by the new astronomy, which revealed to man a universe of infinite possibilities and at the same time raised deeply troubling issues. The new astronomy had deconstructed the neat orderly Aristotelio-Ptolemaic universe and brought into play new structures and new perceptions. Most importantly, it brought an acceptance of fluidity and change. Advancements in physics and mathematics were fundamental to these developments. At the same time, astronomy continued to be closely allied to magic and alchemy, two subjects for which belief in the capacity for change was fundamental. The fact that there was extensive overlapping, although astronomy was a science and magic and alchemy were not, is by now well established. It is clear, for example, that often the same individual was keenly interested in more than one of these areas. Surprising as it may seem today, Tycho Brahe and Kepler also cast horoscopes. But there was another important fundamental force that drew these fields together. Astronomy, magic, and alchemy were three subjects that shared a deep involvement with strategies of empowerment. This might seem more apparent with regard to magic and alchemy than astronomy. Yet a considerable body of astronomical thought was taken up with not just the location and properties of new stars and comets, but also their effects and significance, as well as the moral implications of alternative world systems. The abiding concern with moral and philosophical issues is apparent not only in Tycho and Kepler's interpretation of the significance of the new stars,[28] but also in Kepler's curious attempt to explain the harmony of the spheres by placing the five regular solids within the interplanetary spaces.[29] Kepler employed his visual imagination and mathematical skills to establish the harmony and perfectibility of the universe without which the power of the Creator would be in doubt. Moreover, the debate about the admissibility of knowledge about the new astronomy, particularly with reference to university curriculum, was itself a questioning of power and authority, and dissemination of scientific knowledge often had to be conducted through almanacs and popular encyclopedias with their untenable academic status. In many ways, astronomy thus became a contentious field and the conservative orthodox establishment and the more enlightened spirits of the age were locked in a tussle for acceptance. In spite of its scientific basis, therefore, astronomy participated in strategies of empowerment as much as magic and alchemy. Often, the same event was analyzed or the issue debated with reference to astronomy, alchemy, and magic. The psychological space all three subjects inhabited was like a magnetic field of speculations dealing with astronomical signs and magical and alchemical processes. The question that is often asked is this: Apart from the fact that Milton had a naturally receptive mind, what external evidence is there to support the contention that he was at all interested in alchemy, magic, and the new astronomy? What would be the extent of his familiarity? What would be his sources? After all, he does not discuss these subjects at length in his letters and prose works. In this context, it seems to me to be extremely relevant to note that Harris Francis Fletcher[30] pointed out that Milton's father, the elder Alexander Gil, John Florio, and Giordano Bruno were all at Oxford at the same time. Florio and Bruno were friends and the elder Gil knew Bruno and stated in his *Sacred Philosophy* that "*Iordanus Brunus* a *Neapolitan*" had been "in my time in *Oxford*." Whether Milton's father had met Bruno is not known, but being present in the same university town during Bruno's Oxford debates, he could not have been unaffected by the controversial and charismatic Italian.[31] Fletcher suggests that the elder Milton's acquaintance with John Florio and Bruno would explain why his father urged the young Milton to learn the continental vernaculars, including Italian. It is possible to suggest that Bruno would at least have featured in the conversations of Milton's father and his schoolmaster, and is likely to have inspired interest in the young Milton in Bruno's philosophy, Copernicanism, and magic.

Then there are the factors surrounding Milton's acquaintance with certain key individuals. Three could be singled out for special mention at this point—the younger Alexander Gil, Samuel Hartlib, and Nathan Paget. The younger Gil, son of Milton's high master at St. Paul's School in London, was a controversial figure with whom Milton shared an interest in mathematics. Gil held radical political views, wrote Latin poetry, and was known for his confrontations with authority. Milton's friendship with him continued over many years. At a time when new discoveries in astronomy were constantly being examined from a millennial perspective, Gil's published work demonstrates his interest in both the new astronomy and in prognostications. It is likely that Milton found in him congenial company for sharing his own interest in the new astronomy and its implications as well as his hopes for the Puritan revolution. One does not know what other related areas of interest they shared. The somewhat cryptic Latin letter Milton wrote to Gil on December 4, 1634, is very suggestive as Milton asks Gil to meet him "among the booksellers" at St. Paul's Churchyard "to promote our business with that Doctor, this year's President of the College" and to "go to him immediately on my behalf" (CPW1, 322). It is true that Milton may have been referring to the historical and theological resources in the library of Sion College, the corporate body of ministers in London, or to Gresham College,[32] or, as Campbell and Corns[33] suggest, the library of the College of Physicians, where he would have had access to books on astronomy, optics, and mechanics among other subjects. But it seems to me entirely possible, given the interests of the two young men, that the college referred to may have been one of the earlier nonformal groups in seventeenth-century London, similar to the "Invisible College" set up later, in the 1640s, in the house of Robert Boyle's sister, Lady Ranelagh. Such loosely knit societies and organizations in seventeenth-century London brought together individuals with a shared interest in alchemy and the new astronomy, and in hermetic and cabalistic thought. Whatever the destination of Milton and Gil may have been, the impression of excitement and utmost secrecy Milton's letter conveys can only indicate a shared involvement either in radical politics or in controversial forms of knowledge, or, in fact, in both.

Samuel Hartlib and Nathan Paget were associates of a rather different kind. Lewalski believes that Milton probably became acquainted with Hartlib sometime between April and September 1643.[34] In 1644 Milton addressed to him his treatise on education. He was a man of learning and much respected by his illustrious contemporaries, although he was perpetually in financial difficulties. One of Hartlib's passions was the subject of husbandry, but his publications also included an eight-volume *Clavis Apocalyptica, or A Prophetical Key by which the great Mysteries in the Revelation of St. John and the Prophet Daniel are opened*, dated 1651, as well as chemical or alchemical treatises. Hartlib's circle of associates included Robert Boyle, Lady Ranelagh, and the members of the "Invisible College."[35] The importance of Samuel Hartlib, like Henry Oldenburg, was that he established, in the words of Michael Hunter, "an invaluable intelligence network," keeping alive communications between like-minded individuals as well as informal working groups. Hartlib's own alchemical and millenary interests are likely to have been reflected in his exchanges with Milton and there can be little doubt about Milton's knowledge of the "Invisible College." Equally important is the fact that one finds in Hartlib both an interest in occult subjects and an involvement with the emerging new science. This accounted for his association with groups such as the "Invisible College" on the one hand and Henry Oldenburg and the foundation of the Royal Society on the other. Milton probably found in Hartlib a balance between a scientific outlook and an informed and just appreciation of occult subjects that agreed very well with his own bent of mind.

Dr. Nathan Paget, physician and man of learning, was Milton's friend and a cousin of his third wife. Although Milton's acquaintance with him may have gone back a long time, he probably became Milton's physician much later. He was acquainted with Paget at least in the 1650s when he was writing *Paradise Lost*. Perhaps the single most important fact about Paget relevant to the present context is the eclectic collection of books and manuscripts in his library. Hanford described him as the "English physician book-collector" in the tradition of Sir Thomas Browne.[36] The rich holdings of this personal collection[37] included a wealth of material on alchemy, magic, and astrology. Among the books and manuscripts on alchemy and magic were nineteen of the works of Paracelsus, six attributed to Hermes Trismegistus, the Rosicrucian manifestos, two by Bruno, five by Fludd, and sixteen books and manuscripts of Jacob Boehme. There were books and manuscripts on astrology by Lilly, Gadbury, Wharton, and others as part of the collection, although there is no record of the works of Kepler, Galileo, and others relating to the new science. Paget lent manuscripts to Ashmole and Milton's nephew, Edward Phillips, who was employed as a translator and copyist for Ashmole. For Milton, Dr. Paget's library would have provided access to materials on magic, alchemy, and astrology.

At this point, it is important to define what might be meant by knowledge of the "new astronomy" among Milton and his contemporaries. This is a debated issue and one of the reasons for debate is that there is no clear consensus about the content of this knowledge. It is fair to say, though, that the common minimum base of this knowledge among nonscientific educated men and women in the seventeenth century consisted of an awareness of the different cosmological models of the time—Aristotelio-Ptolemaic, Copernican, and Tychonic—as well as questions about the relative position of the sun and the earth, the possibility of infinite space, the notion of multiple worlds, the possible movements of the earth, and, finally, speculations generated by the appearance of the new stars and comets. Galileo and his discoveries with the telescope would be known to anyone with a more-than-common interest in the subject. In other words, nonmathematical and nontechnical aspects of the new astronomy that were either controversial or had a strong visual appeal soon became part of the general range of knowledge of the average educated individual. Astronomy, one need hardly add, was not the only scientific field to break from tradition and explore new possibilities. Of the other areas of new science of the early modern period, there are two that Milton draws upon in *Paradise Lost*—vitalism and mechanics. However, it is the new astronomy that fascinates Milton most.

In a recent article, William Poole has challenged the "newer school of criticism" that believes in a "much closer engagement" with the new science on Milton's part.[38] Poole cautions us about the inadequacy of documentary evidence and about Milton's apparently only tangential interest in the mathematical and technical developments of the new science. Referring to Milton's contacts with Hartlib and others and his correspondence with Henry Oldenburg, he warns that "contact is not necessarily dialogue, nor dialogue consent." While the caveat is well taken, it needs to be said that the proof of Milton's interest in the new astronomy is to be found in his poetry, in the way in which controversial issues such as infinite space, the plurality of worlds, the movement of the earth, and the implications of the new stars are integrated into *Paradise Lost*. In defining Milton's attitude to the new science, Poole detects an implied distinction between pre- and postlapsarian scientific activity in the Promethean reverberations of Adam ad Eve's gardening tools having been made "guiltless of fire" (*PL*, 9.392). "Consequently, a critical strategy that uses the *prelapsarian* books of *Paradise Lost* as evidence for a *progressive* scientific world-view, as if the Fall had never taken place, is merely the converse of expecting cooked meat in Paradise." To argue for the presence of knowledge of the new astronomy in the prelapsarian books of *Paradise Lost*, however, is not to read the fallen world into Paradise. The integration of concepts of the new astronomy functions in more complex ways in directing political implications and defining character that will be examined in the chapters that follow. The skill with which this is done shows Milton's alertness to the finer points of cosmological distinction between pre- and postlapsarian worlds. Finally, about that crucial meeting with Galileo, Poole writes: "Milton's supposed meeting with Galileo fails to mention, say, dynamics or optics because, as his polemic context dictates, Milton is concerned not with natural philosophy *per se* but with a particular natural philosopher as victim of the state—here a Catholic state." This view that Milton's interest in Galileo was a matter of the meeting of two radical minds is one that has been made earlier. Among others, Donald Friedman noted "the poet's consciousness of the profoundly spiritual resonances of the mind of the revolutionary, empiric, heretic"[39] and Julia M. Walker suggested that "for John Milton, Galileo was a martyr to the cause of intellectual freedom...Milton conferred upon the Tuscan artist a secular, a poetic, an artistic canonization."[40] This assessment of Milton's attitude to Galileo is just, but does not in any way undermine Milton's informed interest in the new astronomy. It is Galileo the oppressed intellectual that Milton sought to meet, but the "victim of the state" was also the person who fired his imagination about sunspots, the surface of the moon, and the possibilities of infinite space.

It has often been suggested that while Milton was familiar with the new astronomy, magic, and alchemy, his poetry avoids such contentious fields by sustaining an orthodox Christian worldview. This is indeed a strange fate for one of the most radical English writers of all time. The pioneering advocate of freedom of speech and of reasoned divorce, the fearless upholder of revolutionary ideals, apparently either lacked the courage to incorporate his knowledge of magic, alchemy, and the new astronomy into his poetical works or failed to assess the significance of these subjects in the intellectual history of the seventeenth century. This is a view of Milton that would not only do him injustice but would also divert attention from one of the most vibrant aspects of his poetry. Perhaps the true picture can emerge once the readers' own inhibitions and presuppositions are set aside and the sophistication and mastery of Milton's handling of these subjects are recognized. In an age in which alchemy and magic were taken up as subjects of serious study by men of science such as Boyle and Newton, and the importance of the new science was recognized in almanacs and popular encyclopedias such as those of Digges and Swan, new science, alchemy, and magic could be integrated into Milton's epic to create a fabric of contextual expectations.

Milton scholarship has long acknowledged the presence of the new astronomy in *Paradise Lost*, though consistently with many reservations.[41] With a primary focus on heliocentricity, Lawrence Babb's analysis of the astronomy of *Paradise Lost* is based on the belief that "Milton was born in a period of intense excitement among astronomical theorists."[42] He dwells briefly on Copernicus, Tycho, Kepler, Galileo, Gilbert, and the Ross-Wilkins controversy, with passing references to Bruno and Campanella. Harinder Singh Marjara's more recent book *Contemplation of Created Things: Science in Paradise Lost*[43] is an exhaustive scholarly work that supersedes the earlier work of A. H. Gilbert, Grant McColley, Marjorie Nicolson, Kester Svendsen, and Lawrence Babb. However, its intention is that of "placing Milton in the mainstream of seventeenth century scientific thought and method" and does not seek to interrogate the strategic ways in which the new astronomy is interwoven into the text. Angelica Duran's *The Age of Milton and the Scientific Revolution*[44] looks more closely at the dramatic texture of *Paradise Lost*, with regard to the interface between the new science and poetry, and examines the roles of Uriel, Gabriel, Raphael and Michael as teachers. The centrality of Milton's angels is further explored by Joad Raymond, who argues that *"Paradise Lost* is a poem about angels,"[45] and points out the significant connections between angelic vision and optics.

The presence of alchemy and magic in Milton's poetry has been largely ignored and sometimes categorically dismissed. Mary Ann Radzinowicz, for example, believes "Milton did not understand poetry as magical and was profoundly skeptical of magic; he used the word *incantation* in a generally hostile tone and the word *oracle* often in a hostile context."[46] Without going into the question of Milton's poetics at this point, it should be clarified that magic, for Milton, was not a matter of classical rituals involving oracles and incantations, but more a reforming movement consistent with the belief in the promised millennium. This explains Milton's own observations,[47] such as his comment in *De Docta Christiana* that "all study of the heavenly bodies, however, is not unlawful or unprofitable; as appears from the journey of the wise men, and still more from the star itself, divinely appointed to announce the birth of Christ, Matt. Ii. 1,2." Of significance, too, is his reference to John Dee in a passage in his *Life of Peter Ramus* as one of the "learned" Englishmen with whom Ramus came into contact. Frances Yates[48] had long ago pointed out that the occult philosophy of the Renaissance is relevant to a study of Milton, and Christopher Hill recognized "Hermeticist and alchemical writers culminating in Robert Fludd"[49] as important sources for many of Milton's ideas, although he suggested that Milton condemns magic and alchemy at critical points in the narrative of *Paradise Lost*. More recently, Michael Lieb has examined the links between cabalism and Milton's poetry.[50] Lyndy Abrahams's meticulous study of the alchemical context of the poetry of Milton's contemporary Andrew Marvell suggests that a similar exploration of Milton's poetry should be undertaken.[51] One scholarly work that needs to be acknowledged in particular for its contribution to our understanding of astronomy, magic, and alchemy in Milton is Alastair Fowler's edition of *Paradise Lost*.[52] In its combination of scholarship and insight, this edition significantly enhances our appreciation of Milton's integration of these areas of knowledge into *Paradise Lost*.

In an incisive study of the period titled *The Matter of Revolution*, John Rogers has examined the connection between Paracelsian vitalism and revolution in the seventeenth century and its relevance to *Paradise Lost*.[53] Rogers relates philosophical vitalism to Milton's depiction of creation from chaos in *Paradise Lost*. He suggests that "the constant pressure chaos is imagined to apply on creation" in the epic signals that "the Vitalist Moment at mid-century was never to be recovered." The "ebullient intellectual ferment" of the mid-century, he believes, was at once political and scientific and Rogers draws attention to the important factor of "the cultural intersections" between the English and the Scientific Revolutions in the seventeenth century. However, it is possible to go beyond an assessment of "cultural intersections" when one takes a close look at Milton's poetry, specially with regard to *Paradise Lost, Paradise Regained*, and *Samson Agonistes*, the poems written from the "experience of defeat," to borrow a term from Christopher Hill.[54] There is an enormous amount of emotional investment in these last poems so that they are not only expressions of a prevailing interconnectedness but also modes of deliberate negotiation.

Milton's epic was written from a position of defeat, but also from a prophetic conviction of ultimate triumph. The inspiration for this belief did not come only from the traditional prophets praised in the invocations in *Paradise Lost*. Perhaps more important as catalyst for the creative process are the disenfranchised figures that haunted the imagination of radical intellectuals in the seventeenth century. Giordano Bruno, the "excommunicated defrocked monk from the Dominican monastery in Nola was burned alive at the stake in Rome"[55] in 1600 for refusing to recant his philosophic principles, which included hermetic and cabalist beliefs, and his scientific convictions, including his acceptance of the Copernican hypothesis. In 1638, as Milton tells us in the *Areopagetica*,[56] he visited Galileo in Florence—"there it was that I found and visited the famous Galileo grown old, a prisoner to the Inquisition, for thinking in Astronomy otherwise than the Franciscan and Dominican licensers thought." For Milton in defeat, blind, for a time under sentence of death, these persecuted but enlightened intellectuals must have seemed to be the prophets of the new age. Milton's poetry appropriates the strength of this new enlightenment—the belief in fluidity, change, and reform intrinsic to alchemy, magic, and the new astronomy. These subjects provided him with a vibrant intellectual resource that Milton utilizes for shaping strategies for construction of character as well as for defining his own epic aspirations.

CHAPTER 2

Invocations: Milton as Moses

The invocations in *Paradise Lost* are, for Milton, the play within the play. As a significant unit, they direct attention to important aspects of the main narrative. The unique status of the invocations as at once fictional and real, dramatic as well as autobiographical, enables Milton to use this device as a means of engaging with fundamental debates raised within the epic narrative. One of the issues constantly debated and questioned in *Paradise Lost* is that of authority and empowerment. The story of the fall of man and the fall of the angels is embedded with notions of empowerment that surface through the words and actions of Satan, the angels, and Adam and Eve. Satan's open defiance of God and his claim to be uncreated are overt declarations of protest, but there are a number of other subtler ways through which his positioning for authority is often conducted. Among other characters, Milton's good angels—Raphael, Uriel, and Gabriel—have their own agenda of extending the limits of authority entrusted to them by God. Within the new cosmos they are prepared to assume positions of intellectual dominance, which might raise uneasy questions about divine control. Adam and Eve, being human, are much less adventurous than the angels, but are equally liable to challenge stereotypes. As a result, the general direction this narrative takes is toward a radical repositioning of traditional notions of authority. The means of communicating these subtle negotiations for power are often fashioned out of a selective incorporation of new science, magic, and alchemy, and sometimes through a questioning of fundamental issues relating to the same fields. While magic and alchemy could be used as resources for individual empowerment, and this was also true of the new astronomy to a surprising extent, the suggestion of a different order of power—a more leveling, radical erosion of authority—could be achieved through vitalism and other forms of early modern science. The persistent interweaving of these exciting areas of early modern thought into the unfolding of the epic narrative can be understood more clearly through the parallel strategies Milton adopts in the shorter—but infinitely significant—narrative of the epic invocations.

Positioning *Paradise Lost* as an epic of significant distinction is one of the vital objectives of the invocations. Milton scholarship has regarded the four strategically placed invocations in *Paradise Lost* as the means through which the poet identifies his Muse and, in the process, distinguishes his epic from that of Spenser and from classical epic. It is possible to suggest that there is, in fact, a further dimension that needs to be explored. In the process of defining the status of this epic, the invocations, from the beginning, identify Moses as the prophet whom Milton, as poet, seeks to emulate. This is the key to a vital strategic component of the invocations. The reference to Moses in the opening lines of the first invocation is not an isolated instance. An analysis of the invocations in Books 1, 3, and 7 reveals the presence of repeated references to the Mosaic tradition. This chain of Mosaic allusions needs to be understood in the light of the prominence given to Moses in much of seventeenth-century thought. There were two converging strands in the configuring of Moses in the early modern period—the cabalistic interpretation of Moses as prophet in Bruno's philosophy and a chemical philosophy, also fundamentally cabalistic, including the controversial Rosicrucian doctrines championed by Robert Fludd. The main arguments of Fludd's philosophy are incorporated in his late work, the *Mosaicall Philosophy*. The chemical philosophy of the seventeenth century, including that of Fludd, argued for a return to the true knowledge of Moses and brought together the creation narrative of Genesis and the Cabala, the secret art thought to have been taught by God to Moses, as two divinely communicated sources of knowledge.[1] While the Rosicrucian doctrines and Fludd's Mosaic philosophy, with their chemical bias, emphasized the central importance of creation narratives in the revelation of true knowledge, Bruno's cabalistic philosophy foregrounded empowerment and invested Moses with extraordinary powers. Both these strands of Mosaic philosophy were debated and discussed during Milton's lifetime. Indeed, the entire seventeenth century might be said to be a period when the Mosaic tradition predominated and even Newton, in the *Principia*, upheld Mosaic atomism as the ultimate *prisca sapientia* on which, he claimed, his own work was based.[2] Milton's identification of Moses as the prophet whom, as epic poet, he wishes to follow, needs to be understood in this seventeenth-century context.

In the invocations, Milton sets up two benchmarks of excellence, one of which is clearly spelled out. Any discussion about the invocations always takes note of Milton's positioning of classical and Spenserian epic as a level of achievement that he intends to surpass. The other benchmark, more intricately woven into the texture of the invocations, has not been commented upon because the contextual data have been forgotten or ignored. This is the framework of empowerment constructed through the series of cabalistic references to Moses and constitutes a much more potent point of reference for the seventeenth century than the classical or Spenserian epic model. This is not to suggest that Milton, very much an early modern in his thinking, sees himself as a Renaissance magus. What the cabalistic framework does is to create a second benchmark, which he wishes to surpass just as he wishes to rise above the Aonian mount. While he identifies the formal excellence of classical and Spenserian models as a mark of achievement that he must improve upon, he also recognizes the model of inspiration and empowerment in the cabalistic narrative of Mosaic prophecy as another benchmark to be surmounted to establish his own more exalted Mosaic aspirations. The framework of the invocations establishes these two benchmarks, one formal and generic, the other relating to the prophetic mode. As Milton eventually distinguishes his own Mosaic aspirations from the cabalistic magical field, he sets a standard for individual empowerment as epic poet that is defined through the surmounting of these two benchmarks. However, in the end, in a characteristic mode of questioning and dismantling, the epic's final invocation challenges the need for empowerment and points instead to a vitalist possibility of self-generative creativity. This suggestive questioning of authority in the final invocation reflects one of the key issues of the epic narrative.

While the invocations end by examining the contested polarities of divine inspiration and vitalist self-generation, they begin by focusing attention on Mosaic empowerment and a cabalistic interpretation of cosmic origins accepted by the chemical philosophers. This strand of chemical philosophy was itself a contested site and historians of science[3] have pointed out how Fludd and the Rosicrucians had to contend with Kepler on the one hand and with Andreas Libavius, Marin Mersenne, and Pierre Gassendi on the other. In understanding this debate, it is also worth remembering that Gassendi had rejected Harvey's views on the circulation of blood, that Fludd had written a reply in defense of his friend Harvey, and that this had led to an attack on Fludd by Gassendi's friend Mersenne. While Fludd's own philosophy relied on a belief in creation through divine agency, his friends and associates urged a vitalist theory of self-generative creativity. It can be argued that Milton engages with these complex strands of seventeenth-century debate and discussion in the invocations, formulating his own individual understanding of the Mosaic tradition, incorporating also references to cabalistic representations of Moses as a powerful point of reference. And if the final invocation of *Paradise Lost* does indeed convey a vitalist account of possible self-generative poetic achievement, such an account could be said to reflect Harvey's later theory of vitalist self-creation.

One other point needs to be made here. Milton's clearly stated desire, in the invocations, to be inspired like Moses should be read in the light of the epic poet's anxiety of self-representation.[4] Crucial to the invocations is the identification of his Muse as well as the construction of authorial identity. The subject matter of the epic is cosmic history, the early phases of human history, and a prophetic vision of the future. The weight and complexity of this subject matter had to contend with the critical historical phase in which *Paradise Lost* was written. The mid-seventeenth century was a time when the radical experiments of the English Revolution had failed and the Restoration was at hand. It was also a time when the scientific revolution was ushering in sweeping changes while currents of hermetic, cabalistic, and alchemical thought persisted. Given the nature of the subject matter and the volatile contemporary situation, a unique and powerful voice was needed to command attention. A prayer for inspiration is an integral part of invocations in an epic poem, but in *Paradise Lost* this is less conventional and more personal. Milton utilizes the formal conventions afforded by the epic invocation to incorporate an eloquent plea for empowerment within a Mosaic framework. Not content with a "middle flight," he positions himself as a supplicant seeking prophetic authority of the highest level for which again the natural analogy is Moses who had communicated directly with God. Conscious of the Mosaic tradition that extends from Bruno to Fludd, Milton sets up a Mosaic framework incorporating some of the resources of cabalism, creating a benchmark of empowerment, only to circumvent it eventually and to identify the status of his own aspiration as belonging to the highest degree, higher than classical and higher than Renaissance magical.

Time and again—as in *Lycidas* and *Comus*—Milton has demonstrated his remarkable ability to reinvent the forms and conventions he uses. This is also true of the invocations. The invocations are unique in that they not only define the special qualities of his epic, but also provide the space within which the poet's own identity is constructed. In *Paradise Lost*, there is a significant degree of self-consciousness with which Milton examines his own role as epic poet. After all, in the poem, he is dealing with a subject of enormous significance, one that had been "unattempted yet in prose or rhyme" (1.16). Milton sees himself as the privileged narrator of human history and cosmic history as well as the interpreter and prophet who can extend his understanding of that history to the contemporary world. The basic narrative components of his epic are deceit, betrayal, and "foul revolt" in the story of the fall of the angels and of man. Examining the moral, ideological, and social fabric of the seventeenth century, he is in a position to see parallels between the epic narrative and the contemporary situation. The political commitment of *Paradise Lost* is very strong and Milton sees his own role in the epic as that of narrator of the most critical phase of human history, the creation of the world and the Fall of man, as well as an interpreter engaged in the diagnosis and discovery of an infinite variety of motivations. This awareness explains the tentative, and at the same time ambitious, stance that Milton adopts through the series of invocations in *Paradise Lost*. In the opening lines of *Paradise Lost*, J. Martin Evans feels, "the self-confident epic narrator who expelled the swain in the final ottava rima of *Lycidas* has disappeared."[5] Instead, he suggests, "The authorial persona (is)...continually vacillating between self-erasure and self-assertion as he struggles to find a place for himself in his own text. But as *Paradise Lost* continues, the speaker gradually begins to assume a rather more stable poetic identity."[6] Without entering into a Foucauldian debate[7] about Milton's "author function," it is possible to suggest that the procedure is not one of self-erasure and self-assertion but rather one of self-construction, generated, for Milton, by a need to explain his own complex role in the unfolding of the epic narrative.

Seeking empowerment in the first three invocations of the epic, Milton turns to Moses and builds up an allusive framework through references to the special powers associated with the Cabala. Cabala, the system of Jewish mysticism and hermeneutics that developed in the Middle Ages,[8] gained prominence in Renaissance Italy with Pico's studies in the Cabala and his efforts to build a syncretic philosophy that included cabalism. With a strong belief in the Christian Cabala, Pico distinguished between "practical" Cabala, the technique of combining divine names and numbers, and "speculative" Cabala, contemplation on the Sephiroth, the divine names of God, which led to metaphysical and theological insights. As cabalism developed through Agrippa, Bruno, and Fludd, certain trends emerged from the complex network of ideas. One was the focus on Moses and the prophetic tradition, in particular the communication that Moses received from God, which was thought to hold the key to the notion of power implied in the Cabala. Another was the fact that cabalism was associated more and more with theories of creation, the history of cosmic creation, and, more importantly, the mystery of the creative process. It is true that in sixteenth- and seventeenth-century England it is difficult sometimes to isolate cabalism. As Marjorie H. Nicolson explained, although cabalism "permeates much seventeenth century literature, it is as impossible to separate it sharply from other ideas of a particular author as it is to define exactly the particular brand of Platonism he held."[9] In fact, speculations on the mystery of creation occupied a common ground between alchemy, chemical philosophy, and cabalistic magic. But the presence of Moses as a figure of empowerment within references to the mystery of creation is unmistakably cabalistic.

Cabalism had been syncretized with hermeticism by Pico, and later by Giordano Bruno. Both Pico and Bruno were Christian Cabalists. The seventh and fourteenth of Pico's Cabalist Conclusions uncompromisingly asserted the truth of Christianity, reading the name of Jesus, Milton's "one greater man," into the Tetragrammaton.[10] Karen Silvia de Leon-Jones, in her study of Bruno and the Cabala,[11] has examined the complexities of the multiple strands of the Cabala and the interplay of cabalism, cosmology, science, and mysticism in Bruno's thought. For Bruno, cabalist meditation led to prophecy and prophecy was "not only a means of establishing a direct mystical relationship with God, but also a means of empowering the mystic, who is transformed by the prophetic experience and acquires God-like qualities."[12] Moses occupies an important position in Bruno's cabalist writings. He is one of the prominent examples of the prophet magus Bruno discusses. The direct link that existed between Moses and the Cabala was based upon a number of assumptions. According to one view, when God gave Moses the Law, He also gave him a code to decipher the secret meaning concealed in the Law. According to another, Moses is said to have brought the secrets of the Egyptian mysteries to the Jews and these are again encoded within Hebrew alphabets, names, and numbers. Manipulation of the Hebrew alphabet and numbers, the study of the secret names of God, and meditation on the Sephiroth were some of the procedures undertaken by cabalists. As Leon-Jones argues,

> The Renaissance magi considered Moses one of their own: he was not only a sage versed in the sciences and secrets of nature, but also one

who had direct contact with God. For these Renaissance magi, Moses
was the bridge between Hermeticism and the Kabbalah. For Bruno,
the figure of Moses represents this syncretic link between the two
traditions.[13]

As she points out, Bruno often calls Moses "il Revelatore," the one
who revealed the divine secrets of the Cabala to his people. In the *De
Magia* Bruno identifies one section of his ninth variety of magic as
prophecy, defining it in cabalistic terms: "Still others make predictions
by using divine things, like sacred names, coincidental locations, brief
calculations and persevering circumstances. In our day, these latter
people are not called magicians, since, for us, the word 'magic' sounds
bad and has an unworthy connotation. So this is not called magic
but 'prophecy.'"[14] Giordano Bruno spent the years between 1583 and
1585 in England, lecturing at Oxford and London and coming into
close contact with Fulke Greville, Philip Sidney, and the entire Sidney
circle. Frances Yates has given a full account of his influence on the
thought and literature of Renaissance England and her work has been
supplemented by that of others.[15] The controversial nature of Bruno's
impact on people belonging to the academic and literary circles ensured
the survival of interest in Bruno's thought well into the seventeenth
century. Milton's father, John Milton senior, and his headmaster at
St. Paul's, the elder Alexander Gil, were at Oxford at the time when
Bruno gave his lectures on heliocentricity, which were received with
both great interest and hostility. Their acquaintance with Bruno may
have inspired Milton's early interest in the Italian scientist and philos-
opher. Such interest would imply an acquaintance with the different
strands of Bruno's philosophy—hermeticism, cabalism, and cosmol-
ogy. This connection apart, the elder Alexander Gil was familiar with
the cabala and may be the inspiration behind Milton's early interest
in cabalism. This would have been intensified in the climate of caba-
list learning at Christ's. Christ's College, Cambridge, as Christopher
Hill has pointed out,[16] was a great center of cabalist studies. Outside
his immediate academic circles, cabalist ideas were current among
Milton's radical contemporaries and Samuel Hartlib, a correspondent
of Joseph Mede, later a friend of Milton and the man to whom his
treatise *Of Education* was addressed, was an expert in the Cabala.
Additionally, Milton's Italian journey, as Christopher Hill[17] suggests,
would have encouraged greater familiarity with Bruno whom Hilary
Gatti regards as the bridge between hermeticism and cabalism.[18]
Both Yates[19] and Hill direct attention to the existence of a European
intellectual underground, extending from Bruno to the Rosicrucians,

with important English links including Robert Fludd. Although the notion of the Cabala was soon to be satirized in the Restoration, especially in comedy,[20] it was still a potent discourse in the 1640s and 1650s. Cabalism, Brunian philosophy, and the construction of Moses within it thus formed an important intellectual corpus, distinct from the chemical philosophy, sometimes channelized through subversive texts, within which Milton's shaping of his authorial identity and his references to Moses should be judged.

To suggest that Milton incorporated references to magic and cabalism in his epic poem does not imply that, in doing so, he was entering an alien world. After all, magic had always been a central component of Milton's thinking as he planned his definitive work. His original project was that of writing a major work on the Arthurian legends, which would have included the figure of Merlin. In the sixteenth and early seventeenth centuries, the fictional Merlin would have found his reflection in the contemporary world, in the life, work, and reputation of the Elizabethan magus John Dee. The charisma and power of Dee was extraordinary. Howard Dobin tells the story of Queen Elizabeth's visit to John Dee in Mortlake in March 1575.[21] She arrived with her Privy Council members and other nobility to see for herself Dee's notorious magic glass. The nature of the magic glass is still debated and this was one of many meetings between Dee and Elizabeth. This episode is immortalized in *The Faerie Queene* Book 3 where Britomart sees the image of her future husband Arthegall in "the glassie globe that Merlin made" (3.2.21). Britomart and her nurse Glauce visit Merlin. As Dobin points out, although Spenser adapted the Merlin cantos from Ariosto's *Orlando Furioso*, the device of the "glassie globe" is original to Spenser's poem and immediately reminiscent of Dee. Spenser blends history and legend, hinting at the vulnerability of an ageing queen without an heir, as he shows Merlin greatly disturbed as he looks beyond the immediate future (3.3.50). As poetry confronts politics, "the latent subversive impetus of prophecy is unleashed. Like John Dee, the textualized legendary figure of Merlin embodied a threat to the normative order as a possessor of a vaguely defined and illicit source of power."[22] Milton's original plan to write a major work on the story of King Arthur belongs to the 1630s and he was eventually to write it, not as poetry, but as *The History of Britain*, published in 1670. In the mid-seventeenth century, when *Paradise Lost* was written, Merlinic prophecy was an important part of discussions and predictions of the end of British monarchy. Thomas Heywood's *Life of Merlin* and William Lilly's prophetic anthologies were part of these discussions. With the Restoration at hand, all such predictions, including Merlinic prophecy itself, were discredited. Milton's movement away from Merlinic prophecy was only natural. Merlinic prophecy had ceased to command authority. Besides, it is possible to conjecture that Lilly's consistent representation of himself as the English Merlin in his widely circulated almanacs in the 1640s would have made Merlin an inappropriate figure for Milton's great epic. In any event, Merlinic prophecy did not have a place within the changed narrative framework and this initiated the need for an alternative. Contrary to Dobin's view,[23] the collapse of Merlinic prophecy did not mark a disjunction between politics and prophecy. Only the equations changed as Milton moved from Merlin to Moses, from an illicit source of power to an authentic voice, in the act of defining his own prophetic role in an epic poem in which political reverberations are unmistakable.

The early drafts of *Paradise Lost* as tragedy in the Trinity manuscript, written around 1640, show the appearance of Moses as one of the chief characters of the dramatic work and his subsequent replacement. First among the dramatis personae in draft i is Michael and in draft ii "Moses or Michael." In draft iii Moses, a pure and incorruptible being, speaks the prologue. In draft iv, *Adam Unparadized*, Moses is replaced by Gabriel. In *Paradise Lost*, Michael and Gabriel join the dramatis personae but Moses, who cannot have a role within the narrative structure, remains outside the direct action. However, the importance of Moses remains and he is referred to in the invocations and again in the visionary closing books of the epic. Apart from Bruno and Fludd, there were several established sources Milton could have drawn upon and several versions of Moses were available to him. The Moses tradition has been traced by Hanford and Allen to Philo and Josephus and by Rosenblatt to the patristic writers.[24] In Philo, Moses is the supreme prophet and in Josephus he is author, editor, and legislator. At all times the emphasis is on Moses's exemplary life and his role as a mediator. Milton was undoubtedly familiar with these individual traditions, which incorporated also the theme of Exodus in the Moses story, and he uses these details in the concluding books of *Paradise Lost*. Moreover, the tradition of Puritans regarding themselves as the second race of God's chosen people was a well-established one. Writing *Paradise Lost*, Milton could have relied upon this while aspiring to be in the line of Moses showing the way forward to the Promised Land. However, his intention is not one of assuming leadership but of aspiring for a much more complex role as prophet. What is relevant for the invocations is the vibrant tradition of cabalism in which Moses was a central figure. Milton acknowledges

Moses's legislative function in *Reason of Church Government* and his prophetic role generally, but the construction of Moses in the invocations repeatedly draws upon, as a point of reference and comparison, the cabalistic tradition that regarded Moses as a symbol of empowerment and placed him in the context of the mystery of creation. This enables him to define his own role as poet and prophet, while simultaneously investing his Muse with multiple accretions of meaning.

The identification of Milton's Muse in the opening invocation of *Paradise Lost* centers around the heavenly Muse's act of "inspiring" Moses, the "shepherd" who first narrated to the Israelites the story of creation out of chaos. The reference to "shepherd" here carries with it the weight of the multiple meanings of that word that emerged out of *Lycidas*. The swain in *Lycidas* is not only shepherd, priest, and prophet—the roles traditionally recognized in critical readings of the poem—but historian, too, as he traces the history of the pastoral poet's past associations with Lycidas, and provides a sociohistorical analysis of the contemporary situation. In *Paradise Lost*, therefore, Moses as shepherd is empowered to narrate past history, including the story of creation, analyze the present, and look forward to the future. These are ideally the roles Milton would wish for himself. Moses's initiation takes place on the "secret" top of Mount Horeb and Milton's carefully chosen word "secret"[25] has strong cabalistic connotations. It is worth noting also that although Sinai is mentioned as another location where Moses was granted admission to the divine presence, his role in the opening invocation of *Paradise Lost* is not the legislative one of communicating the Ten Commandments or indeed introducing any moral issue. This would have been equally appropriate in the context of "disobedience" had the focus of attention on the role of Moses been toward that of Moses as Lawgiver. Instead, he is defined by his act of interpreting to his people divine knowledge about the mystery of creation: "That shepherd, who first taught the chosen seed, / In the beginning how the heavens and earth / Rose out of chaos" (1.8–10). The mystery of creation permeates the entire invocation in Book 1, from the account of the heavenly Muse inspiring Moses to narrate the story of creation in Genesis to the reference to the Spirit who was both present at and was the prime cause of creation. At the same time, the connections between Creator-creation-creator cannot be missed—the initiation Milton seeks is that of elevation to a prophetic role, which will give him mystical insights and enable him to reveal and interpret history. The mystical nature of the experience explains the "tentative, conditional" way in which, as William B. Hunter and Stevie Davies[26] astutely noted, this invocation moves from God (Oreb and Sinai) to the Son ("or if Sion hill") to the Holy Spirit ("dovelike"). "The distinctions between the persons of the Trinity are not experienced as discrete boundaries, but as subtle transitions mysteriously integrating the perception of the Godhead, as the narrator's vision pauses on each in turn."[27] Milton is conscious of the depth and extent of the recesses of power that he is trying to access in this invocation.

Writing an epic that contains two accounts of creation—those of Uriel and Raphael—it is not surprising that Milton should turn to Moses, the narrator of the *Book of Genesis*. But *Paradise Lost* not only gives an account of creation, it also engages with creation theory, alchemy, and a chemical explanation of the cosmos. Of the many strands of the chemistry of creation explored in the seventeenth century, the invocations pay careful attention to two—the question of cosmic origins and the function of light. In the invocations in *Paradise Lost*, the replacing of darkness with light is prioritized and special attention is focused on the chemistry and functions of light. This framework of references to light incorporates materials that have recognizable cabalistic associations. Light and Moses are closely associated in Bruno who incorporates the mysticism of light into his philosophy even as he establishes the equation of prophecy with cabalistic magic. Fludd also placed great emphasis on the act of creation through the agency of divine light, identifying light with the vital spirit that impelled all life and motion and needed to be understood with regard to both macrocosm and microcosm. Also, the three Mosaic principles Fludd emphasized in *Mosaicall Philosophy* are darkness, light, and the "waters."[28] These factors suggest that as the figure of Moses evolves through the invocations in *Paradise Lost* with sustained allusions to light, it should be examined in this cabalistic context.

The plea addressed to the Holy Spirit in the opening invocation is "What in me is dark / Illumine" (1, 22–23). The prayer is repeated in the invocation to light in Book 3. In view of the fact that the series of invocations opens with Milton identifying the inspired Moses as the prophet he wishes to emulate, the connections between images of light and Moses need to be looked at. The cabalist tradition associated with Bruno invested Moses with an aura of light, sometimes represented as the horns of Moses, which was the effect of his admission to the radiant presence of God. As one who has been touched by divinity, divine light emanates from Moses leading to the images of the veiled Moses or the horned Moses, the veil being necessary to screen this light from ordinary people. Light, in this context, is a sign of empowerment. This equation of light and empowerment is also to be found in the other strand of Mosaic philosophy, the chemical philosophy of Robert Fludd. Fludd, defining the "true Mosaicall principles," in his *Mosaicall Philosophy,* identified light with plenitude calling it "the formall principle."[29] This form-giving or creative significance of light is also at the core of Fludd's earlier work, as in *Utriusque Cosmi Maioris,* where he explains the first appearance of light thus: "Moses, Plato and Hermes all agree on calling the first act of creation one of light. This light, neither uncreated or created, is the intelligence of the angels, the vivifying virtue of the heavens, the rational soul of man, and the life-force of the lower realms."[30] Light is empowerment and the essential creative principle.

In the invocations in *Paradise Lost,* the prayer for light is rightly interpreted primarily with reference to Milton's own blindness. However, it is equally important to recognize allusions to cabalistic projections of light. The invocation to light can be interpreted both as Milton's prayer for empowerment, through divine inspiration, and his desire for recognition. Light would then be both enlightenment—a reception of inspiration—and an investiture transforming the epic poet and aligning him with Moses. Not surprisingly, considering the ambitious nature of the enterprise, as he aspires to be recognized as belonging to the prophetic tradition of Moses, Milton describes his epic as an *"advent'rous* song" (1.13; italics mine). The extent of Milton's aspirations, as well as his own consciousness of the immense disparity of levels between himself and the inspired Moses, hinted at through the epithet "advent'rous," becomes clearer through the play on light and blindness. His brief prayer for light in the invocation in Book 1 is expanded in the one in Book 3, dwelling with great poignancy on his physical blindness. He laments his loss of eyesight through the analogy of the veil as obstruction—"So thick a drop serene hath quenched their orbs, / Or dim suffusion veiled" (3.25–26). This needs to be read in the context of cabalist implications and references to the veil of Moses. While Moses needs a veil to hide his radiance, the image of the veil has only negative connotations of darkness for the poet. For Milton, the "veil" is a sign of his disability, while for Moses "veil" signifies an acknowledgment of empowerment. The reference to "veil" is therefore a means of indicating the polarities of empowerment and deprivation that mark the disparity of levels. The invocation to light in Book 3 juxtaposes aspiration with reality, underlining Milton's desire to transcend his material physical limitations to reach the level of prophecy so that he "may see and tell / Of things invisible to mortal sight" (3.54–55) as Moses once did.

When one turns to Robert Fludd, a wide spectrum of meanings of light becomes apparent. While Fludd's Mosaic chemical philosophy invested light with creative potency, he also incorporated the Brunian tradition of empowerment, and the representation of light and prophecy in his illustrations and writings is particularly relevant in this context. An illustration in the second book of *Utrisque Cosmi Maioris* shows a shaft of light directed from heaven on to a kneeling figure who is being initiated into prophecy by another prophet who anoints him while the Spirit, in the form of a dove, appears within the band of light. Fludd, citing the names of prophetic figures from Hermes Trismegistus to Merlin, writes: "Examples are to be found in many biblical figures, and also in those of Antiquity...Just as the Sun shines perpetually on all men, so God incessantly offers his pearls of wisdom, and those who receive them become prophets."[31] The *Philosophia Moysaica,* published posthumously, further states

> The most secret theologians and those most expert in true Cabbala say that just as Mind has domination in the human Soul, thus does Mettatron in the celestial world, where he rules from the Sun...And to the degree to which the active intellect of the Mind is the light of the soul, even so the light of that same Mettatron or World's Soul is Sadai, and the light of the Messiah's soul is Elchai, which signifies the living God, and the light of Adonai is Ensoph, signifying the infinity of Divinity. The world's soul is therefore Mettatron, whose light is the Soul of the Messiah or of the Tetragrammaton's virtue, in which is the light of the living God, in which is the light of Ensoph, beyond which there is no progression.[32]

This passage deserves to be quoted at length because the cabalistic gradations of light it cites seem to be an appropriate gloss on the lines in *Paradise Lost* Book 3 where God explains to his Son the nature of the light He has placed within Adam. "And I will place within them as a guide / My umpire conscience, whom if they will hear, / Light after light well used they shall attain" (3. 194–96). Taken in conjunction with the placing of "umpire conscience" within man, the reference to light here is very close to the recurring metaphor of the "candle of the Lord" in the writings of the Cambridge Platonists.[33] However, "light after light" may also have precise cabalistic implications if the suggestion of gradations of light in the phrase can be understood to imply a series of steps leading to the ineffable or the infinite. This would indicate strong affiliations with the cabalistic philosophy of light leading to the Ensoph. Although outside the invocations, such allusions confirm the presence of cabalist thought in *Paradise Lost* and direct attention to allusions to the cabala and to light in the invocations.

Cosmology has always been at the heart of all forms of magic including cabalism. The cosmology of Bruno's *Cabala del cavallo pegaseo*, together with his *Eroici furori*, shows his delineation of orders of blindness transformed into orders of enlightenment in a series that is connected to cosmology. Bruno's cabalistic dialogues evolve an interlocking system of hierarchical levels involving the Sephiroth, the Muses, and the celestial spheres. These, together with the causes of blindness and the different orders of insight or enlightenment, are accompanied by different musical instruments. As Leon-Jones demonstrates through the charts she presents,[34] the eighth sphere shows the alignment of Hocma or Wisdom with the Muse Urania and the celestial sphere of the fixed stars. In Bruno's presentation, Hocma translates into Sapienza or Wisdom. Bruno may have derived his tabular form from a variety of sources including the *Zohar*, Pico, and Agrippa. With this in mind, and remembering the upsurge of interest in the cabala in the seventeenth century, it seems fair to assume that when references to Wisdom, Urania, and light appear in conjunction, there is every likelihood that what is emerging is a pattern of cabalistic thought.

When one turns, therefore, to the third invocation in *Paradise Lost*, in Book 7, the conjunction of Urania, wisdom, and the ethereal or empyreal sphere of light and air do not seem to be accidental.

> Descend from heav'n Urania, by that name
> If rightly thou art called, whose voice divine
> Following, above the Olympian hill I soar,
> Above the flight of Pegasean wing.
> The meaning, not the name I call: for thou
> Nor of the Muses nine, nor on the top
> Of old Olympus dwellst, but heav'nly born,
> Before the hills appeared, or fountain flowed,
> Thou with eternal wisdom didst converse,
> Wisdom thy sister, and with her didst play
> In presence of the almighty Father, pleased
> With thy celestial song. Up led by thee
> Into the heav'n of heav'ns I have presumed,
> An earthly guest, and drawn empyreal air,
> Thy tempering; with like safety guided down
> Return me to my native element. (7.1–16)

This invocation appears embedded with cabalistic thought. Even the qualifications "by that name / If rightly thou art called" (7. 1–2) and "The meaning, not the name I call" (7.5) point in the direction of cabalism with the emphasis on "name" and "meaning" fitting in with the concept of the Sephiroth. The "celestial song" (7.12) sung by Urania is also consistent with the musical associations of Bruno's cabalistic system. So pervasive is the presence of cabalistic references in this invocation that it can be argued that the reference to Pegasus may in fact hint at the title of Bruno's cabalist dialogue *Cabala del cavallo pegasio (Cabala of the Pegasean horse)*. Indeed, there is a strong case for arguing the validity of this allusion, which would mean that the invocations have reached a critical point where two strands of Mosaic allusions separate. The magical prophetical role of Moses that belongs to cabalism is distinguished from a purer prophetic strand of Mosaic philosophy. Milton soaring "above the flight of Pegasean wing" is not only rising above the level of classical epic as generally understood, in a conflation of "Olympian hill" and "Peagasean wing," but also rising above the level of prophecy constructed in Bruno's cabalism. Milton implores this Urania, a name that is not a simple reference to the classical Muse of Astronomy, but one with much greater accretions of meaning, and a much more sublime figure than the model of prophecy constructed by Bruno, to help him find a song for a "fit audience...though few" (7.31). In the changed context, these lines might be an ironic reference to Renaissance magic, to the exclusivity and esotericism implied by the cabala, which would fit in with the idea of a restricted audience similar to a group of initiates. His own "fit audience," Milton seems to suggest, belongs to a different order.

What conclusions, then, can be drawn from the invocations in Books 1, 3, and 7? All three invocations are a search for empowerment through enlightenment, the allusive texture deeply embedded with references to cabalism and the Mosaic tradition. If Milton takes great care to identify his "heavenly Muse" (3.19), he is equally conscious of the need to achieve an elevated status as poet to do justice to his great theme. The desire for empowerment is consistently accompanied by references to notions of creativity—the Holy Spirit impregnating the vast abyss in Book 1 and initiating creation, light as the first creation of God and itself the creative spirit in Book 3, and specifically poetic creation in Book 7. But while the invocations in Books 1 and 3 configure prophetic power through the matrix of wide-ranging Mosaic allusions that include cabalism, the invocation in Book 7 functions differently. This invocation that marks a return to earth from the unfamiliar regions of hell, chaos, and heaven also marks the point when Milton separates his configuring of Moses from areas of Renaissance magical philosophy. The distinction he is thereby able to confer on his version of the poet-prophet marks the end of a series and is a prelude to a reassessment of the entire notion of privileged poetic status in the invocation in Book 9.

Also, throughout the first three invocations, the plea for inspiration and enlightenment is represented in terms of the desire for movement. The comparatively conventional "what is low raise and support" (1.23) of the invocation in Book 1 may signify moral upliftment, a contrast with the Fall. But the journeys referred to in the invocations in Books 3 and 7 configure movement in more specifically physical terms, as cosmic voyages. Book 3 describes his flight "Through utter and through middle darkness... / Taught by the heavenly Muse to venture down / The dark descent, and up to reascend" (3.15–16, 19–20). He is referring to his imaginative journey through the realms of Chaos and Night. In the invocation in Book 7 he describes his space flight into other regions:

> Up led by thee
> Into the heaven of heavens I have presumed,
> An earthly guest, and drawn empyreal air,
> The tempering; with like safety guided down
> Return me to my native element. (7.12–16)

These are imaginative space travels plunging into the depths of chaos and hell, flying up again to cover an astonishing distance and reach heaven, returning to the safe haven of the earth. As such, they mirror the great cosmic voyages undertaken by Satan and the angels in *Paradise Lost* and incorporate, as indeed those other voyages do, the excitement and sense of exhilaration released by the discoveries of the new astronomy. Invocations deeply embedded with cabalistic allusions are simultaneously alive to the new science of the early modern period.

The invocation, if it may be so called, with which Book 9 begins, reiterates the position assumed in the opening invocation and in fact even echoes some of the earlier phrasing. The references to disobedience, the tasting of the fruit, and the loss of Eden in Book 1 are reiterated in Book 9.

> Of man's first *disobedience*, and the fruit
> Of that forbidden tree, whose *mortal taste*
> *Brought death into the world, and all our woe.* (1.1–3; italics mine)

> Disloyal on the part of man, revolt,
> And *disobedience*: on the part of heaven

Now alienated, distance and *distaste,*
Anger and just rebuke, and judgment given,
That *brought into this world a world of woe.* (9. 7–11; italics mine)

The deliberate echoes of the words and phrases of the opening invocation in the closing invocation of the epic bring about a strategic closure of the sequence of invocations. They also draw attention to a critical difference between the two. First, the nature of the Muse invoked in this final invocation of the poem appears to be different from the Muse invoked in the earlier invocations. In Book 1, Milton's invocation had been addressed to the divine presence on Horeb and Sinai and the Holy Spirit present at Creation. In Book 3, the invocation was addressed to Holy Light and in Book 7 to Urania. To all of them Milton had addressed his prayer for empowerment. The final invocation identifies the Muse as the "celestial patroness" (9.21) who inspires his "unpremeditated verse" (9.24) and dictates to him in his sleep.

If answerable style I can obtain
Of my celestial patroness, who deigns
Her nightly visitation unimplored,
And dictates to me slumbering, or inspires
Easy my unpremeditated verse. (9.20–24)

With the passage of time in the epic, Milton's Muse, earlier clothed in a blaze of glorious light in Books 1 and 3, had become a spirit of the stellar world in Book 7 and now becomes a nocturnal presence in Book 9. From Heavenly Muse to Holy Light to Urania to celestial patroness—Milton's Muse evolves through the epic invocations until, in the invocation in Book 9, she takes on a more familiar role. As Mindele Anne Treip perceptively observes in her study of the iconography of Urania and the role of Urania in *Paradise Lost,*

We may not be wrong in thinking that while "Patroness," "deigns," and "visitation" are all words implying a royal condescension, "unimplor'd" reverses perspective, transforming the commercial transactions of political patronage into the free visitations of celestial grace. The lines revive for us the ambivalent situation of the radicalized poet who in 1654 could say with perfect truth (if not without a certain bitterness) that no one had ever seen *him* soliciting advancement or, with "supplicatory" looks, lobbying at the assemblies or doors of the powerful and great.[35]

The steady erosion of power for the Muse through the evolving identities projected in the invocations can be said to synchronize with a concomitant increase in the epic poet's sense of empowerment. From the role of a supplicant in the invocations in Books 1 and 3, Milton had progressed, in the invocation in Book 7, to a position of empowerment when he could declare his intention to rise above both Mount Olympus and the flight of Pegasus. Having reached this empowered position, he then goes on to consider, in the invocation in Book 9, the possibility of writing his epic without divine intervention and assistance of any kind.

In the poem's final invocation, there is the constant tug of a vitalist inclination through "unimplored" (9, 22) and "unpremeditated" (9, 24) and the very suggestive

> Me of these
> Nor skilled nor studious, higher argument
> Remains, *sufficient of it self to raise*
> That name, unless an age too late, or cold
> Climate, or years damp my intended wing
> Depressed, and much they may, if all be mine,
> Not hers who brings it nightly to my ear. (9.41–47; italics mine)

This invocation seems to raise fundamental questions about empowerment, identity, inspiration, and the privileging of the epic voice—indeed all that the earlier invocations had sought to achieve. The vitalist thrust of this invocation needs to be read in the context of the intellectual movement that John Rogers defines as the mid-seventeenth-century "Vitalist Moment"[36] when a philosophy of monistic vitalism emerged, which sought to establish a science of self-motion and self-generation of material bodies that was then extended to the functioning of the body politic. Rogers sees vitalism as "a broadly motivated resuscitation of Paracelsian philosophy,"[37] so that, interestingly, it shares the same roots as Fludd's chemical philosophy. The difference is that vitalism is a politically charged attempt on the part of mid-seventeenth-century radical intellectuals "to distance themselves from the rhetoric of arbitrary authority at the heart of determinist discourse,"[38] while Fludd's chemical philosophy argues for a mystical distribution of power and vitality throughout the macrocosm and the microcosm. Vitalism viewed the causes of motion as inherent within matter so that all matter is intrinsically active and self-organizing. The development of vitalist ideas culminated in William Harvey's theory of reproduction, *De generatione animalium (Anatomical Excitations, Concerning the Generation of Living Creatures)*, printed in March 1651 by Milton's printer William Dugard. In this new work, with the motto "*ex ovo omnia*" on the title page, Harvey declared that the female ovum was not passive but active, and required no direct contact with the male sperm for conception. In a daring, however unscientific, assertion of gynocentric generation, Harvey, impelled by his vitalist convictions, put forward his thesis of fermentative as opposed to impregnate origins. This controversial vitalist philosophy of self-creation that is debated in the creation narratives in *Paradise Lost* appears also in this final invocation. Questioning the notion of a divinely inspired epic, the invocation in Book 9 offers, in its place, a radical view of the epic being generated by the materiality of events, as if the ferment of the "higher argument" energizes a self-generative creativity. But immediately the vitalist claim is tempered with the acknowledgment of "much they may, if all be mine, / Not hers who brings it nightly to my ear" (9, 46–47), a point that touches on the crux of the vitalist debate, which seems to hinge on the question of first causes and the belief in a philosophy of disengaged self-generative continuity. In effect, what happens in the final invocation in *Paradise Lost* is that a countervoice is produced, which opposes the privileging mode of the earlier invocations. The doubts and hesitations released by a sense of venturing into a formidable field, together with Milton's feeling of isolation and of being surrounded by hostile forces, had prompted the appeal for empowerment and the integration of a benchmark of cabalistic magic, eventually transcended and excelled. The final invocation suggests that by the time the last segment of the epic is reached, the theme itself is recognized as being powerful enough to produce an epic poem.

Such dismantling of modes already set up within the poem that one sees in the invocations is typical of the way *Paradise Lost* operates. Milton never hesitates to put forward conflicting alternatives, not because he does not wish to take up a position but because his mind is open to the possibility of the authenticity of alternative systems of belief. The difficult question in the invocations is Milton's own position as poet—does he wish to suggest a transference of vitalist beliefs to the poetic impulse? There is a need to look closely at the invocations, to notice the changes that take place, and to relate that to the seventeenth-century interest in cabalism and to the vitalist debate in early modern science. It may be simplistic to believe that the continuing role of divine authority in the form of the Muse's inspiration is central to Milton configuring himself as epic poet. It may be equally problematic to believe that Milton moved to a position of independent self-creation in the epic's final invocation. Perhaps all one can say about the final invocation in *Paradise Lost* is that, just as Milton is conscious of belonging to the "vitalist moment," setting up accounts of creation in his epic remarkable for their modernity and for a radical approach, he is equally conscious that the same analogy could be extended to the mode of writing with problematic consequences. While the invocations provide the space for the construction of authorial identity, the identity of Milton's Muse has perplexed readers because his Muse appears to be masculine in the invocations in Books 1 and 3 and feminine in the invocations in Books 7 and 9. Michael Lieb, in his analysis of the integration of the cabalistic concepts of *maaseh merkabah* (work of the chariot) and *maaseh bereshit* (work of creation) into Milton's poetry, has offered an explanation of the change of sexes in Milton's Muse.[39] Pointing out that "the feminine element in Milton's *maaseh bereshit* assumes paramount interest in his rendering of the Son's role as creator,"[40] Lieb suggests that the key to this apparent contradiction is to be found in the fact that androgyny is implicit in Milton's perception of God. The conflation of brooding and impregnation is not a mixed metaphor but is consistent with Milton's view of God as both masculine and feminine. Lieb's reading of androgyny in this context of the epic needs to be related to the fact that androgyny is implicit in the other coordinate of the story of creation—Milton's Chaos—and the implications of this will need to be worked out later. In the immediate context what is relevant is that Milton's Muse is predominantly masculine in the invocations in Books 1 and 3, where the Muse is associated with a blaze of light by day, and predominantly feminine in the invocations in Books 7 and 9, where the Muse is associated with the light of the stars at night. These gender distinctions are consistent with the traditional cosmic pattern that Milton follows generally in *Paradise Lost*, based on ideas drawn from Pliny and other sources, according to which the sun is masculine and the moon feminine. Given the androgyny of Milton's God, it is not surprising that the concept of the Muse in *Paradise Lost* is a composite one and accommodates within it the change of sex.

It is worth speculating on the reasons as to why Milton creates a cabalistic benchmark in the invocations in *Paradise Lost*. This great poem is a work filled with a sense of belatedness. Milton wrote this epic, he says, "long choosing and beginning late" (9. 26) and hopes his poem will succeed "unless an age too late, or cold / Climate, or years damp my intended wing" (9.44–45). As the work of a "survivor," a term used by Goldberg and Orgel,[41] it is not a poem that exults in the excitement of esoteric knowledge and subversive ideas like the poems of the 1645 volume. The references to magic in poems such as the *Nativity Ode, L'Allegro*, and *Il Penseroso* are youthful, adventurous excursions into new areas of learning, the allusions themselves being more in the nature of ornament or embellishment. The compulsions behind the references to cabalism in the epic invocations are different. Like *Lycidas*, *Paradise Lost* "by occasion foretells" the history of the nation as well as human history. This exceptional attempt could truly succeed only if divinely inspired. In the closing years of the Renaissance such an empowered role had been represented through the concept of magic and the figure of the magus. Milton had explored hermetic magic in his early poems and he now turns to cabalism and its construction of Moses as "il Revelatore." The magic of the cabala had been Christianized and was therefore readily acceptable both for Milton and for his readers. It was also widely discussed in the seventeenth century. The essential difference between Merlinic prophecy, similar to Dee's reading of the crystal ball, that would have been part of his original project, and the tradition of Mosaic cabalistic prophecy, both magical, is that the former is speculative and the latter divinely inspired. The initial reference to Moses, "that shepherd" (1.8), in the epic's opening invocation, initiates a network of references to the cabalist tradition of Mosaic prophecy not as a tour de force or rhetorical flourish, but as a conscious engagement with a discourse of power.

Once Milton's self-construction into the mode of Mosaic prophet is understood, the nature of his Muse in *Paradise Lost* becomes clearer. In the poem's opening invocation the "heavenly Muse" and the Holy Spirit are invoked in association with the beginnings of cosmic history. Later, we are reminded that God spoke to Moses from a "radiant shrine" hiding the "full blaze" of His "glorious brightness" (3.375–82), and later still the Muse is addressed as a celestial being. Milton invokes this "heavenly Muse" and the "holy light" that is a manifestation of God. The enlightened Moses had not only learnt the story of creation but the mystery of creation itself. It was this knowledge that invested the figure of Moses with the touch of divine radiance leading to the representation of the veiled or horned Moses. Creativity itself is empowerment. The first two invocations of the epic carry forward the projection of Moses and empowerment along recognizable cabalistic lines. But once Milton's inner vision becomes sharper and more intense, the cabalistic tradition of Moses takes its place as a benchmark that needs to be circumvented making way for the emergence of the figure of an unencumbered divinely inspired Moses. The intervention of the divine Urania, in the invocation in Book 7, acts as a catalyst for separating the cabalistic tradition of Mosaic empowerment from a Mosaic prophetic role of a higher order, ensuring, for the epic poet, a privileged position. Later, as he reconsiders the inherent power and dynamism of the subject of his epic poem, Milton is led eventually to reassess his search for empowerment. The invocations mark a learning curve through which the notion of creativity is explored.

The setting up of a network of cabalistic allusions to establish a framework of empowerment that he wishes to surpass is, in part, Milton's own private engagement, a process of identifying and establishing his own identity within the epic. But it is also a structure of thought that would have been recognized in the intellectual ferment of Milton's age. In the atmosphere of mid-seventeenth-century debate and controversy, the network of cabalist allusions to light would have been understood by readers familiar with the tradition flowing from Bruno to Fludd and beyond. The epic poet could engage with this cross-section of readers of the early modern period and draw upon their understanding of his positioning of himself as a second Moses invested with greater power and authority than a cabalistic magical status. Restoring contextuality to the chain of Mosaic allusions in the invocations enables us to understand better the complexities of Milton's self-representation in the invocations as well as the dramatic character of the invocations themselves.

Milton wished to bring together questions of empowerment, enlightenment, and creativity in the invocations. Cabalism and chemical philosophy, and the figure of Moses within it, on the one hand, and vitalism on the other provided him with the polarities within which such issues could be debated and explored. Milton's positioning of himself as Moses in the opening invocation of *Paradise Lost* is the beginning of a narrative of inspiration, worked out through the epic's invocations, culminating in a radical, vitalist understanding of creation, the implications of which cannot be fully understood without reference to the resources of both cabalism and early modern scientific thought.

CHAPTER 3

"Unoriginal Night" and Milton's Chaos

Chaos is a deeply troubling presence in *Paradise Lost*. While the immense power of the opening books of the epic can be attributed in large measure to Milton's portrayal of Satan, there can be no doubt that the other significant factor that contributes to this sense of a strong beginning is his depiction of chaos. Milton's chaos is powerful because it is enigmatic. Chaos is a dynamic entity, simultaneously a place and a person. It is evil and terrifying in its indefinable shapelessness and immensity—"formless infinite" (3.12)—and in its destructive potential, while at the same time it is recognized as the residuary of good first matter. It is submissive to God but always suggests subversive tendencies. This essentially fluid identity holds immense imaginative power and opens up questions about many aspects of the epic narrative. Although chaos occupies only a brief segment of the second book of *Paradise Lost*, it makes an enormous impact. A recovery of the contextual data for Milton's depiction of chaos helps us uncover nuances and suggestions embedded in this brief description. This, in turn, reveals Milton's strategies for defining character in the epic.

Milton scholarship has sought to explain his chaos primarily with reference to *De Doctrina Christiana* and the account of first matter in the patristic writers. Yet the chaos of *Paradise Lost* has an imaginative life of its own whose roots are far more complex. John Leonard has argued that "Milton's conception of Chaos and Night is deeply indebted to Lucretius."[1] Just as Milton's fascination with infinite space reminds us of the wonder and terror of boundless space in Lucretius, the threatening chaos of his epic, Leonard suggests, with its "belligerent atoms rising from the void,"[2] shows the impact of Lucretius. If Lucretius inspired the imaginative intensity of Milton's exploration of

infinite space within the cosmos and outside it, including the "illim-
itable ocean" (2.892) of chaos with its hyperactive atoms, there is
another source Milton draws upon for his depiction of chaos and
Night that demands greater scrutiny as its graphic illustrations are
almost replicated in *Paradise Lost*. This is the account of chaos in
the hermetic philosophy of Robert Fludd. Although the connections
between Milton and Fludd have been commented upon, the full
implications of this for Milton's depiction of chaos have not been ade-
quately explored. The Mosaic framework that Milton constructs as
a benchmark in the invocations incorporates allusions to the Mosaic
tradition in seventeenth-century chemical philosophy that includes
Fludd, but the borrowings from Fludd for Milton's depiction of chaos
are much more specific. Robert Fludd was a controversial figure in
the seventeenth century. His copious use of illustrations made him
the object of ridicule among scientists such as Kepler and Mersenne.
But for a poet like Milton, who had an unusually strong visual imagi-
nation, the writings and illustrations of Robert Fludd must have been
of absorbing interest. Many copies of Fludd's two-volume history of
the macrocosm and the microcosm were printed in the 1620s and, as
Edgar H. Duncan suggests, "it is not unlikely that the young Milton
had access to them, perhaps owned them, and that they had their part
in feeding the intellectual and visual imagination of the future author
of *Paradise Lost*."[3] However, to establish the relevance of Fludd as
a source of critical importance, one would need to revisit first the
unresolved debate as to whether Milton's chaos is good or evil and
reexamine the significance of Night.

In a uniquely decisive gesture in *Paradise Lost*, Milton places the
new cosmos right in the middle of chaos. It is a significant divergence
from Ptolemaic and Copernican models of the universe that there is
no powerful enveloping outermost region providing a sense of secu-
rity. Illustrations of the Aristotelio-Ptolemaic model of the universe
in encyclopedias and textbooks would have familiarized contempo-
rary readers with the reassuring presence of the empyrion girdling
the cosmos. For the Copernican model, this would be replaced by
the sphere of the fixed stars. In either case, the eye would be invited
to look upward and outward to a radiant world. In *Paradise Lost*,
Milton deliberately moves the empyrion away from the circumference
and places heaven not around but above the created universe and at
a distance from it. The stars as possible worlds have immense power
in Milton's epic, but beyond them is a circular opaque shell within
which the cosmos is held and beyond that again is the blustery region
of chaos. The hard outer shell itself is lifeless, "dark, waste and wild"

(3.424), and provides no light or sustenance. Moreover, it has an aperture on top offering open access to the angels as well as to Satan and his associates. There is, in fact, always the provocative possibility of chaos invading the cosmos. Consequently, one has the feeling that the new universe is thrust into the middle of a hostile region making the created universe entirely vulnerable. The spatial expanse within which the epic's action takes place is so constructed that between the bottomless depths of hell below, secured by the rusty gates guarded by Sin and Death, and the infinite expanse of heaven above, with its apparently unguarded automatic gates ("the gate self-opened wide / On golden hinges turning, as by work / Divine the sovereign architect had framed" [5.254–56]), the intermediate region is that of chaos and Night with the new universe suspended in its middle. Indeed, as Leonard rightly points out, hell may not be the lowest region of this epic expanse as chaos may very well extend beyond it.[4] Or, from a different perspective, had chance not intervened and Satan kept falling "to this hour" (2.934), the spatial definition of chaos would have been indefinitely deferred. When Satan reaches the cosmos after his long journey from hell and walks on the hard outer shell of the universe, the outside of the new world appears thus:

> a globe far off
> It seemed, now seems a boundless continent
> Dark, waste, and wild, under the frown of Night
> Starless exposed, and ever-threatening storms
> Of Chaos blustering round, inclement sky. (3.422–26)

The function of the outer shell, the "firm opacous globe / Of this round world" (3.418–19), is to protect the new universe from the inroads of chaos and Night. Yet, as its defensive capabilities invite instant comparison with the encircling walls of Paradise, we are reminded that both prove to be barriers unable to keep out evil. Both, in fact, serve only to enhance the essential vulnerability of that which is sought to be protected. Unlike the impregnability of heaven and the solid fortifications of hell, the hard outer shell provides unhindered access through the aperture and is thus essentially a less-than-satisfactory means of separating chaos from cosmos. Not surprisingly, the universe suspended from its golden chain in the middle of chaos is perceived as "this frail world" (2.1030). While Satan does enter through the aperture, and the immense bridge from Hell constructed by Sin and Death extends to this aperture, the question of whether chaos is able to enter or is resisted is a more difficult one and needs to be assessed in the context of Milton's perception of the power of the created universe and the events that take place within it.

The complexity of Milton's chaos is in large part due to the fact that chaos is both a place and a person. As a place it is a dark, wild, blustery region through which Satan makes his somewhat uncertain journey in search of the new world. As a place, again, it is neither an ally nor an enemy of Satan who experiences the turbulence of air pockets and gale force winds as he flies upward through chaos. As a person, Chaos is a natural ally of Satan with their common agenda of bringing ruin and devastation. The identity of chaos as place and person is fluid and indeterminate. While chaos as place subsists at all times, a shape or figure emerges out of this chaotic mass for a while and engages in a conversation with Satan. Chaos as animated matter and Chaos as persona often overlap, but are still distinct. In the complex dynamics of the poem, while chaos is prime matter out of which God created the cosmos, it is also a potentially subversive "other" who is sometimes submissive, sometimes displays a self-generative capability that subverts authority, and sometimes assumes an overtly defiant attitude threatening the orderliness of creation. It is this subversive "otherness" that is projected not through the hostile form of the allegorical Chaos but in Milton's depiction of chaos as place. In this intensely dramatic epic, the ambivalent role of chaos has a major impact and becomes a tool with which much of the interpersonal relationships in the epic can be understood. It is also worth noting that, in the spatial canvas of *Paradise Lost*, it is the middle region of chaos that is distinct from heaven and hell in being animated matter, place-as person, and person-as-place. In this essential fluidity, while there is a constant transference of qualities between place and person, chaos as place has no definable character, being both good and evil, while Chaos as person is combative and threatening but in the end ineffectual.

From the very beginning it becomes clear that chaos is a threatening entity. However, debates regarding the identity of chaos as prime matter, questions of whether chaos is inherently good or evil, refuse to die down. "Wild abyss" (2.910, 917) is one of the most prominent epithets used to describe Milton's chaos and it is surprising how, in spite of this, Miltonists, by and large, are reluctant to consider chaos in *Paradise Lost* as being possibly hostile. Robert M. Adams's comments, with its parentheses and hesitations, are symptomatic of the kind of defensive reaction to chaos that is dictated by traditional Christian considerations: "Chaos is neutral as between good and evil; all he likes is disorder. That inclines him to evil, of course, but not all

the way, for evil is itself a principle of order; and Chaos is, so to speak, beyond good and evil."[5]
Much more forthright is A. S. P. Woodhouse's remark that

> it must, for example, be plain to every reader of *Paradise Lost* that the description of the Chaos there throws a very much heavier emphasis on its formlessness and disorder than does the account of the original matter in the *De Doctrina,* so that it is difficult to escape the inference, denied in the treatise, that this disorder is, or at all events has some affinity with, evil.[6]

The primary reason for hesitations in regarding chaos as evil involves troubling questions raised by the identification of God with prime matter that seems implied in *Paradise Lost.* How can good prime matter possibly be hostile? The perception of chaos as prime matter out of which the cosmos was created is central to the debate about Milton's monistic materialism. It is also at the root of the difficulty of accepting Milton's chaos as potentially evil. Rumrich, who separates divine potency from chaos as good prime matter, explains that, in his view, "the realm of Chaos is good only in the sense that it is materially sufficient for God's creative purposes."[7] His earlier suggestion that chaos contains "the potential for otherness"[8] argues for both the possibility of the freedom of the will and the existence of evil in chaos. Chaos, in other words, as the matter of creation, is good, but as the state of the self-willed disordered "other," it is potentially evil. However, arguing for a hostile chaos, Leonard points out that chaos in *Paradise Lost* is governed by chance, not free will, which makes it arbitrary and denotes the absence of responsibility.[9]

The solution to these debates may lie in Juliet Cummins's suggestion of "the paradox that Milton's God at once is, and is not, the matter of chaos."[10] For Cummins, God at once is and is not the matter of chaos because "in *Paradise Lost* Milton draws a distinction between prime matter and chaos, a distinction given allegorical form in the characters of Night and Chaos."[11] Paradox is also the answer for Regina Schwartz when she puts forward the case for a hostile chaos and declares that she finds "the inference of an evil chaos so difficult to escape that it is not worth trying."[12] Toward the end of her analysis of chaos, Schwartz extends the idea of *felix culpa* to explain the apparent dichotomy between theology and poetry.

> It is here, in a redemptive creation, that we find the seeds of reconciliation between Milton's description and his doctrine of chaos. *Felix culpa* is not an after-the-fact rationalization for Milton. We know

good by knowing evil. Milton reads the logic of that fortunate fall
back into his cosmology: a fallen chaos is also fortunate, for it issues in
creation...Paradoxically, Milton's hostile chaos becomes a "good first
matter" after all—but then, paradox is the pivot upon which the whole
of Christian theology turns.[13]

While admitting the hostility of Milton's chaos in *Paradise Lost*,
Schwartz still finds herself in a dilemma as she faces the difficult task
of reconciling description and doctrine. She, like Cummins, finds her
answer in the rich corpus of Christian paradox.

A further exploration of possible sources can throw some light on
the troubling ambiguities of chaos that continue to perplex Milton
scholarship. It can be argued that the roots of the ideas Milton used
to construct his account of chaos and creation are embedded not
in traditional Christian doctrine, but in the interpretation of it in
Renaissance occult philosophy. Seventeenth-century hermetic phi-
losophy provided Milton with an explanation of chaos and creation
that acknowledges chaos as the matter of creation, even as it admits
the undeniable hostility of chaos. Milton's decision to incorporate
this tradition in *Paradise Lost* was perhaps dictated by his perception
of the possibilities that it offered for an exploration of character and
motivation in the epic. Milton both utilized and modified this mate-
rial to make his own construction more meaningful. His chaos, at
once a hostile presence and good first matter, also encompasses an
immense complexity of gendered relationships that connect with the
human protagonists of his epic. These gender equations are the direct
result of his modification of the representation of chaos he found in
the hermetic philosophy of Robert Fludd.

"The womb of nature and perhaps her grave" (2.911): Milton's
description captures the essential ambivalence of chaos. Chaos is not
only hostile, but it also has undeniable alliances with Satan. Chambers
made out a convincing case for the similarities between chaos and
Satan who has to contend with a "hateful siege of contraries" within
him, and between Satan and Adam and Eve in their state of discord
after the Fall.[14] Milton's chaos, to whom we owe the phrase "confu-
sion worse confounded" (2.996), shares with Satan and with fallen
man a condition of perpetual discord. While disharmony in chaos
has its devilish parallel in Satan, for Satan this discord is a condi-
tion of the mind. But in his presentation of chaos, Milton gives this
discord a physical dimension. Michael Lieb has drawn attention to
the "organicist polemic"[15] in *Paradise Lost*, one instance of which
is Milton's Chaos, presented as a huge person. Referring to David

Masson's reading of the principles of hot, cold, moist, and dry striving for mastery within Chaos as none other than the humors of a gigantic elemental body in a state of perpetual strife, Lieb points to the proliferation of images of digestion and decomposition in the middle books of *Paradise Lost*. As part of this group of metaphors, the endless conflict of the four contending elements of earth, air, water, and fire within Chaos is presented through the image of "intestine broils" (2.1001) within Chaos. It was the ordering of these discordant elements that took place during creation. In Uriel's brief account of this great event, "the cumbrous elements, earth, flood, air, fire" (3.715) disentangled themselves from their state of disordered confusion to occupy orderly positions when the cosmos came into being. But discord is not the only point of similarity between chaos and Satan. The allegorical Chaos's agenda of wreaking "havoc and spoil and ruin" (2.1009) is identical to that of Satan, and Chaos's unproductive bluster throws into sharp focus Satan's success in bringing about the Fall of man.

Chaos is a vast region, a "wild abyss" (2.910), "wide on the wasteful deep" (2.961). It exists as

> a dark
> Illimitable ocean without bound,
> Without dimension, where length, breadth, and hight,
> And time and place are lost. (2.891–94)

It is a region without bounds, without limits, without shape, and without determinable features. Chaos shares in the terrifying indeterminateness of Milton's portrayal of Death in *Paradise Lost*: "If shape it might be called that shape had none" (2.667). While harmony and exactness, almost a mathematical precision, mark the details of the universe within its hard outer shell, the region of chaos and Night shares with hell and with Death the quality of indeterminateness. Its combination of boundlessness with wastefulness and wildness makes chaos recognizably evil. There is undoubted hostility in Milton's chaos, and the new created universe needs to be protected from it. The vulnerability of the new cosmos becomes apparent from its situation "under the frown of Night / Starless exposed, and everthreatening storms / Of Chaos blustering round..." (3.424–26). Yet the universe itself was formed out of chaos. Cosmos and chaos thus have strong filial connections. The threatened assault of chaos on the cosmos, therefore, is a violation of the sanctity of this relationship and has its hellish parallel in the relationship between Satan,

Sin, and Death. It is to Satan that the allegorical figure of Chaos confesses his ultimate desire: "havoc and spoil and ruin are my gain" (2.1009)—a desire that again reveals psychological resemblances between the two.

In its state of "eternal anarchy" (2.896), Chaos is throughout accompanied by a silent partner, Night. On one occasion Night and Chaos are together presented as the ancestors of Nature (2.894–95) and again, later, Night is the consort of Chaos (2.963). As companion, partner, spouse, Night and Chaos share at least equal status, a compatibility of temperament, and a commonality of attributes. But, more importantly, there is a sustained emphasis on the fact that Night is ancient, primordial. She is never mentioned without a stress on her antiquity. She is not only "old Night" (2.1002) and "darkness old" (3.421); she is "ancient Night" (2.970, 986) and indeed older than Chaos, for she is "eldest Night" (2.894) and the "eldest of things" (2.962). As a condition prior even to Chaos, she appears to be the only entity Milton admits to being coeternal with God. In a climactic passage in Book 10, Milton gives ancient Night, one of the ancestors of Nature, the unique distinction of being uncreated. This is when Satan, seeking to invite acclaim from his followers, describes his hazardous journey through the regions of "unoriginal Night and Chaos wild" (10.477).[16]

It is at this point that we begin to realize the importance of the separation of chaos and Night as two distinct entities and the implications of creating Night as an ancient and consistently silent figure. Seeking to interpret the question of cosmic origins, Milton visualized the beginnings of the universe as a condition involving the coeternal presence of darkness or Night, "unoriginal Night," as an image of divine alterity. Into this area of primeval darkness there entered an added presence, that of chaos. Night, therefore, was the original condition of complete privation, the absolute negative, silent, motionless. Chaos followed with its discordant sounds and elemental motions. After chaos came the creation of the cosmos. Creation involved, to return to Uriel's account, the expulsion of darkness ("darkness fled," [3.712]), the separation of chaos and Night.

This pattern of thought reflects the account of Chaos and Night, particularly its visual representation, in Robert Fludd. Ever since Denis Saurat drew attention to the possible connections between Milton and Fludd, scholars have examined the similarities between not only Fludd's philosophy and Milton's ideas, but also Fludd's illustrations and Milton's images and imaginative constructs.[17] One area that has remained largely unexplored is Milton's indebtedness to Fludd for his depiction of chaos and the beginnings of creation. A. B. Chambers does consider Fludd in his survey of classical and Renaissance sources while raising the important question of "why chaos, with its puzzling details, occupies so prominent a position in Milton's narrative."[18] More recently, Juliet Cummins[19] also refers to Fludd while analyzing Milton's presentation of chaos. But the similarities with Fludd are much more pervasive than such brief references may lead us to believe.

In the first part of his *History of the Macrocosm and Microcosm*, first published in 1617, Fludd presents his version of the great darkness that prevailed at the time of the beginning of the universe. Diagrammatically, this is presented as a totally black square stretching from infinity to infinity, with the words *Et sic in infinitum* inscribed on the margin on all four sides.[20] Fludd notes: "What was there before creation? Some first state of unformed matter (*material prima*), without dimension or quantity, neither small nor large, without properties or inclination, neither moving nor still. Paracelsus calls it the Great Mystery (*Mysterium Magnum*) which he says is uncreated; others claim it as God's first creation."[21] The original state before creation is thus an absolute negative, represented visually as an endless darkness. Chaos is presented by Fludd as a separate stage that belongs to a later phase of cosmic history than the original darkness, although still a part of his account of the beginnings of the universe. Chaos is shown as a confused and undigested mass in which the four elements fight against each other, and Fludd's diagram depicting this state bears a marked resemblance to the human intestines.[22]

Milton's "unoriginal Night" and the "intestine broils" of his Chaos appear to be a reworking of these images in Fludd. In this reworking, however, Milton allows the coexistence of Fludd's two entities. Instead of presenting Night and Chaos as two entirely separable states existing at different points of time as in Fludd, he has brought them together as partners. Night is the uncreated, ancient, primordial being, but she coexists with Chaos. The effect of this companionship is to deepen the horror of Chaos by imparting an added dimension of total privation to the hostility of Chaos. The change from sequentiality to coexistence also achieves a transference of power from "unoriginal Night" to Chaos. Sitting enthroned beside "sable-vested Night, eldest of things, / The consort of his reign" (2.62–63), Chaos can claim to share equal power with an entity in whom power resides naturally as one who is coeternal with

God. Although as consort or spouse Night should be inferior to Chaos in the gender equation the epic follows consistently, Satan instinctively recognizes her superior natural power as he tries to impress Chaos and Night with the announcement that his intention is to seek out

> if some other place
> From your dominion won, the ethereal king
> Possesses lately, thither to arrive
> I travel this profound, direct my course;
> Directed no mean recompense it brings
> To your behoof, if I that region lost,
> All usurpation thence expelled, reduce
> To her original darkness and your sway
> (Which is my present journey) and once more
> Erect the standard there of ancient Night. (2.977–86)

It is the restoration of the rule of Night and not the rule of Chaos that Satan announces as his declared intention, perhaps because he can sense Night's greater power. Her total silence throughout this scene is remarkable. The reply to Satan's offer of restoring the rule of Night is given by Chaos, not Night. Her silence, which contrasts with Satan's loquacity, may seem at first to be a sign of decrepitude as the phrase "weakening sceptre of old Night" (2.1002) seems to suggest, but, more appropriately, it is a mark of her status of total privation and a sign of her power as absolute negation.

"Unoriginal Night" also reminds us of another strand in Fludd's cosmic theories, which envisaged the existence of a God with a dual power—God who can remain in a state of potentiality or God who can act. These two states are referred to by cabalists as the "Dark Aleph" and the "Light Aleph." Since *Paradise Lost* consistently follows the structural principle of setting up sets of contraries, the presentation of Night as absolute negation and of Chaos as ceaseless but discordant activity may be understood as negative images opposed to God as Dark Aleph and as Light Aleph. Milton's acceptance of God's choice to act or to desist from action is clear from the statement in Book 7.

> Boundless the deep, because I am who fill
> Infinitude, nor vacuous the space.
> Though I uncircumscribed my self retire,
> And put not forth my goodness, which is free
> To act or not (7.168–72)

Night, as absolute negation, can be seen as the contrary of that state of the Dark Aleph, God's chosen state of inactive vitality.

In her essay on silence and darkness in Milton's *Paradise Lost*, Shirley Sharon-Zissar examines "the attachment of silence to darkness in many of Milton's images" in the poem, as in the scenes in Paradise (7.106, 7.444, and 8.163), and locates this association in Platonic and Augustinian traditions and in the tradition of the *Theologia Negativa*.[23] She looks, in passing, at the positive aspects of silence—as in Christ's and God's injunctions to silence in the epic—and examines closely the darkness of Hell and Chaos, the two realms external to creation. However, she makes no reference to Night, that Miltonic entity in which her two central concerns, silence and darkness, in fact converge. In a discussion that ends by focusing on textuality, she concludes,

> Thus, it seems that though Milton balances and juxtaposes silence and darkness throughout the poem, placing them both as conditions for knowledge and conditions of evil—as both good and evil on the psychological, epistemological, and physical dimensions of his universe—he ultimately tilts the balance and projects silence as the greater evil.

Night, the consort of Chaos, personifies the absolute negative values of silence and darkness. Translated into the terms of a failed revolution, it would not be out of place to suggest that Milton would have regarded, in retrospect, the revolutionary years with its passions and deceptions, its hopes and betrayals, as inherently chaotic, but the restoration of monarchy, already in preparation in the 1650s, as the ultimate negative, the return of the reign of Night.

Since the crisis at the heart of *Paradise Lost* is the possibility and imminence of uncreation, the opening books appropriately begin with Chaos and Night because they signify the state of uncreation into which creation might regress. There is an undeniable urgency felt in the epic, located in a belief in the possible reversal of creation. Even Belial, in the debate in Pandemonium, can sense the possibility of total extinction, a reduction to the state of absolute negativity, total darkness. He describes to the assembled devils the possible repercussion of open war against God: "To perish rather, swallowed up and lost / In the wide womb of uncreated night, / Devoid of sense and motion" (2.149–51). Satan, similarly, describes the possibility of annihilation by being sucked into an abyss of darkness.

> These passed, if any pass, the void profound
> Of unessential night receives him next

> Wide gaping, and with utter loss of being
> Threatens him, plunged in that abortive gulf. (2.438–41)

Milton's use of that phrase "abortive gulf" combines the tragedy of an untimely termination of life with the suggestion of disappearance or extinction contained in the Latin root of "abortive."[24] The region of unessential night is like an immense black hole swallowing up stars. Throughout the debate in Pandemonium, in fact, apart from Mammon's mocking reference to "Chaos judge the strife" (2.233), the fear expressed by Satan and his followers is the fear of Night, not Chaos. It is almost as if they recognize the power of Night as divine alterity while Chaos as an entity of similar temperament poses no threat to them.

The allegorical presentation of Night and Chaos, in fact, both undermines and enhances the power of chaos. The allegory identifies the ambivalent nature of chaos as at once terrifying in its threat of a regressive capacity and yet essentially blustering but powerless. As a personified figure, Chaos is hostile, raging but decrepit and ineffective. Night, on the other hand, provides the dimension of power. The essential ambiguity of Milton's chaos is graphically projected through this dual representation. "Milton's complex, multidimensional, enigmatic chaos," as Mary F. Norton defines it,[25] becomes clearer to us through the allegorical presentation of Night and Chaos. The complex amalgam of power and powerlessness, regressive endlessness, and material ferment that characterizes chaos is separated, identified, and represented through the allegorical forms of Night and Chaos.

Yet Milton scholarship at times seems unclear in its interpretation of the allegorical figure of Night. Juliet Cummins believes that "Milton uses the allegorical figure Night to represent God's base, material identity." When Milton refers to the "dark materials" (2.916) of chaos out of which God might create more worlds, there is an explicit connection being made, she feels, between darkness and prime matter. Milton's use of allegorical Night to represent prime matter, she argues, is part of a philosophical tradition in which matter is dark, unessential, passive, and feminine.[26] She then connects "unoriginal" (10.477) night with "increate" (3.6) light as an equation that partly dissolves the opposition between them and represents both as inherent in God.[27] But John Leonard sees Milton's Night as a much more sinister figure. Arguing that Milton "nowhere implies that Night is matter,"[28] he concludes that "Night is dark, infinite, uncreated space, identical with the deep, the abyss, the void."[29] In his response to Leonard, Rumrich points out that Milton does not uniformly present night and darkness as threatening. Night in heaven and within the cosmos can be soothing and restorative.[30] These arguments seem to be engaging in separate debates without focusing on the key issue. Leonard is looking at Milton's allegorical Night, companion of Chaos, and not at night and darkness generally as Cummins and Rumrich appear to do. In this, Leonard is surely right as the allegorical figure of Night has an identity of its own quite distinct from the general pattern of light and darkness in the epic. If one were to thus separate allegorical Night from the physical and metaphorical representation of light and darkness in *Paradise Lost*, the further question remains, should one regard Night as a dimension of prime matter?

What complicates Milton's presentation of chaos and night in *Paradise Lost* is what might be termed a preoccupation with the womb—chaos's fecundity and the suggested fecundity of Night ("the wide womb of uncreated Night" [2.150]). Chaos is a state of potentiality, which God impregnated with His creative energy to bring the cosmos into existence. It is this that makes chaos "the womb of nature" (2.911). Chaos is the *ancestor* of Nature (2.895), the *womb* of nature (2.911) in which *embryon* atoms (2.900) swarm *populous* (2.903) and all the elements are in their *pregnant* causes mixed (2.913). The idea of generation is reinforced through Milton's description of the moment of creation as one in which

> Darkness profound
> Covered the abyss: but on the watery calm
> His brooding wings the spirit of God outspread,
> And vital virtue infused, and vital warmth
> Throughout the fluid mass... (7.233–37)

In this context if one now returns to the visual image of the hard outer shell enclosing the created world within chaos, the image of the womb becomes immediately apparent. The created universe, the cosmos, is at once within the womb of chaos almost in a prenatal state, and simultaneously an independent entity, newborn, needing protection from a parent threatening to violate the innocence and integrity of the child.

The "womb" of chaos/Night has also been at the center of scholarly debate. Rumrich's reading[31] that chaos is the "womb of nature" (2.911) was challenged by Leonard who felt that the phrase refers to Night instead. Relying also on two other passages—"the wide womb of uncreated Night" (2.150) and "plunged in the womb / Of unoriginal Night and Chaos wild" (10.476–77)—he configures chaos as in fact being in the womb of Night.[32] Rumrich disputes this, pointing out that "the womb of nature and perhaps her grave" (2.911) refers clearly to the abyss of chaos.[33] That there is an ambiguity in Milton's use of "womb" in the context of Night and chaos can hardly be disputed. The words "the womb of nature and perhaps her grave" (2.911) come in a context where Milton is describing the "wild abyss" (2.910) of chaos into which Satan is about to venture. The "wide womb of uncreated night" (2.150) is part of Belial's gloomy prediction in the debate in Pandemonium before Night as an entity actually appears in the epic. The syntactically challenging "plunged in the womb / Of unoriginal Night and Chaos wild" (10.476–77) presents both Night and Chaos as "womb." However, this ambiguity can be explained if one looks at Fludd's depiction of Night and Chaos as the likely source of Milton's configuration of Chaos and Night. If Milton is following Fludd as his source, he regards Night as the womb of chaos, as chaos came into being from the original darkness. If that is indeed so, it creates an unnatural relationship between Night and Chaos with Night as both parent and partner of Chaos. The suggested flawed relationship between Night and Chaos would then be seen as having its parallel in the relationship between Satan and Sin. Chaos, in turn, is the womb of nature. Chaos is prime matter, and it is from the "dark materials" of chaos that God created the cosmos. Since Milton refers to Night and Chaos as "ancestors of Nature" (2.895), it seems safe to assume Night and Chaos represent the two stages through which matter evolves before creation takes place. The suggested flawed relationship between Night and Chaos does not morally impact the nature of prime matter. Prime matter, in any event, as the matter of chaos, was troubled, disorderly, disruptive, until God's power and goodness transformed it into a harmonious cosmos.

The essential fecundity of chaos extends beyond the moment of generation into a continuum, which is a curious amalgam of submissiveness and independent productivity. Chaos exists in a state of continuous ferment in which the very essence of the four elements, though not the elements themselves, are "in their pregnant causes mixed" (2.913), thus holding out the possibility of self-generation, the creation of multiple worlds. Read within the vitalist context, the continuous ferment that characterizes chaos might lead to alternate cosmoses, which, in fact, not being created by God, might not share the orderly condition of the first cosmos. This suggests the intriguing possibility of a series of disconnected cosmoses scattered through the vast expanse of chaos, self-begot and of undetermined shape and composition. The debate about a possible multiplicity of worlds that

Milton explored in relation to the solar system, while describing Raphael's voyage within the cosmos, is here presented from a different perspective, speculating on the possibility of multiple cosmoses within the limitless expanse of chaos. The effect, again, is that of deepening the potentiality and power of chaos. However, these possible multiple cosmoses within chaos are never generated because what is posited in *Paradise Lost*, in the context of the fecundity of chaos, is the need for divine intervention and chaos's submissiveness to God. Chaos admits the possibility of God creating other worlds. The matter of chaos will continue to be in a state of confused ferment "Unless the almighty maker them ordain / His dark materials to create more worlds" (2.915–16). The ultimate powerlessness of chaos is underscored through this projection of a chaos with self-generative potential who yet has to wait for God to infuse "vital virtue" and "vital warmth" (7.236).

In the light of chaos's submissiveness to God and the vocabulary of chaos as the "womb" of nature, it is not surprising that Milton's chaos should be perceived as feminine. The metaphoric representation of chaos provides a strong case in favor of just such a reading. The problem arises as soon as one engages in a close textual analysis, for Milton, in uncompromising terms, asserts the masculinity of the allegorical Chaos. "Chaos umpire sits, / And by decision more embroils the fray / By which *he* reigns" (2.907–909; italics mine). Chaos sits presiding over his domain sometimes as a masculine anarch, sometimes as an umpire. When Satan and Chaos first meet and Chaos speaks to Satan, this personification of prime matter is presented as an "anarch old / With faltering speech and visage incomposed" (2.988–89). His role here is that of a patriarch deeply conscious of his own property rights, resentful of the territories he has had to surrender, without the power or confidence to resist the encroachment and therefore willing and eager to enter into a pact with Satan against the common enemy.

In the ultimate analysis, Milton's chaos is neither male nor female but androgynous. While this provides an additional dimension of indeterminacy to chaos, making possible its combination of potentiality and submissiveness, it also connects with Milton's assimilation of the Renaissance idea of androgyny into his epic. Examining androgyny in *Paradise Lost* in the context of Adam, Eve, and the separation scene in Book 9, Marilyn R. Farwell points out the pervasiveness of ideas of androgyny in Hermeticism, Cabalism, and magic as sources Milton draws upon. Reading *Paradise Lost* in this context, Farwell suggests that "individuality...is a postlapsarian experience."[34] This contention can be extended to fit in with Milton's description of chaos. Chaos is submissive, pliable, fecund, though without creative energy, yet simultaneously aggressive, hostile, predatory, with destructive inclinations and powers. Considering this simultaneity of "dual hierarchized oppositions,"[35] it is perhaps paradoxical that chaos is more powerful and positive in its female role as the womb of creation—and powerful also in the negative dimensions of power he shares with his consort and partner Night—while merely decrepit, raging yet defenseless in its role of a masculine anarch.

As the repository of the matter out of which God created this cosmos, chaos is the submissive, fecund progenitor of a possible multiplicity of orderly cosmoses. At the same time, chaos is also a perpetual threat to the orderliness of the cosmos. This ambivalence of Milton's chaos radiates nuances that bring in unexpected resemblances to Milton's Eve—the last of creation just as chaos was the first, herself the agent who "Brought death into the world and all our woe" (1.3) and at the same time the "great expectation" (12.378), the seed of future immortality. The story of Eve's creation in Book 4, in sharp contrast to Adam's in Book 8, shows Eve's attraction for darkness and shadows. Eve's initial behavior is in fact regressive and self-involved. She is unwilling to face the "real" world. This proclivity for shadows, reflections, and self-absorption is perhaps enhanced later by the sense of self-importance generated in her by the first temptation. This makes Eve, at the beginning of Book 9, sensitive to the presence of wildness even in Paradise. Regressive self-absorption, unwillingness to admit the dominance of an orderly objective reality, association with darkness—these are character traits in Eve that display atavistic connections with chaos. It is almost as if the root cause of Eve's tragic flaw is inherent in the character of prime matter. The moral destruction of the cosmos, for which Milton ultimately makes Eve responsible, is the result of a tragic duality in Eve, which can be traced back to the basic materials out of which both she and the rest of the universe were created, but which, in her case, was a dominant character trait. In its way, one aspect of the Chaos-Night relationship also throws light on the relationship between Adam and Eve. Apart from the group of Satan, Sin, and Death, Chaos and Night is the only representation of a gender equation in the epic other than Adam and Eve. If Milton intends the allegorical Chaos and Night to be a miniature drama that makes explicit the oppositions implicit within chaos as place, the unexpected suggestions they portray are that of Night as a silent but immensely powerful woman and Chaos as a blustering, aggressive, but ultimately ineffectual man. In its way, this prepares us for a rendering of a similar relationship, though infinitely of a higher plane, sublime and sophisticated, the relationship between Adam and Eve. Eve's silences in the epic are remarkable. It is there in her creation story where she does not speak at all, and this is unlike Adam's creation story with its eloquent process of reasoning and naming. Indeed, throughout *Paradise Lost*, until Book 9, it is a fact that Eve never initiates a conversation, preferring always the role of a listener. It is always Adam who speaks, the same Adam who is shocked and distressed when, in Book 9, Eve opens the conversation and announces her decision to separate. Adam's chaotic thoughts pour out into a series of unconnected arguments in his futile attempt to prevent the separation. Eve prevails. The structure of gender authority so carefully built up, in which Eve was designated the submissive, inferior partner, falls apart and Eve emerges as the dominant, subversive "other." Milton prepares us for this critical questioning of traditional notions of authority through his presentation of chaos and the unfolding of its complexities and contradictions through the narrative of Chaos and Night.

Milton's presentation of chaos also impacts the angel conversations in the epic. Chaos refers to the noise and confusion that characterizes this region as "our intestine broils" (2.1001) and later the realm of chaos is described as the "boiling gulf" (2.1027). The suggestion of indigestion that this conveys reminds us of the visual representation in Fludd's diagram where chaos appears like the human intestines in which the four elements fight against each other. The condition of chaos is sharply antithetical to the ideal physiological state described by the angel Raphael to Adam in Book 5. Explaining angelic and cosmic digestion as the turning of "corporeal to incorporeal" (5.413), Raphael puts forward an ideal of digestion as sublimation that contrasts with the distempers that afflict Adam and Eve after the eating of the fruit, but contrasts more with the perpetual discord within chaos.

Finally, the act of allowing chaos to surround the cosmos, permitting them to coexist in close proximity, is both an admission of the family relationship between chaos and cosmos and the means of indicating imminent threat, almost providing for the prelapsarian universe of *Paradise Lost* a cosmic parallel to the presence of the serpent in Paradise. Interpreting *Paradise Lost* through his watercolors, William Blake changes Milton's narrative by showing an upright serpent coiled around Eve rather than confronting and addressing her. A similar suggestiveness can be seen in Milton's description of chaos surrounding the cosmos. The visual image of "this pendent world" suspended from heaven by a golden chain surrounded by "ever threatening storms / Of Chaos blustering round" is like an ancient hieroglyph or Renaissance emblem that can be used as a visual shorthand capable of conveying an immense complexity of meaning. The politics of chaos in *Paradise Lost* is not one of containment. Chaos is not a hostile force to be evaded or shut out. Rather, it is confronted, its family relationship uncovered, its potential for good and evil recognized, its paradoxical potential for creation and uncreation identified. As a powerful presence in the opening books of *Paradise Lost* it provides a key to the pressures and counterpressures within the epic narrative and the epic characters. The immense depth and complexity of Milton's chaos, very different from the linear, though intelligent and devious, character of Satan, becomes evident once the Fludd context is put in place and the importance of Night is recognized. When one looks at the series of diagrams in Fludd's *History of the Macrocosm and Microcosm*, from the representation of the great darkness to chaos to creation, Milton's representation of these states become much clearer. Vitalism, always one of the focal points in Milton's range of interests, and the means of interrogating authority in the invocations, is also suggested in his depiction of chaos. The vitalist implications of chaos become more significant when examined in the context of his representation of creation in *Paradise Lost*.

Milton's assimilation of Hermetic philosophy into the text of his epic in his depiction of chaos and Night, and his modification of it to fit into the texture of his poem, enabled him to indicate a negative version of spatial expansion into infinity. Thomas Digges's diagram of the Copernican model of the universe had, in 1576, introduced the concept of an infinite universe by visually extending the sphere of the fixed stars beyond the margins of the printed page.[36] Milton's own incorporation of the concept of infinity into his created cosmos was achieved through other modes, which will be discussed later. Spatial expansion within the cosmos has a strong positive resonance. On the other hand, the immensity of the region of chaos and Night, the "dark / Illimitable ocean without bound" (2.891–92), by its sheer expanse and formlessness, its suggestions of a terrifying regressive endlessness, provided, in contrast, a negative version of infinity. At the same time, Milton's presentation of chaos and Night also prefigure the depiction of character in the epic narrative and help us to understand motives, structures, and tensions that underline the negotiations of power within the epic. The assimilation of materials from Fludd into an exploration of the traditional Christian theme of creation out of chaos contributed its own subversive edge. It is not, of course, as a curiosity, an entity created from esoteric sources, that Milton's chaos makes such a strong impact on the readers' consciousness. That impact is largely due to the ambivalence of his chaos as both place and person, the relationship between Chaos and Night, and the complex ways in which chaos in *Paradise Lost* acts as an index to character and as a paradigm for vital interpersonal relationships in the epic.

CHAPTER 4

"This Pendent World": The Cosmos of *Paradise Lost*

At the end of his long journey from hell through chaos, Satan arrives within sight of "the empyreal heaven, extended wide / In circuit" (2.1047–48) and sees "fast by hanging in a golden chain / This pendent world" (2.1051–52). As readers, this is our first encounter with Milton's new cosmos, one of the most remarkable innovations in *Paradise Lost*, and the suggestive phrase—this "pendent world"—captures the essential ambiguity in the epic poet's imaginative depiction of the universe. The range of possible meanings of "pendent" expands through its homophonic association with "pendant" to signify both the state of the new cosmos as being contingent and uncertain, as well as the appearance of the new cosmos as a jewel hanging from heaven on a golden chain. The associated "pendant" urges us to consider the new cosmos as a precious gem as well as a work of art. We are invited to look at it as an auxiliary visual object just below heaven, like a pendant painting below that grander canvas. However, the perspective on its size as being like "a star / Of smallest magnitude close by the moon" (2.1052–53) is a deeply troubling one as the moon, to which heaven is apparently being compared here, has no light of its own and shines with borrowed light unlike a star, even the least significant one with which the cosmos is being compared, which has light of its own. This reversal is perhaps a sign of the confused state of Satan's mind as it is from his visual experience that the image is generated. The visual appeal of the sight of the new cosmos hanging like a perfect jewel in the middle of chaos, suspended from heaven by a golden chain, is immense. But perhaps more powerful is the other axis of meaning where the adjectival value of "pendent" defines the new cosmos as essentially undecided and uncertain. This problematic status of the cosmos is reinforced through a significant physical detail. The cosmos, we are told, is enclosed within a "firm opacous globe" (3.418), a hard shell, and it is on this opaque surface that Satan lands at the end of his journey through chaos.

> Mean while upon the firm opacous globe
> Of this round world, whose first convex divides
> The luminous inferior orbs, enclosed
> From Chaos and the inroad of darkness old,
> Satan alighted walks. (3.418–22)

This hard outer shell enclosing the cosmos is suspended from heaven by a golden chain, which sometimes changes its formation into a staircase. At the top of this shell, directly below the gates of heaven and at the foot of the golden staircase, there is a wide passage, open and accessible, and it is through this that Satan first views the inside of the new cosmos.

> The stairs were then let down, whether to dare
> The fiend by easy ascent, or aggravate
> His sad exclusion from the doors of bliss.
> Direct against which opened from beneath
> Just o'er the blissful seat of Paradise,
> A passage down to the earth, a passage wide...
> So wide the opening seemed, where bounds were set
> To darkness, such as bound the ocean wave.
> Satan from hence now on the lower stair
> That scaled by steps of gold to heaven gate
> Looks down with wonder at the sudden view
> Of all this world at once. (3.523–28, 538–43)

It is remarkable that while both heaven and hell have gates, the new cosmos, suspended in the middle of chaos, is totally unprotected, perpetually offering open access to all. Almost ironically, Paradise is encircled by a wall and has an entry gate guarded, however ineffectually, by Gabriel. If the one entry point at the top of the otherwise impenetrable hard outer shell did have gates, perhaps with the angels given the power to open and shut them, the cosmos would have been almost totally secure from intrusion by evil spirits, requiring greater ingenuity from Satan in devising a means of entry. Instead, not only does the aperture provide easy access to the angels, it is also the point through which Satan, Sin, and Death enter the cosmos.

Why does Milton deliberately create a cosmos carefully enclosed within an opaque shell and yet leave it vulnerable by not providing it with secure gates so consistently provided for heaven, Paradise, and hell? Perhaps the open aperture is a mark of distinction showing the innate power of this divinely inspired harmonious cosmos that can keep chaos at bay. Milton's cosmos in *Paradise Lost*, although fluid and indeterminate, is remarkable for the precision and harmony of its imagined structure and celestial movements. Milton configures the new universe as at once uncertain, contingent, ambiguous, admitting various cosmological possibilities, and at the same time incredibly precise as a mechanism in terms of diurnal movement. The clockwork mechanics of this cosmos coexists with conflicting possibilities and suggestiveness. This enriching experience of the simultaneously precise and imprecise gives the cosmos of *Paradise Lost* its recognizable vitality. Although it is suspended amid threatening chaos, and has an open aperture, at no point does chaos enter and corrupt its orderliness. Yet the possibility remains, and makes the cosmos seem defenseless and vulnerable. The open passage also provides the perfect means of communication between the gates of heaven, the "doors of bliss" (3.525), and the "blissful seat of Paradise" (3.527); and the echo in the two lines so close to each other draws our attention to this. Human eyesight is not powerful enough to look upward through interstellar spaces into the abode of angels, but angels can and do look down from the gates of heaven and see the cedars growing in Paradise (5.253–61). Tragically, it is not only the angels but also Satan, Sin, and Death who look through and enter through the aperture. The only conclusion one can draw from this is that the ontological significance of the device of the open aperture is to provide a physical image of the notion of free will, the presence of good and evil as options. Milton's cosmos in fact has a curiously amoral stance, offering neither help nor hindrance to good or evil. It allows both the good angels and the infernal trinity equally easy transit. Also, although it holds its own harmonious structure till the very end of the epic narrative and is able to resist any intrusion of chaos, the threat of possible contamination always remains. It is this uncertainty that is reflected in the opening phrase "pendent world" and captured in the physical image of a cosmos enclosed within a hard outer shell with an aperture on top. In his *Philosophical Enquiry*, referring to Milton's presentation of Death in *Paradise Lost* as "if shape it might be called that shape had none" (2.667), Burke had remarked, "With what a significant and expressive uncertainty of strokes and colouring Milton has finished his portrait."[1] Milton's cosmos is, in its way, the exact antithesis of Death in *Paradise Lost*. If Death is terrifying in its indeterminateness, the cosmos is impressive in the precision of its diurnal structure. Yet the remarkable combination of openness and closure that Burke's oxymoron of "finished" and "uncertainty" holds out regarding the depiction of Death is also true of Milton's imaginative presentation of a unique cosmos in *Paradise Lost*, perfect yet uncertain and vulnerable.

As Satan lands on the hard shell, the cosmos is no longer a luminous star-like object. Seen from a distance, it had perhaps reflected the light it received from heaven and appeared like a shining celestial sphere. On nearer view, it seems a dreary continent.

> A globe far off
> It seemed, now seems a boundless continent
> Dark, waste, and wild, under the frown of Night
> Starless exposed, and ever-threatening storms
> Of Chaos blustering round, inclement sky;
> Save on that side which from the wall of heaven
> Though distant far some small reflection gains
> Of glimmering air less vexed with tempest loud. (3.422–29)

John Leonard has suggested that Lucretius may be Milton's source for this extraordinary opaque shell.[2] In *De Rerum Mundi*, volatile atoms rise up beyond the celestial spheres to form the walls of the world. Milton's opaque shell, however, unlike that of Lucretius, is static, unchanging, lifeless. Lucretius's shell made of atoms admits constant change and renewal. This dynamism is absent from the shell of Milton's cosmos whose "dark, waste and wild" form ominously reflects epithets that are used to describe chaos: "wild abyss" (2.910), "wide on the wasteful deep" (2.961), and "a dark / Illimitable ocean without bound" (2.891–92).

The question of which contemporary astronomical model Milton follows in shaping the cosmos of *Paradise Lost* has been much debated, particularly since he never commits himself when required to state his position. Alternatives such as

> whether the bright orb,
> Incredible how swift, had thither rolled
> Diurnal, or this less voluble earth
> By shorter flight to the east, had left him there (4.592–95)

always serve to hedge the question. When one looks closely at the astonishing cosmos Milton creates, it might be said that his cosmos is Ptolemaic in having a stationary earth with Paradise always facing heaven and the sun apparently circling around it. But it is Copernican in projecting a sense of infinite space and Tychonic in dispensing with the idea of solid orbs. There can be little doubt that conformity with any of these models is not the primary objective. The contours of the cosmos are dictated by the compulsions of the epic narrative. With "man's first disobedience" as the primary focus, it is important that human habitation, the earth, should be at the center, and important also that Paradise always faces heaven. But the urgent need for this did not mean that Milton had to confine himself to a Ptolemaic model. Imagining space is also of critical importance as indeed is unrestricted free movement through space. For this, accommodating Copernican and Tychonic notions was imperative.[3] Indeed, the image of a series of concentric spheres that was an essential part of the design of both the Aristotelio-Ptolemaic and the Copernican models is never a feature of Milton's cosmos. The only occasion when these spheres are mentioned is in the context of the Paradise of Fools. "They pass the planets seven, and pass the fixed, / And that crystalline sphere whose balance weighs / The trepidation talked, and that first moved" (3.481–83).

In the history of astronomy, all cosmic systems had been imagined as circular, but not always concentric. It was the Greek mathematician and philosopher Eudoxus (403–355 BC), a younger contemporary of Plato, who first introduced the idea that all the spheres are concentric to the earth.[4] According to Eudoxus, there were seven "planetary" spheres—Moon, Mercury, Venus, Sun, Mars, Jupiter, and Saturn— and an eighth sphere of the fixed stars that acted as the primum mobile. Aristotle accepted this with slight modifications while Ptolemy, in the second century AD, added a ninth sphere to account for the precession of the equinoxes. This was when the primum mobile was separated from the sphere of the fixed stars, with the cosmos now thought to have nine spheres. Later, Arabian astronomers believed that precession was variable and one of them, Tabit ben Korra (826–901 AD), added a tenth sphere, the crystalline sphere, to account for variable precession, often popularly referred to as "trepidation." This model of ten concentric spheres revolving around a stationary earth was familiar to Milton and his contemporaries as the Aristotelio-Ptolemaic system. Milton's allusion to the specifics of this astronomical model, however, comes in a context in which he is describing the cosmos after the Fall and these spheres are traversed by those journeying to the fool's paradise. In contrast, the prelapsarian cosmos of *Paradise Lost* is not multitiered. Within the hard outer shell of the cosmos there are vast spaces within which the sun, moon, planets, and stars are located, but nowhere does one encounter either the crystalline sphere or the primum mobile. Nor is there a consciousness of a graded position-ing of individual planets followed by a band of fixed stars. In Uriel's account of creation, the planets "each had his appointed place, each his course" (3.720) and Raphael, too, assigns the individual plan-ets "their stations" (7.563). This recognition of specific locations for individual planets still avoids the notion of fixed positions within solid spheres or even an acknowledgment of their relative positions in a graded series of concentric spheres. Not surprisingly, Adam and Eve, in their morning prayers, refer to the five planets as "wander-ing fires"[5] (5.177). While the phrase draws upon the etymological meaning of planets as errant stars, it is a strategic usage suggesting Adam and Eve's empirical assessment of the freedom of movement that the planets appear to enjoy. The sphere of the fixed stars is rec-ognized as a circling band ("the rest in circuit walls this universe" [3.721]), but even that acquires fluidity and expansiveness with Satan and Raphael weaving their way through the stars, speculating on the possibility of multiple worlds. The notion of a structured system of concentric spheres is carefully avoided. Seventeenth-century English poetry, even when it was conscious of the intellectual agility of the astronomer, was bound by the structure of concentric spheres that was a feature of both the Aristotelio-Ptolemaic and the Copernican diagram of the cosmos. George Herbert, for example, paying tribute to the intellectual power of the astronomer, still relies on the system of concentric spheres.

> The fleet Astronomer can bore,
> 	And thred the spheres with his quick-piercing minde
> He views their stations, walks from doore to doore,
> 	Surveys, as if he had design'd
> To make a purchase there: he sees their dances,
> 	And knoweth long before
> Both their full-eyed aspects, and secret glances. (*Vanitie* 1)

In contrast, Milton's cosmos is astonishingly modern in its fluid-ity, in the absence of fixed borders, and its consciousness of ever-expanding spaces. While the notion of circularity remains, and the cosmos of *Paradise Lost* is energized by a highly charged dynamism and continuous movement, that movement is complex and its details are debated. Raphael's much discussed conversation with Adam at the beginning of Book 8 on the subject of astronomy intriguingly sug-gests complex possibilities regarding the position, movements, and properties of celestial phenomena. However, Milton does retain the stylized notion of "cosmic dance" that was a feature of early modern poetry. In *Paradise Lost*, the harmonious movement of the angels as cosmic dance as they sing their hymn of praise circling God (3.344–417) is repeated in the movement of the constellations in their "starry dance" (3.580) and of the planets in "mystic dance" (5.178). This careful choreography of celestial movement establishes a consciousness of harmony as the single most powerful determining factor characterizing Milton's cosmos and firmly secures a contrast with chaos. At the same time, although the cosmos of *Paradise Lost* is a harmonious entity, it accommodates within its overall simplicity and grandeur unexpected deviations and complexities. It is possible to suggest that this ambiguity in the macrocosm is an index to similar nuances in Milton's presentation of the human pair at the center of his epic, Adam and Eve.

One of the unexpected alterations Milton makes in his presentation of the newly created world is in relation to the compass points of his cosmos. Positioning Paradise on the east and aligning Paradise directly with the aperture and the gates of heaven, Milton, as Alastair Fowler noted,[6] turns his cosmos on its side. East and west are above and below and north and south are on two sides. Landing on the hard outer shell of the cosmos at the end of his long journey through the region of Chaos and Night, Satan looks down in wonder through the aperture surveying the newly created world for the first time.

> Round he surveys, and well might, where he stood
> So high above the circling canopy
> Of night's extended shade; from eastern point
> Of Libra to the fleecy star that bears
> Andromeda far off Atlantic seas
> Beyond the horizon; then from pole to pole
> He views in breadth. (3.555–61)

The irony of the situation is that in his first survey of the new cosmos Satan, unknown to himself, is directly facing Paradise. It is again into this part of the cosmos, the region immediately above Paradise, that Satan will escape on his expulsion at the end of Book 4. Standing at the aperture, close to the point where the golden chain extending down from heaven secured the cosmos suspended in chaos, Satan finds himself above the conical shadow of the earth and in the region of Libra. As Marjara points out, in *Paradise Lost* there is "an extensive use of mathematical symbols and images related to geometrical configurations of the heavens"[7] and one of these is the cone. In Milton's universe, the sun being larger than the earth, a conical shadow of the earth is projected on the side opposite the sun. This moving cone is invested with a special significance and one of its chief functions is to act as a marker of specific hours in the universe.[8] Satan enters the cosmos at the moment when the cone touches the aperture. It is also the moment when Libra is at the eastern point. Traditionally, the world was created at the vernal equinox and in Milton's cosmos the sun is fixed in Aries. The position of the constellation Libra is diametrically opposite to that of Aries. As Satan looks down from the eastern point of Libra toward the "fleecy star" Aries, he is looking down the length of the universe, but from east to west. He then turns his attention to the two poles, north and south, which he views "in breadth."

The primary effect of this rearrangement of the compass points[9] of the cosmos of *Paradise Lost* is to align Paradise directly with heaven. Confirming the *Genesis* account "the Lord God planted a garden eastward in Eden"[10] in which He placed Adam and Eve, Milton tells us "For blissful Paradise / Of God the garden was, by him in the east / Of Eden planted (4.208–10). He goes on to locate Paradise as extending from the eastern point of Israel (Auran/Haran) to "great Seleucia" (4.212) in Syria, on the Tigris, south east from Auran.[11] Writing in an era of great debate regarding the exact location of Paradise,[12] Milton appears to situate it in what we would today call the Middle East. The circling canopy at Satan's feet as he enters the cosmos is at the "eastern point" and Paradise is unquestionably in the east facing the aperture as Raphael, standing at the gates of heaven, can look down directly through the aperture toward the earth and see the cedars growing in Paradise. Positioning the east at the top rather than on one side of the cosmos has other implications too. It places Paradise, as a garden in the east, as much in alignment with heaven and the angels as with the aperture and chaos. Should chaos intrude, Paradise would immediately be under threat. But there is another detail that needs to be factored in. As Fowler has pointed out,[13] in the cosmos of *Paradise Lost* before the Fall, the two great cosmic circles of the equinoctial, or the celestial equator, and the ecliptic, or the path of the sun, coincided. They were separated only after the Fall.

> Some say he bid his angels turn askance
> The poles of earth twice ten degrees and more
> From the sun's axle; they with labour pushed
> Oblique the centric globe: some say the sun
> Was bid turn reins from the equinoctial road
> Like distant breadth. (10.668–73)

Before this change, the most powerful celestial object within the cosmos, the sun, circling in an east-west direction, moved along the same plane as that of the celestial equator and in line with the aperture above Paradise. When one looks at the totality of this visual image, the dramatic significance of the rearrangement of the compass points of Milton's cosmos becomes clear. The vulnerable garden of Paradise finds its protective anchor in its direct alignment with the gates of heaven, while perpetually under threat from all who enter through the aperture, including Satan. There is always also the possible incursion of chaos. In this situation the sun, in the role of a protector, appears to circle the earth and Paradise, its trajectory taking it along a wide sweep past the aperture in the hard shell of the cosmos. As if to intensify the drama, while the sun lights up the space between Paradise and the aperture for at least 12 hours of the day from sunrise to sunset, its movement also creates a conical shadow over Paradise when it is on the other side of the earth. True, in this dark zone, the moon "in her pale dominion checks the night" (3.732), but she is only a mild "fair star" (3.727) shedding borrowed light from mid-heaven and lacks the authority of the sun. The dark shadow of the cone of night provides a safe haven within which Satan can hide after his expulsion from Paradise at the end of Book 4. Extending to the aperture, this cone of night also becomes an ominous zone that reflects the darkness of the region of Chaos and Night outside the opaque shell and almost provides a bridge or link with it.

In view of this highly charged cosmic drama, it is hardly surprising that the walls and gates of Paradise play such an insignificant role until the scene of the expulsion of Adam and Eve at the end of the epic. For the human pair at the center of the epic narrative, Paradise is a gated property. They feel secure within its walls until the first temptation of Eve instills in her a sense of claustrophobia. At the end of the epic, the walls and the gates are the cause of deep anguish as Adam and Eve are shut out from Paradise forever. Unlike the human pair, the angels and Satan are cosmic players for whom the walls and gates of Paradise do not matter. The fact that Gabriel sits guarding the gates of Paradise and patrols around the walls with his band of angels is nothing but a charade as these fortifications are totally ineffective and irrelevant for Satan. As a seasoned cosmic voyager, Satan approaches Paradise, climbs over the wall "at one slight bound" (4.181) and enters, flies out of Paradise and into the cone of night at the end of Book 4. He returns to earth and reenters Paradise through a subterranean river in Book 9 and wings his way up into the sky and into one of the constellations after the Fall. For Satan, avoiding the walls and gates of Paradise is a means of demonstrating his skill. But it is not only to evil spirits like Satan that the boundary walls and the gates do not matter. Two of the more effective good angels, Raphael and Michael, appear not to notice the walls and gates at all as they enter Paradise. Neither of them wastes time in decorously announcing their presence at the gate. They simply fly straight into Paradise. The fact is that, in Milton's epic, while there are great events that take place outside the cosmos, such as the war in heaven and the expulsion of the rebel angels, within the opaque shell of the cosmos there are not one but two distinct locations where events unfold. One is no doubt Paradise, the central stage on which "man's first disobedience" is enacted. The other is the larger cosmos, the space within the hard outer shell in which the earth is but a spot, where Satan deceives Uriel, where Raphael and Satan configure infinity, and where Satan finds a dark space within which his plans for uncreation can be fine-tuned. Indeed, configuring the status of humans through an understanding of his own condition and that of the angels, Satan had at first thought of man as capable of cosmic voyages. He asks Uriel,

> Brightest seraph tell
> In which of all these shining orbs hath man
> His fixed seat, or fixed seat hath none,
> But all these shining orbs his choice to dwell. (3.667–70)

Uriel corrects him and guides him toward Paradise.

All this seems to suggest that the earth is a static inconsequential spot in the universe. And yet, as the significant center of the epic action, Milton does give the earth its own vibrancy. True, both Adam and Raphael acknowledge the fact that the earth is insignificant in size in comparison with the vast expanse of cosmic space and the powerful celestial bodies within it. Looking up into cosmic space from Paradise, Adam comments on the negligible size of the earth— "this earth, a spot, a grain, / An atom, with the firmament compared" (8.17–18)—and Raphael diplomatically agrees that the earth indeed is "in comparison of heaven, so small" (8.92). When the earth is first identified in *Paradise Lost*, however, in Uriel's conversation with Satan, it is seen from a different perspective, from Uriel's vantage point in space. From this position in space the earth is a visible cosmic object, a globe that reflects the light of the sun, and it is Paradise that is "that spot" (3.733) on it toward which Uriel points. Later, as Raphael flies toward Paradise, he sees the earth as "not unconform to other shining globes" (5.259), the planets and stars. Although it is still an inferior cosmic body as it has no light of its own, the earth is given greater recognition by the two angels from their position in space. Indeed, in Raphael's detailed account of creation in *Paradise Lost*, the earth is given a position of strategic importance. As the story of creation unfolds, the initial stages record the formation of the globe of the cosmos and that of the earth at the center. In his account of creation in Book 5, Raphael explains "As yet this world was not, and Chaos wild / Reigned where these heavens now roll, where earth now rests / Upon her centre poised" (5.577–79). Continuing his account of the initial phases of creation, he describes how the globe of the cosmos was formed with the earth at the center:

> Then founded, then conglobed
> Like things to like, the rest to several place
> Disparted, and between spun out the air,
> And earth self-balanced on her centre hung. (7.239–42)

The formation of the earth is a critical phase of the creation story and given due recognition independent of the other celestial bodies. Details of the creation of the stars and planets emerge later. Moreover, the idea of the earth resting while in equipoise, or in a state of being "self-balanced," admits the possibility of its motion. As Marjara shows, both Gilbert and Galileo argued that the fact of the earth's being balanced in equilibrium facilitated its motion.[14] Milton's choice of the words "poised" and "self-balanced" seems to suggest a moment of stasis, as if the earth, motionless and perpetually facing heaven at this point, yet holds out the possibility of motion. If the Fall initiated a separation of the planes of the ecliptic and the equator leading to the loss of perfection of an eternal spring and a new experience of the change of seasons, may it not also lead to a moving earth? Yet movement is not in itself a negative factor, and, within the framework of the cosmos Milton creates, the possibility of the earth's participation in cosmic movement enhances rather than decreases its stature. Simultaneously, the possibility of a moving earth hinted at by Raphael through the suggestive "poised" and "self-balanced" deepens the uncertainty of Milton's cosmos.

In *Paradise Lost*, Milton's engagement with the cosmos is not confined to an account of the physical details of the universe but extends also to a consideration of creation theory. This enables him to accommodate a vitalist perception of creation that addresses fundamental questions of authority and empowerment central to an understanding of Milton's position on these critical issues in his epic poem.

Vitalism, which engaged people's minds during the period from 1649 to 1666 that John Rogers defined as the "Vitalist Moment,"[15] viewed the causes of motion as inherent within matter so that all matter is intrinsically active and self-organizing. Rogers draws attention to Milton's note dated March 5, 1651, in the Public Records Office in London, addressed to the Examinations Committee of the Council of State. It is a recommendation to the committee in two parts—the first, that there should be a reprint of one of Milton's recent political tracts—presumably the *Defence of the English People* published a few weeks earlier—and second, that due cognizance should be taken of Milton's complaint about the unauthorized translation of a Latin text whose patent was owned by Milton's printer, William Dugard. The text referred to was Francis Glisson's 1650 work *De rachitude, or, A Treatise of the Rickets*, which Glisson wrote in collaboration with Milton's friend Dr. Nathan Paget. Milton's interest in Glisson's work has puzzled many biographers. Other than the Paget connection, it seems difficult to account for his interest in the treatise. It is a fact that Dr. Nathan Paget, a cousin of Milton's third wife, Elizabeth Minshull, was someone with whom he was well acquainted from the 1650s if not earlier, and Paget's library had a wealth of books and manuscripts on alchemy, magic, and astrology, which was for Milton an important resource considering his interest in these subjects. But Paget's involvement was not the sole cause of Milton's interest in the treatise on rickets. An additional factor may have been that Glisson, as Hanford points out, "was a senior member of the body of 'learned and inquisitive persons' who from about the year 1645 constituted the philosophical society or 'Invisible College' in London"[16] and so would have been within the radar of Milton's interests. But Rogers suggests that the real reason for Milton's interest in this treatise is Glisson's vitalist agenda.

Glisson's treatise on rickets focuses attention on "random, disparate masses of bodily tissue that find themselves capable of actions and reactions independent of any efferent center of command."[17] He begins with a provisional dualism of "solid parts" or bodily substance and the energy force of "Vital Spirit." Once infused with the Vital Spirit, the bodily substance acquires the capacity for participating in, what Glisson calls, the "Nature of Life"—self-healing, self-renewing. For the royalist Glisson there is still a monarchic structure with his reliance on the central control of the heart over the movement of the blood. However, significantly, he believes in a decentralized determination whereby an individual group of tissues may on its own volition "sparingly sip that blood" and so become diseased.

Glisson's friend William Harvey had published his treatise on the cir-
culation of the blood a year before, in 1649—*De circulatione san-
guinis*—*On the Circulation of the Blood*. In an account of animated,
self-moving blood, Harvey dismantles the monarchic paradigms of
the brain, heart, and stomach as traditional centers of bodily control.
In fact, he goes beyond the parameters of medical science to pres-
ent his account of the circulation of blood as a paradigm of the ideal
body politic. Earlier, in 1628, in *De motu cordis* (*On the Movement
of the Heart*), he had presented the circulatory system as a solar sys-
tem. In the dedication to this work he had addressed Charles I as
the sun—like the king, the heart's duty is to provide nourishment to
all parts of the bodily kingdom. Twenty years later, however, in *On
the Circulation of the Blood*, Harvey revises his entire position. The
heart is no longer at the center of importance because, as he says,
blood has its own "native heat, call'd innate warmth" and circulation
occurs by the "meer impulsion of the blood." Blood itself, in this
new text, "is the very soul of the body." In a remarkable figurative
change, the heart is no longer the sun of the microcosm, the source
of power, but now "the heart is to be thought the Warehouse... of
the blood"—no longer a prince but a mere receptacle. Two years later,
Harvey published his theory of reproduction, *De generatione anima-
lium* (*Anatomical Excitations, Concerning the Generation of Living
Creatures*), printed in March 1651 by William Dugard, the printer of
Milton and Glisson. In this new work, with the motto "*ex ovo omnia*"
on the title page, he declared that the female ovum was not passive
but active, and no direct contact with the male sperm was needed for
conception.[18] In a daring, however unscientific, assertion of gyno-
centric generation—a theory that earned him plenty of ridicule from
other scientists and from conservative thinkers such as Alexander
Ross—Harvey, impelled by his vitalist convictions, put forward his
thesis of fermentative as opposed to impregnate origins. Returning
to his theory of circulation, he suggested that an act of fermentative
heat, rather than the dictates of the heart, motivates the revolution of
the blood. Vitalist philosophy seems to have reached its farthest limits
through this assertion of a science of self-creation.

Milton's suggestion of a vitalist account of creation needs to be
read in this context. Satan's words to his followers early in *Paradise
Lost*—"Space may produce new worlds" (1.650)—traditionally taken
as Satan's devilish denial of divine creativity, can take on a new mean-
ing in the vitalist context. Its significance emerges when it is placed
alongside the accounts of creation given by the angels Uriel and
Raphael. In Uriel's account of creation in Book 3, the Word of God

acts as an initial infusion of divine virtue into chaos, but thereafter, creation proceeds in a self-generative process as the matter of chaos takes on a life of its own.

> I saw when at his word the formless mass,
> This world's material mould, came to a heap:
> Confusion heard his voice, and wild uproar
> Stood ruled, stood vast infinitude confined;
> Till at his second bidding darkness fled,
> Light shone, and order from disorder sprung:
> Swift to their several quarters hasted then
> The cumbrous elements, earth, flood, air, fire,
> And this ethereal quintessence of heaven
> Flew upward, spirited with various forms,
> That rolled orbicular, and turned to stars
> Numberless, as thou seest, and how they move;
> Each had his place appointed, each his course,
> The rest in circuit walls this universe. (3.708–21)

The passage records two fiats or commands given by God, but, as Christopher Kendrick notes, the creative fiats are less causal than occasional in nature.[19] And indeed, after the first appearance of light, the movement of the elements and of the ethereal quintessence is marked by a suggestion of autonomy and self-generative vitality. This vitalist account of creation in Uriel's excited narrative appears to be somewhat tempered in Raphael's more structured account in Book 5.

> O Adam, one almighty is, from whom
> All things proceed, and up to him return,
> If not depraved from good, created all
> Such to perfection, one first matter all,
> Indued with various forms, various degrees
> Of substance, and in things that live, of life;
> But more refined, more spirituous, and pure,
> As nearer to him placed or nearer tending
> Each to their several active spheres assigned,
> Till body up to spirit work, in bounds
> Proportioned to each kind. (5.469–79)

Raphael's explanation might seem at first to be a straightforward lesson to Adam about the Neoplatonic hierarchical gradations of the Great Chain of Being. Yet, if one reads the passage with attention, his carefully inserted suggestion of matter infused with spirit has a sharper vitalist impact. A little later, when Raphael gives Adam an account of the first appearance of the earth in Book 7, the vitalist implications are unmistakable.

> The earth was formed, but in the womb as yet
> Of waters, embryon immature involved,
> Appeared not: over all the face of earth
> Main ocean flowed, not idle, but with warm
> Prolific humour softening all her globe,
> *Fermented the great mother to conceive,*
> Satiate with genial moisture. (7.276–82; italics mine)

The image of a parturient earth giving birth to itself in an act of self-generation is the closest one could get to Harvey's vitalist account of gynocentric generation—generation as a fermentative process.

The crux of the vitalist debate seems to hinge on the question of first causes and the belief in a philosophy of disengaged self-generative continuity. If one looks at representative seventeenth-century writings, such as Van Helmont's extensive discussions of fermentation as the essence of the creative process[20] or Gerard Winstanley's literalization of the "woman's seed" of the Book of Genesis (3:15) in his *Fire in the Bush* as capable of sprouting on its own and flourishing into a tree that can bruise a serpent's head,[21] there is a range of assertions of a vitalist materialism of the second kind that is essentially radical in its formulation of an auto-generative agenda. Endorsing this belief in vitalism, Milton, however, keeps faith in a divine First Cause. The result is that Milton's account of creation throws open the vitalist debate rather than provide a closure. The accounts of creation given by Uriel and Raphael, while admitting a divine First Cause, urge a vitalist infusion of body and spirit with the generative impulse taking on an independent existence. This is most strikingly present in Uriel's account and in Raphael's description of the earth creating itself. To take this a little further, in an epic that engages in a fine balancing of opposites, the paradigm of self-motion and self-generation of material bodies that emerges from Uriel and Raphael's accounts of creation finds its negative image in Milton's chaos where the continuous flux of all the elements in their "pregnant causes mixed" (2.913) has to wait perpetually for divine command—"Unless the almighty maker them ordain / His dark materials to create more worlds" (2.915–16). On the one hand the self-generating and self-moving of good material bodies and on the other the submissive protocol of a volatile chaos.

In *Paradise Lost*, response to the cosmos is one of the ways of defining character. For Chaos, there is no sense of wonder that the new cosmos generates, only deep resentment at what seems to be an encroachment into his territory. For the angels Uriel and Raphael, what matters most is the process of creation, and their accounts reveal not only their great admiration for a spectacular phenomenon but also their scientific attitude, their engagement with creation theory. They are fascinated also with the internal mechanism of the cosmos, in particular celestial movement, and the possibility of multiple worlds. But this is an area of interest with complex implications that reveal significant differences between the angels and will be examined later.[22] Response to the cosmos is also measured in terms of response to cosmic movement and this becomes one of the primary ways of marking the difference between the angelic and the human.

Paradise Lost is an epic with an astonishing number of space flights. The epic poet's own explorations are charted through the invocations. They take him down into the depths of hell, up through the realm of Chaos and Night into heaven, and finally through the new cosmos to earth where he finds firm ground beneath his feet on arriving in Paradise. Outside the hard outer shell of the cosmos, there is Satan's journey from Hell through chaos in search of the newly created world and many angelic flights in the aftermath of the war in heaven. For instance, on the sixth day of creation, Raphael and his band of angels are sent down to the gates of Hell by God to make sure that no evil spirit interrupts the final stages of the creation process. Within the cosmos, there are four space flights that Satan undertakes—his initial plunge from the aperture to the sun, his journey from the sun to Paradise, his seven-day orbit in space between the two temptations, and his journey back to the aperture after the Fall. Uriel's less adventurous but still spectacular two flights gliding down sunbeams to the earth and back to the sun are followed by his flight back to heaven, together with Gabriel and other angels, to report to God on their failed mission. And then there are the space flights undertaken by the powerful angels Raphael and Michael who are sent on special assignment by God. Their space flights take them from heaven to the aperture in the hard outer shell, then through the great spaces of the cosmos to Paradise. All of these flights reveal not only Milton's own fascination with the opening up of cosmic space in the early modern period, but also his perception of the nature of angelic minds and ability. The angels have an awesome power to negotiate infinite space and enormous velocity.

It is precisely this unquantifiable speed that he senses, not in angelic space flights, but in celestial movement, that troubles Adam. Watching the sun, moon, and stars that apparently circle the stationary earth he and Eve inhabit, he seems to suffer from vertigo. He experiences a sense of deep discomfort at the thought of such celestial "speed, to describe whose swiftness number fails" (8.38). Adam's questions to Raphael on the revolution of the spheres, although philosophically centered on the subject of disproportion, yet reveal his deep anxiety about the dizzying movement imposed upon the sun, moon, and stars.

> How nature wise and frugal could commit
> Such disproportions...
> ....and on their orbs *impose*
> Such *restless revolution* day by day
> Repeated. (8.26–27, 30–32; italics mine)

This "incorporeal speed" (8.37) unsettles him. It is almost as if he feels that the sun, moon, planets, and stars are trapped into this diurnal round of unimaginable swiftness. Raphael's interpretation of "the swiftness of those circles" (8.107) as a sign of divine omnipotence that could invest corporeal substances with speed that is spiritual fails to calm Adam's nerves. All the more so as Raphael pointedly refers to the astonishing velocity of his own journey from heaven to Paradise through unfathomable distances:

> Me thou think'st not slow,
> Who since the morning hour set out from heaven
> Where God resides, and ere mid-day arrived
> In Eden, distance inexpressible
> By numbers that have name (8.110–14)

and then goes on to suggest to Adam that the comforting belief in a stationary earth may be a myth and the earth in fact might have three different movements. What about Eve? From the beginning, Eve is as conscious of diurnal movement as Adam, but her curiosity is primarily directed to the need for a witness to justify celestial splendor. The feeling of self-sufficiency that Eve's account of her own creation reveals perhaps insulates her from the fear of uncontrollable cosmic movement and immense cosmic spaces that troubles Adam. Her intensely lyrical account of diurnal movement in Book 4 betrays no anxiety regarding enormous speed, but in Adam's reply there is real urgency as he explains, "Those have their course to finish, round the earth, / By morrow evening" (4.661–62). In the dream temptation that she relates to Adam next morning, Eve experiences the thrill of a space flight although it is abruptly terminated. Perhaps it is this that instills in her a new consciousness of dizzying heights and swiftness similar to that of Adam. As she and Adam pray together the morning after, their words are shot through with a sense of continuous diurnal movement of astonishing velocity. Rising, climbing, falling, meeting, flying, running, circling—the momentum built up by the verbs that shape the text of their prayer imparts a sense of movement, swiftness, and urgency.

There is no doubt that the incredible swiftness of celestial bodies within the cosmos generates greater discomfort in Adam than in Eve and it is possible to see this as an index to character. Milton invests Adam with a more powerful imagination as well as greater sense of stability and responsibility than Eve. This makes Adam more sensitive to great heights and velocity, which inspire anxiety. Adam's alertness to space and time—the "spaces incomprehensible" (8.20) and "incorporeal speed" (8.37) he discusses in his conversation with Raphael—reveals also his sharper intellectual power in contrast with that of Eve for whom diurnal movement within the cosmos is invested with a lyrical charm. Eve, on her part, being by nature self-involved, is less sensitive to cosmic space and velocity until after her experience of an aborted space flight in the first temptation. For Adam and Eve, response to space and to velocity within the cosmos is one of the means of marking differences in their character. Both are passionately moved by the visual appeal of the cosmos they inhabit, its beauty and grandeur, but their human limitations, their negative experiences of stress and discomfort, are revealed through their responses to the cosmos, which contrast sharply with those of the nonhuman participants in the action of the epic. Although there are shades of difference that define their character, unlike Adam and Eve there is a general sense of tremendous exhilaration felt by Satan as well as the good angels in their experience of cosmic movement.

Finally, the careful rearrangement of the compass points and the precision of celestial movement might suggest a purely mechanistic universe. Yet, the cosmos of *Paradise Lost* is an animated one. The energy generated by the incredibly swift movement of celestial bodies hurtling through immense spaces invests it with an extraordinary dynamism. This is enhanced when the accounts of creation inject vitalism into the materials of the cosmos and the narrative configures varying perceptions of space by speculating on the possibility of the stars being worlds. Finally, the cosmos is inhabited not only by Uriel,

Gabriel, and Gabriel's band of angels, but perhaps by other sentient beings, too, whose presence Adam senses.

> Millions of spiritual creatures walk the earth
> Unseen, both when we wake, and when we sleep
> ....how often from the steep
> Of echoing hill or thicket have we heard
> Celestial voices (4.677–78, 680–82)

These multiple presences invest the mechanics of the cosmos with a mystical quality, reminiscent of Plato's *Timaeus*. The animated cosmos of *Paradise Lost* is a constantly moving, evolving entity. It is not just the stage on which the drama of the clash of angels and the Fall of man is enacted, but appears to have a life of its own. The animism and vibrancy of Milton's cosmos is suggestive and enhances its richness, while deliberately stopping short of assigning the cosmos the kind of proactive role that is played by the personified Chaos. For Milton, the process of configuring his cosmos in *Paradise Lost* is the means of defining, rather than creating, character. It is remarkable to what extent their own individual understanding of the most basic cosmic movement—diurnal movement—becomes the means of defining the character of Uriel, Gabriel, and Adam. Diurnal movement within the cosmos brings together a consciousness of space and time, the two parameters that determine the very notion of the cosmos. Milton's engagement with space and time is very specific and evolves out of the many ideas generated by the intellectual ferment of his time that included traditional cosmology as well as the new astronomy.

CHAPTER 5

"The Visible Diurnal Sphere": Space and Time

Within the cosmos of *Paradise Lost*, space and time are not absolute but relative, constructed through the perspectives of individual characters. In the vast region between Heaven and Hell, where Chaos and Night reign, space is an objective reality. The immensity of that region is repeatedly projected through phrases such as "wild abyss" (2.910, 917), "vast vacuity" (2.932), and "wild expanse" (2.1014). The realm of chaos combines the terrifying void of atomism with the endless darkness of Fludd's Night to project a palpable sense of space as immense, unquantifiable, but real. The cosmic spaces of Milton's epic, on the other hand, are dynamic and animated, equally immeasurable and undetermined, but constantly configured and reconfigured. Drawing attention to the intertexture of notions of "space" and "place" in *Paradise Lost*, Maura Brady suggests that Milton's contribution to the understanding of modern space "lies in imagining what it would be like to inhabit a world whose governing physical concept is space."[1] Imagining space in their own individual way, Adam and Eve, Satan, and the angels who make their way through the cosmos contribute to the configuring of space, creating multiple perspectives, projecting space as exhilarating, infinite, and essentially uncertain.

In view of the varied resources Milton draws upon in the invocations and in his depiction of chaos and the cosmos[2]—magic, alchemy, and the new sciences—it is remarkable how, in the innovative details of his depiction of space and time, Milton's imagination seems to have been fired by science alone rather than an amalgam of sources. The new astronomy and mechanics provided him with enough material, often controversial, that enabled him to present a fresh and challenging view of space and time. With his evident interest in cabalism, Milton would have been familiar with the cabalist philosophy of space that percolated through the Lurianic Cabala, Henry More, and Joseph Raphson to Newton.[3] But while this tradition highlighted the Hebrew concept of *maqom* (place) to convey an understanding of infinite space permeated by God, it did define an outer boundary of divine presence within which the whole of creation was contained. If one turns from cabalism to chemical philosophy, alchemical presentations of the cosmos, as in Fludd, are based on a Ptolemaic model. The charts in *Utriusque Cosmi Maioris*, representing the universe, nature, and the arts,[4] show a structured format with an outer boundary of the sphere of the fixed stars. Milton's more fluid universe within the hard outer shell needed a less-structured model for the configuring of space and time. Also, the powerful suggestion of uncertainty inherent in his imaginative concept of a universe contained within a hard outer shell with an aperture on top that barely separates cosmos from chaos—and is in fact breached by Satan, Sin, and Death—would have been lost had he incorporated the traditional diagram of the cosmos with an outer circle of divine presence as in cabalistic, hermetic, and alchemical writings. More congenial for Milton's purposes were the doubts and debates initiated by the new discoveries in astronomy, which released new perceptions of cosmic possibilities. For these reasons, and perhaps because of his specific millenarian agenda, Milton found the dynamic, changing spatial expansion of the new astronomy more relevant and invigorating.

Space within the cosmos, in Milton's epic, is constructed, altered, and expanded through the perspectives of Satan, Raphael, and Adam and Eve. In the early modern period, the understanding of perspective was sharpened by developments in optics. In the mid-sixteenth century, John Dee's *Propaedeumata aphoristica* (1558/1568) and the *Monas hieroglyphica* (1564) had combined optical theories with astrology and magic. Dee's discussion of parallaxes and the behavior of light, his belief that rays are dispersed by both the immanent and the occult, and that the angels traveled to the natural world with the help of rays constituted a prelude to his later angel conversations.[5] The seventeenth century was an age of significant developments in scientific optics leading up to Newton's great work on the subject. Early in the century, in addition to his major contributions in astronomy and mathematics, Kepler experimented in optical theories and Stephen Hawking believes that "the publication in 1611 of his book *Dioptrices*, changed the course of optics."[6] This was followed by investigations with the telescope[7] or the "optic glass" by Galileo, Thomas Harriot, and others, which fired the imagination of poets such as Donne and Milton. After the Restoration, in 1668–69, Isaac

Barrow delivered a set of lectures on optics at Cambridge University, later published as *Optical Lectures* (1669). Newton attended these lectures and had many private discussions with Barrow about optics. Newton's own defining work, *Opticks*, was published in 1704. Although the publications of Barrow and Newton postdate *Paradise Lost*, much of the developing ideas on optics was known well before these publications.[8] Investigations into light and sight had become an exciting field. It is therefore perhaps not surprising that the directing of the gaze—of looking up or down or looking beyond—is a device Milton constantly uses to define and extend the perception of space within the new universe.

Infinite space was not a new discovery of early modern science. As far back as the fifth century BC, Democritus, the disciple of Leucippus, believed that the universe was made up of an infinite number of minute, indivisible, finite bodies or atoms, which moved in a void. "In infinite space, this infinite number of atoms produced an infinite number of worlds, which were subject to continual change."[9] Atomist philosophy, including the belief in infinite space, was given a new, imaginative rendering by Lucretius in the first century BC, and the recovery of the text of *De rerum natura* in 1417[10] ensured its impact on the Renaissance mind. Although Aristotle had argued for a finite universe, rejected the possibility of a void, and attacked the notion of a plurality of worlds, the atomic view of the universe was not forgotten and these issues continued to be debated. The decisive point was reached with the introduction of the Copernican system, which provided compelling reasons for the acceptance of infinite space. When Copernicus put forward his heliocentric hypothesis, however, he did not directly address the question of infinite space. It was in interpretations of the Copernican system by Bruno, Digges, Kepler, and others that infinite space emerged as a necessary corollary to the Copernican hypothesis. Giordano Bruno's perception of infinite space needs to be understood in the context of his belief in atomism. Indeed, Hilary Gatti suggests that the two are interconnected, affirming the existence of an "essential link between Bruno's infinite cosmology and his development of an atomic theory of matter."[11] Unlike Democritus and Epicurus though, for whom the infinite universe was filled by atoms interspersed with empty space, for Bruno the interstices between the infinite numbers of atoms of his infinite space is filled with a substance called "ether." Again, unlike Democritus and Epicurus who contemplate a variety of shapes, all atoms in Bruno's philosophy are circular. These atoms, as Gatti explains, "are seen as each invested with the total power of the infinite cause" and the indivisible, impenetrable atoms touch one another at indivisible distances, making up the forms of the infinite whole.[12] Bruno's atomism, remarkable for its vitality and its portrayal of an animated universe, is the natural counterpart to his belief in infinity. When one looks carefully at the space within Milton's cosmos, it is difficult to avoid the conviction that the animated spaces of his cosmos incorporate and extend Bruno's model. The "pure marble air" (3.564) through which Satan flies during his first exploration of the cosmos and the "vast ethereal sky" (5.267) along which Raphael sails on his way to Paradise are not the daunting empty spaces of atomism. These are the ethereal spaces of traditional cosmology but invested with animism, like that of Bruno, incorporating also the very modern sense of space filled with celestial objects that connect and intersect through light rays.

The philosophy and science of space was a conceptually exciting and evolving field in the intellectual history of the early modern period. However, for those unfamiliar with the intricacies of Renaissance mathematics and astronomy, the connection between the Copernican model and infinite space was not immediately apparent. Copernicus's new diagram of the universe in *De Revolutionibus*, published at the time of his death in 1543, still maintained the overall Aristotelio-Ptolemaic system of concentric spheres while interchanging the position of the earth and the sun—a neat series of concentric circles with a marginal increase in the space between spheres as one moved outward. Also, the diagram retained a circular outer boundary, the sphere of the fixed stars. In visual terms, this comforting stellar zone encircling the universe provided security and definable limits to the universe. Then, in 1576, Thomas Digges, son of almanac maker Leonard Digges and a pupil of John Dee, published an appendix to his father's almanac entitled *A Perfit Description of the Celestial Orbes*[13] in which he argued for the acceptance of the Copernican system and, in support, produced a diagram of the Copernican universe in which, instead of a finite outer circle of stars, the sphere of the fixed stars was extended into infinity. Visually, in the diagram, this sphere stretched to the outer limits of the margins of the page, the stars seemingly spilling over the margins into endless space. Almanacs were an essential tool in the daily lives of people, providing information regarding feast days, the weather, harvesting times, and other essential aspects of everyday life.[14] Digges's almanac and its appendix would have been consulted by people from varied walks of life. Here finally was a work that would have brought to sixteenth-century minds a new consciousness of the possibilities of infinite space. This is perhaps the first published document that visually impressed the idea of infinity implicit in Copernicus.

Response to the possibility of infinite space in late sixteenth- and seventeenth-century Britain was complicated by the association of this idea with the controversial figure of Giordano Bruno.[15] As with John Dee, Bruno was admired by some as scientist and Copernican, but despised by others as charlatan and imposter, and viewed with suspicion by many as cabalist and hermetic magus. However, acknowledging Bruno's contribution to science, Stephen Hawking credits "Giordano Bruno, an Italian scientist and avowed Copernican," with being the person "who suggested that space might have no boundaries and that the solar system might be one of many such systems in the universe."[16] Renaissance scholars, including Frances Yates, have generally regarded Bruno primarily as an occult philosopher.[17] However, in a searching examination of the many aspects of the life and career of Bruno, Hilary Gatti has tried to disentangle Bruno from an exclusive identification as Hermetic magus and emphasize his scientific interests. But she has also drawn attention to the importance of Bruno for Henry Percy, ninth earl of Northumberland, named the "wizard earl," and his three "magi," the astronomer Thomas Harriot, the mathematician Walter Warner, and the geographer Robert Hues, an association that contributed to the doubts and questions about Bruno's genuine scientific interests. Giordano Bruno visited England between 1583 and 1585 and is credited with introducing the idea of infinite homogenous space. He came into close contact with Sir Philip Sidney, Fulke Greville, and others and may have encouraged their speculations about infinite space. The Sidney circle, as well as Marlowe, also had known links with the Northumberland circle. Bruno's advocacy for infinite space was connected with his belief in the controversial notion of a plurality of worlds. This, as well as Bruno's links with the Northumberland circle, help to explain why the concept of infinite space he advocated became a somewhat risqué, though familiar, subject in the late sixteenth and early seventeenth centuries. At the risk of oversimplification, one might argue that the notion of infinity implicit in Copernicus was made explicit in philosophical terms by Bruno and rendered through a mathematical visual image by Digges. Milton's portrayal of infinite space in his epic may not rely on any one of these specific sources, but shares common ground with them to a remarkable extent. Bruno's occult philosophy had provided him with a discourse of empowerment that could be fashioned into a benchmark of achievement in the epic invocations, only to be eventually rejected. His Copernicanism, on the other hand, encouraged cosmic possibilities

that Milton found more congenial. The cosmos of *Paradise Lost*, as
the earlier chapter has shown, is clearly an animated one that might be
said to reflect the version of atomism one finds in Bruno. However,
there is also a remarkable clarity of vision in Milton's representation of
infinity, which is reminiscent of Digges.
Paradise Lost incorporates this early modern excitement regard-
ing infinite space. And, writing nearly a century after Digges, Milton
adds to the consciousness of space the dynamism of an expanding
universe. The experience of spatial expansion is an integral part of our
understanding of the mechanism of the new cosmos of *Paradise Lost*.
This is first presented through Satan's visual exploration. Standing
on the lowest step of the golden staircase that links the new cosmos
to heaven, Satan

> Looks down with wonder at the sudden view
> Of all this world at once…
> Round he surveys, and well might, where he stood
> So high above the circling canopy
> Of night's extended shade; from eastern point
> Of Libra to the fleecy star that bears
> Andromeda far off Atlantic seas
> Beyond the horizon; then from pole to pole
> He views in breadth. (3.542–43, 555–61)

The sense of distance created by "looking down" is checked by "sud-
den," a word that carries the impact of Satan's amazement at this awe-
some visual encounter. The next moment "view" widens the range of
vision. These verbal devices constantly changing perspective bring in
a sense of space. Remembering that Milton presents his universe as
being on its side, Satan's visual trajectory extends first down into the
depths of the universe from east to west, and then along the breadth
of the universe from north to south. Entering the cosmos at mid-
night, when Libra would be at the east, his eye follows the constel-
lations Aries and Andromeda as they move west beyond and to the
other side of the earth. He then examines the universe from side to
side, from north to south. Since creation took place after the fall of
the angels, this is Satan's first view of the new cosmos. The changes
in visual perspective, involving constant adjustment of Satan's eye in
his exploration of "all this world," convey a sense of space. "Far off"
and "beyond" do suggest extension of that space, but not infinite
space. Satan's visual exploration establishes the immensity of the cos-
mos, but infinite space has to wait for a more dramatic moment of
discovery.

The astronomical image most effective in creating a feeling of infinite space and an expanding universe in *Paradise Lost* is the image of stars as worlds.[18] The idea of the plurality of worlds had fired the imagination of other seventeenth-century poets also. In "Donne the Space Man," William Empson points out that Donne "was interested in getting to another planet—he brought the idea into practically all his best love-poems."[19] As Empson shows, Donne's excitement about the subject comes out through his play upon words such as "world" and "sphere." In the lines in *The Good-Morrow*, "Let sea-discoverers to new worlds have gone, / Let Maps to others, worlds on worlds have showne, / Let us possess one world, each hath one, and is one," the maps are star-globes with the planets and stars, the "worlds on worlds," marked on them.[20] One finds in the "worlds" here adventure and discovery, but the spatial expansion cannot quite come off since the "worlds" are there only in maps. The cosmic dimension and dramatic structure of Milton's epic makes a different kind of treatment of this idea possible. As Satan and Raphael undertake their great cosmic voyages approaching the new universe, and traveling within it toward Paradise, their speculative gaze examines, experiences, conjectures, and imaginatively extends the space within the cosmos.

In *Paradise Lost*, the idea also inspires a special kind of word play, which helps to create a tremendous sense of space. This can be seen particularly in three passages where the stars/worlds comparison occurs. The first of these is the astronomical image describing the universe as first seen by Satan at the end of his journey through chaos. "Fast by hanging in a golden chain / This pendant world, in bigness as a star / Of smallest magnitude close by the moon" (2.1051–53). The immediate effect is a sense of wonder as Satan suddenly discovers the new universe. The main point of the image is the comparison of the world to a star beside the moon. It is an image in which a whole is being compared to a part of itself—the universe to a single star—a process that is reversed in later descriptions of Satan and of Raphael sailing between the stars as sailing between "worlds." The comparison is double-edged. First of all, it achieves a great reduction in size. The whole universe, which contains mankind, the earth, the sun, moon, planets, and stars, is, from one point of view, no bigger than a star in the night sky. At the same time, a star is really immense in size, so that, although visually reductive for the moment, the image keeps alive simultaneously the possibility of immense enlargement. This is partly achieved by the juxtaposition of "magnitude" with "smallest" since one normally associates "magnitude" with great rather than small size. In astronomy, "magnitude" also has the technical meaning of "degree of brightness" according to which stars can be arranged. From that point of view, again, "smallest magnitude" has a reductive effect. The splendor of the sudden vision of the universe hanging like a star from the golden chain—so dazzling to the eye after the journey through chaos—is diminished by its being of comparatively inferior luminosity. Perhaps it is only right that to a fallen archangel, still retaining his memories of Heaven, the new universe should seem to be no more than an inferior star. The richness of this astronomical image derives from the complex wordplay in the passage: the clash of bigness/smallest/magnitude, the self-infolding of world into star, and the simultaneous expansion of star into world. Helen Gardner in *A Reading of "Paradise Lost"* commented on the continual swing between the precise and the vague, the measurable and the immeasurable, in Milton's presentation of the universe.[21] It is perhaps more true to speak of not a continual swing between the measurable and the immeasurable but a continual dissolving of the apparent contradictions between the two, so that it might be quite valid to speak of the world as at once "spaces incomprehensible" and a definable area circumscribed by a pair of compasses.

Three space fights within the universe are described in detail in *Paradise Lost*. They are Satan's initial exploration of the universe in Book 3, Raphael's journey to Eden in Book 5, and Satan's seven-day orbit in space in Book 9. In the first of these, Satan

> Down right into the World's first region throws
> His flight precipitant, and winds with ease
> Through the pure marble air his oblique way
> Among innumerable stars, that shone
> Stars distant, but nigh hand seemed other worlds,
> Or other worlds they seemed, or happy isles. (3.562–67)

In the second, Raphael "Down thither prone in flight / He speeds, and through the vast ethereal sky / Sails between worlds and worlds" (5.266–68). In the two passages Milton is not simply handling a potentially explosive issue, the possibility of a plurality of worlds. He is using an idea that the astronomy of the early modern period had provided him with and expressing that idea through a particular form of wordplay in order to create a sense of tremendous space. It is the close juxtaposition of "worlds" and "worlds" in both passages that is responsible for the effect. In both passages there is the multiplication of worlds within worlds. It is the simultaneous magnification of an object as at the same time a world and a star and the multiple presence of such objects within the universe that suddenly enlarges the space involved.

There is a significant difference in technique between the two passages. The earlier passage is the first description of the inside of the universe. Here the effect of the stars as worlds is directly related to Satan. It is he who sees them as such, and indeed the two "worlds" are played off against each other with a sense of wonder generated by personal encounter. "Seemed other worlds, / Or other worlds they seemed"—there is remarkable felicity in the way the two statements are constructed so that "worlds" faces "worlds." There is first excitement at the seeming appearance of other worlds followed by hesitation as the line-ending supported by the comma invites us to pause. But immediately the excitement is repeated in the next line with "Or other worlds" and indeed repeated with a heightened sense of awareness that comes out through the special emphasis on "seemed" in this line, an emphasis that "seemed" in the previous line does not have. By the time we reach the second passage, the immensity of the universe is an accepted fact. And yet at that point in the narrative Raphael, standing at heaven's gate, sees through the aperture in the shell not only earth and Paradise but even the cedars growing in Paradise. Angelic vision thus effects a sudden reduction of space. But almost at once the immeasurability of this, for a time, limited universe is stressed with Raphael moving "between worlds and worlds."

There is a clear line of development in these three passages. In the first, the "pendent world" is *like* a star; in the second, the stars are *like* worlds; in the third, the stars *are* worlds. This seems to be deliberate poetic strategy. Each passage reaches across to the next. We move from the astronomer's observation, which gives us the image of the world as a star, to the astronomer's speculations, which give us the image of stars as worlds, to the astronomer's theoretical assertion of the stars as worlds. In doing so, we move progressively into an imaginative sense of an expanding universe.

The complexities of Milton's presentation of multiple worlds and infinite space need to be clearly understood. Raphael's construction of infinite space through the stars/worlds analogy may be read in the context of the suggestion that such a perception comes with divine sanction. In their song of praise after the six days of creation, the angels call attention to the possibility of multiple worlds:

> Witness this new-made world, another heaven
> From heaven gate not far, founded in view
> On the clear hyaline, the glassy sea;

> Of amplitude almost immense, with stars
> Numerous, and every star perhaps a world
> Of destined habitation. (7.617–22)

Perhaps the stars are worlds and perhaps those worlds will one day be inhabited. Multiple worlds, here, is a sign of divine omnipotence. By projecting the possibility of plural *inhabited* worlds into a foreseeable future, and not as part of the present, Milton skillfully avoids the theological debates regarding multiple worlds. It is understood in heaven that the stars might in fact be worlds that will one day be inhabited and it is this knowledge that Raphael brings with him. A notion acknowledged as controversial in the early modern period is at the same time being invested with legitimacy. For Satan, this is not shared knowledge but conjecture and reveals his imaginative and intellectual strength. And embedded in the Satanic conjecture is a suggestive phrase—"other worlds they seemed, *or happy isles*" (3.567; italics mine)—that seems to hint at the radical possibility of those other worlds as already inhabited. Also, multiple worlds is a possibility both within the cosmos and outside it. The matter of chaos, we are told, can provide God "His dark materials to create more worlds" (2.915–16). Presumably these would one day be new cosmoses, like the "pendent world" in which the Fall of man is about to take place. Radical as this might seem in the early modern context, it is still less problematic than the notion of multiple worlds within the cosmos. This is because Milton creates a universe with a finite outer boundary—the hard shell—and yet explores the possibilities of infinite space within it through the stars/worlds analogies. The precision and clarity of Milton's imagination urged him to enfold the epic action of his poem within a definable cosmic stage to ensure narrative coherence. At the same time, his fascination with the new ideas thrown up by the new astronomy led him to explore the challenging possibilities of infinite space. The concept of multiple worlds becomes, for Milton, one of the ways of engaging with seventeenth-century debate and also one of the tools for defining character in *Paradise Lost*.

The projections of infinite space in the stars/worlds passages arise out of visual explorations made by Satan and Raphael. Satan's enquiring gaze is fueled by curiosity and guided by his diabolical intelligence. Reminding us of the scientifically advanced prediction he had made early in the epic—"Space may produce new worlds" (1.650)—before he had any knowledge about the new cosmos, Satan's speculative feel of the stars as worlds significantly enlarges the space within the cosmos. Raphael, too, contributes to the sense of infinite space and an expanding universe by regarding the stars as worlds, although, in the passage presenting him sailing between "worlds and worlds," there is no clear individual optical contribution that he makes to the construction of the stars as worlds. He creates a sense of infinite space not through visual experience, but through a projection of knowledge. His confident belief in the stars as worlds makes a greater impact than Satanic speculation. Raphael's visual contribution to the creation of the immensity of space is to be found elsewhere in the epic, in his perception of distances, the distance between the gates of heaven and Paradise and the distances within the cosmos. In Book 8 he impresses on Adam the immensity of the physical distance between heaven and earth through the measure of time:

> Me thou think'st not slow,
> Who since the morning hour set out from heaven
> Where God resides, and ere mid-day arrived
> In Eden, distance inexpressible
> By numbers that have name. (8.110–14)

If it took the winged angel half a day to cover the distance from heaven's gate, past the golden chain, into the aperture and through cosmic spaces to Adam's bower in Paradise, the distances must be immense. At the time when he had set out, the earth and other cosmic spheres had appeared to him to be "small" (5.258) because of the great distance. In Book 5, Raphael's awareness of the immensity of space is underlined by the interwoven reference to "the glass / Of Galileo" (5.261–62), the telescope, recognized in the seventeenth century as an essential tool for negotiating vast cosmic distances. As Raphael looks down at the earth, he is compared with Galileo looking at the moon through his telescope. To this extent, Raphael's gaze is as important, operationally, as Satan's, in creating a sense of space.

However, in spite of these similarities between Satan and Raphael, their perceptions of space reveal diametrically opposite intentions. In so far as the extensions of space are the result of Satanic perspective, the attempt seems to be to demolish distinctions and integrate the new cosmos into a seamless fabric of space that includes chaos too. It was in the middle of chaos that Satan had seen this "pendent world" (2.1052) appearing like a "star / Of smallest magnitude" (2.1052–53). Within the cosmos, he sees the "innumerable stars" (3.565) that look like "other worlds" (3.566). This reversal has a sinister suggestiveness as it appears to blur and erase the distinction between what lies within the opaque shell of the cosmos and what lies outside. Satan's opening up of space through the possibilities of multiple worlds thus subverts the orderliness of the cosmos. It also constitutes an invasion of space that makes the complex intertexture of space in the poem at once exhilarating, expansive, liberating, and at the same time open to tragic possibilities. The image of Raphael sailing "between worlds and worlds" has implications of a different kind. Raphael's sight is more "assured" than that of Galileo, his flight path through the ethereal sky controlled and steady, and his understanding of the stars as worlds is positive and compelling. The crucial differences between Raphael and Satan need to be clearly stated. To Satan, the entire cosmos suspended in chaos had appeared to be like a star, and so when the stars seem to him to be like worlds the entire analogy is fraught with anxiety as it brings with it associated resonances of chaos. Raphael's perception of the stars as worlds, on the contrary, expands and extends the richness of the cosmos, pushing chaos further back.

One of the crucial factors that engages Milton's attention in *Paradise Lost* is angelic eyesight. Joad Raymond cites two alternative theories of vision of the early modern period—the extromissive theory of vision, which suggested that the eyes emit rays that are reflected by objects and return to the eye, and the intromissive theory, which argued that "the eye saw by apprehending light that was reflected from objects and return to the eye."[22] He makes the point that Satan's fall has not diminished his eyesight. In Book 1 Satan's eyes that "sparkling blazed" (1.194) emitting light are directed in a survey that takes in the wide expanse of hell. Cast down from heaven, visual knowledge is indeed one of his key resources and it is remarkable with what frequency he is asked to direct his gaze. Having made his first survey of the new cosmos through the aperture, almost in the manner of an astronomer looking through a telescope, Satan makes his way to Uriel in the guise of a cherub and conveys to him his "Unspeakable desire to *see*, and know / All these his wondrous works" (3.662–63; italics mine). He asks Uriel to show him the way to the seat of man "That I may find him, and with secret *gaze*, / Or open admiration him *behold*" (3.671–72; italics mine). In reply, Uriel commends just this desire "To *witness with thine eyes* what some perhaps / Contented with report hear only in heaven" (3.700–701; italics mine). Uriel, himself the sharpest-sighted angel, privileges the sense of sight over hearing. In *Paradise Lost*, it is remarkable to what extent Satan looks and thinks with his eyes. At the end of Book 4, Gabriel will ask Satan to "look up" (4.1010) at Libra, Satan will comply and will then begin his seven-day journey in darkness. Presumably, while looking up, he sees the dark cone of night above Paradise, conjectures that that would be the safest place to hide from the sun and from Uriel, and flies into it. Earlier, flying through the air on his way toward the sun, his searching gaze had picked out the stars and speculated on their being "other worlds" (3.566) but he did not stay to investigate further as the sun "allured his eye" (3.573). Arriving there,

> Here matter new to gaze the devil met
> Undazzled, far and wide his eye commands,
> For sight no obstacle found here, nor shade,
> But all sunshine, as when his beams at noon
> Culminate from the equator, as they now
> Shot upward still direct, whence no way round
> Shadow from body opaque can fall, and the air,
> No where so clear, sharpened his visual ray
> To objects distant far. (3.613–21)

Light and sight come together in this remarkable moment of viewing as Satan's eyes are not blinded by the sun and in fact, for clarity of sight, he needs, like human eyesight, "all sunshine" and no clouds. This, indeed, seems to be a requirement for angelic eyesight. In Book 5, as Raphael looks out from the gates of heaven toward Paradise, he is able to see clearly because there are no clouds. Milton further imagines him to be looking through interstellar space

> From hence, no cloud, or, to obstruct his sight,
> Star interposed, however small he sees,
> Not unconform to other shining globes,
> Earth and the garden of God, with cedars crowned
> Above all hills. (5.257–61)

Raphael's situation is strikingly similar to that of Satan looking through the aperture in Book 3. For both, it is telescopic vision, as the comparison with Galileo's telescope in Book 5 suggests. Both Satan and Raphael's viewing of the new cosmos from their respective vantage points are compelling statements about the immensity of cosmic space revealed by the telescope.

Adam and Eve's consciousness of space is related to celestial movement and to time. This becomes apparent in their conversation (4.657 ff.) regarding the function of the sun, moon, and stars at night, their morning prayers (5.153 ff.), and in Adam's troubled questions to Raphael (8.13ff.) about the disproportion of the stars and planets moving in "restless revolution" around "the sedentary earth" (8.31–32). Their consciousness of space is God-centered and earth-centered, firmly based on a belief in order, and limited to this one world. But from their position in Paradise, they can sense the immensity of the cosmos. As Adam explains to Raphael,

> When I behold this goodly frame, this world
> Of heaven and earth consisting, and compute
> Their magnitudes, this earth a spot, a grain,
> An atom, with the firmament compared
> And all her numbered stars, that seem to roll
> Spaces incomprehensible (for such
> Their distance argues and their swift return
> Diurnal) merely to officiate light
> Round this opacous earth, this punctual spot,
> One day and night. (8.15–24)

He is unable to quantify the "incorporeal speed" (8.37) with which the sun and the stars complete their diurnal cycle. But, without entering into speculations about multiple worlds, human perception of "spaces incomprehensible" does create a sense of infinity within the cosmos.

While Adam and Eve configure space and time in terms of celestial movement, for them, too, sight is of critical importance. As night descends and moonlight and starlight fill Paradise, Eve questions Adam about the function of the moon and stars: "But wherefore all night long shine these, for whom / This glorious sight, when sleep hath shut all eyes?" (4.657–58). Part of Adam's answer addresses the question of sight. He explains to Eve the life-generating power of the sun and stars and then continues,

> These then, though unbeheld in deep of night,
> Shine not in vain, nor think, though men were none,
> That heaven would want spectators, God want praise;
> Millions of spiritual creatures walk the earth
> Unseen, both when we wake, and when we sleep:
> All these with ceaseless praise his works behold. (4.674–79)

The critical significance of the difference between "unbeheld" and "behold" is signaled by the urgency with which Adam argues that the moon and stars are viewed by others, even though the human pair and the birds and animals of Paradise may be asleep. It is almost as if their very existence depends upon a need to be perceived.

For Adam and Eve, then, their understanding of space is related to their perception of time, and both derive from their visual experience of the sun, moon, and stars in their diurnal course. The story of the Fall of Man in Milton's epic shares with other mythic narratives a sense of eternity. As the earliest part of human history, the narrative exists in time. But, as a mythic story, it has a timeless quality as a whole although separate events exist within definable moments. The story of the Fall thus invites us to think of a double time scheme including both eternal and sequential time. Within the particular structure of Milton's poem another aspect of time can be noticed. The new universe, where the greater part of the direct action of the epic takes place, is suspended between the eternity of heaven and the timelessness of Hell and Chaos (where "time and place are lost" [2.894]). In the new universe there is no annual movement of time. The sun is fixed in Aries and it is eternal spring in Paradise. In sharp contrast to this, there is a very real sense of diurnal movement. Eve's question to Adam as to why the moon and stars shine when all are asleep is prefaced by a lyrical rendering of the diurnal cycle that moves from the song of birds at sunrise, to the play of sunlight on fields, trees, fruits, and flowers during the day, to a gentle sunset, to the moon and stars and the nightingale's song at night. Adam's reply, explaining the movement of the moon and stars, encapsulates the diurnal course that Eve's description had dwelt upon in detail: "Those have their course to finish, round the earth / By morrow evening" (4.661–62). Later, Adam tells Raphael in words that convey both his sense of the immensity of space and the diurnal movement of time: "We have yet large day, for scarce the sun / Hath finished half his journey, and scarce begins / His other half in the great zone of heaven" (5.558–60). In spite of this consciousness of diurnal movement, there is, in Adam and Eve, a sense of timelessness. To them the "diurnal round" exists, but exists as part of an eternal cycle—after all, there is also the "change delectable" (5.629) of evening and morning in Heaven. This perception of time may have its metaphysical roots in Plato's *Timaeus*, which examines the question of time and its measurement and defines time as "an eternal moving image of the eternity which remains for ever at once."[23] Time originated at the moment of creation and its visible embodiments are the heavenly bodies. When Plotinus interpreted the *Timaeus* passage in the *Enneads*, he argued that while the soul and intellect are derived from the One, the soul produces the world and time is a characteristic of the world. The soul's contemplation of the intellect expresses itself in a movement that is a fragmentation. "Time is the life of soul in the movement of passage from one mode of life to

another."[24] Into the Platonic continuum of time, Plotinus thus intro-
duced the idea of fragmentation and fundamental change. In spite
of this, the perception of time in the Platonic tradition maintained
overall the image of time as an expression of eternity. In Aristotle,
the universe is intrinsically eternal and time within it is measured by
motion. The Renaissance, with its prevailing Platonism, contested the
Aristotelian position but the general belief was that time is measured
by the movement of celestial bodies and therefore belonged to the
created universe. It is this image of time that is incorporated into
Adam and Eve's initial perception of time in *Paradise Lost.* For St.
Augustine, time began with creation, not before, and, as such, there
is no time in heaven,[25] but, as R. D. Bedford pointed out, Milton
deviated from the Augustinian tradition in presenting the existence
of time prior to creation.[26] In Raphael's account,

> As yet this world was not, and Chaos wild
> Reigned where these heavens now roll, where earth now rests
> Upon her centre poised, when on a day
> (For time, though in eternity, applied
> To motion, measures all things durable
> By present, past, and future) on such day
> As heaven's great year brings forth...(5.577–583)

Perhaps, as Bedford suggests, "in *Paradise Lost*, a timeless stasis
before the Creation would make action utterly intractable, eliminat-
ing or rendering inconceivable of execution any dramatic or narrative
possibilities depending upon suspense, movement, and sequence."[27]

In the seventeenth century, both the Platonic and the Aristotelian
assumptions were significantly altered by the work of Galileo and
Newton. Stephen Hawking has identified two basic factors respon-
sible for this change.[28] One of these is the revolution in observation
introduced by the telescope and the other the new laws of motion.
Time acquired a dimension of relativity and, with it, a new sense of
urgency. Newton's laws of motion may have been formulated after
the composition of *Paradise Lost*, but the range of ideas on which
they were based were in circulation much earlier, and Newton drew
upon the fundamental work done by Galileo to which Milton and
his contemporaries had access. Galileo's work was well-known in
contemporary Britain. An early seventeenth-century treatise such as
Galileo's *Sidereus Nuncius* was avidly read not only by mathematicians
in Britain but also by poets such as John Donne.[29] As knowledge of
these new developments was absorbed into the intellectual life of the

times, it initiated a fundamental change in the existing world picture. As Michael S. Mahoney explains, "during the seventeenth century the world became a machine, and mechanics became the mathematical science of motion...The world machine of the late seventeenth century could be comprehensible and yet transcendental."[30] Milton, for whom mathematics was a passion, would have understood this. It is this change of perception that provides the basis for a different sense of urgency and consciousness of diurnal movement that is felt very keenly at the two points of crisis in the narrative, the first and second temptations.

In the prelapsarian universe of *Paradise Lost* the ecliptic and the equator coincide, and days and nights are of equal length, 12 hours each. In this astronomical system the sun apparently circles the universe. As it does so, it creates two astronomical phenomena by which the passing of time can be accurately measured. First, the rays of the sun striking the earth from various angles act like the hands of a clock. Second, the sun being larger than the earth, a conical shadow of the earth is cast on the side away from the sun. As the sun circles the universe, so does the cone. The effect, again, is like that of a gigantic marker of exact time, the negative image of a dark sundial. Time is related to motion. In *Paradise Lost*, the movement of the sun, moon, and stars across the sky marks the passing of time in the new universe. The movement of these stellar objects, however, merely indicates in a general way the part of day or night such as morning or evening. But the marking of definite hours such as six and nine is achieved by the two images of the cone of night and the moving sunbeams.

Satan, after his close observation of Adam and Eve in Book 4, withdraws with the ominous "live while ye may" for "long woes are to succeed" (4.533–35). Between Satan's threat to man and the first temptation, there is the marking of definite hours by means of astronomical images. The first of these fixes the exact time:

> Meanwhile in utmost longitude, where heaven
> With earth and ocean meets, the setting sun
> Slowly descended, and with right aspect
> Against the eastern gate of Paradise
> Levelled his evening rays. (4.539–43)

The rays of the sun strike the vertical gates of Paradise at right angles. The position of the sun is at the exact midpoint between its place at noon and at midnight. The time is now six o'clock. This is further supported by the image that follows: "Thither came Uriel,

gliding through the even / On a sun beam, swift as a shooting star"
(4.555–56). As Empson points out, there is a pun here on *even*—
"the angel is sliding, choosing a safe gradient, down a nearly *even*
sunbeam."[31] By the time Uriel finishes his conversation with Gabriel,
the sun has set so that its rays now point upward to the earth.

> Uriel to his charge
> Returned on that bright beam, whose point now raised
> Bore him slope downward to the sun now fallen
> Beneath the Azores. (4.589–92)

Six o'clock, the hour of twilight, has just passed.

Twilight is a critical hour in Paradise. In the epic, there are three
versions of twilight. At the two extremes are the "grateful twilight"
(5.645) of Heaven and the "disastrous twilight" (1.597) of Hell,
though the latter is present only by association through an image. In
between, there are the descriptions of twilight upon earth. Twilight
is that time when light and darkness upon earth are held, for a brief
period, in a difficult balance. The power of the twilight image derives
from the sense of precariousness generated by the dynamic time-
scheme of the poem. Twilight, as part of continuous diurnal move-
ment, is a transient phase. And so it is at one point described as "short
arbiter / Twixt day and night" (9. 50).

Night comes to Paradise and Adam and Eve fall asleep. As we wait
for the next phase of the action, again the exact time is accurately
marked. This time it is done by the circling cone of night. "Now
had night measured with her shadowy cone / Half way up hill this
vast sublunar vault" (4.776–77). As Alastair Fowler points out, the
cone would reach the meridian at midnight.[32] Now it is only half-
way up. The time is nine o'clock. Gabriel and his legion now begin
their search for Satan. When they ultimately find him, engaged in the
first temptation, the time is midnight. This is indicated by the fact
that Libra, whose position is just opposite the sun and in the cone of
night, is now directly overhead. Gabriel and Satan have to look up to
see Libra. And Libra reaches the zenith at midnight.

Satan thus leaves immediately after midnight. Six hours now remain
before sunrise and, as Satan flees, the shades of night also begin to
flee. The image of the shades of night fleeing becomes clearer when
we remember that the cone of night is the darkest part of the uni-
verse. This cone was above Paradise at midnight. As Satan leaves, the
cone of night also moves (indeed, Satan moves with the cone for the
next three days) and the shades of darkness continue to cross through

Paradise for the next six hours. *Shades* then would be a pun meaning not only shadows but also the various degrees of darkness from midnight to sunrise.

Six o'clock, the exact hour of sunrise, is again carefully marked. In Book 5, Adam and Eve, after discussing Eve's dream, come out for morning prayers. At that time one can see "The sun, who scarce up risen / With wheels yet hovering o'er the ocean brim, / Shot parallel to the earth his dewy ray" (5.139–41). The time is six o'clock in the morning and this passage is "parallel" to the one in Book 4, which describes twilight at six o'clock.

In the 12-hour period that contains the first temptation, the passing of time is thus clearly marked. Seven days intervene between the two temptations. The passing of time during these seven days is again marked astronomically in the description of Satan's orbit in space in Book 9.[33]

> The space of seven continued nights he rode
> With darkness, thrice the equinoctial line
> He circled, four times crossed the car of Night
> From pole to pole, traversing each colure. (9.63–66)

Here again Satan's three circlings along the equinoctial line in darkness—three journeys around the earth in which Satan keeps within the cone of night—and the four specific crossings of the cone (here called the "car of night") along the colures indicate the movement of time. Significantly, in *Paradise Lost,* Satan's movements in the universe exist within a framework of sequential time. In contrast with Adam and Eve's sense of time as the diurnal cycle, for Satan the reality of time is not simply diurnal movement but the marking of definite hours. The intrusion of Satan into Paradise is itself the intrusion of time into eternity, a new perception of finite time with an urgency of its own. The associations of time with mutability, tragedy, and termination are introduced through the experience of definite hours after Satan's entry into Paradise. There are numerous descriptions of continuous diurnal movement in *Paradise Lost.* But the marking of definite hours in relation to this movement through the images of the moving sunbeams and the cone of night take place only between Satan's first threat to man and his second and final temptation.

Indeed, the corruption of eternity into time may be considered one of the consequences of the Fall and this is prefigured in the ominous marking of specific hours between the time of Satan's entry into

Paradise and the second and final temptation. Commenting on "the fluidity of unfallen temporal boundaries," Amy Boesky points out that "one consequence of the Fall for Adam and Eve's experience of temporality is that time begins to be felt as a measure in a new way."[34] In postlapsarian Paradise, the burden of time configured as "fruitless hours" (9.1188) marks a new consciousness of the computation of time and the relation of time to productivity.

The time/eternity equation so central to the cosmos of *Paradise Lost*, and the precise but symbolic astronomical clock that Milton conceptualizes to mark time in Paradise, might remind us of Marvell's *The Garden*:

> How well the skilful gardener drew
> Of flowers and herbs this dial new,
> Where from above the milder sun
> Does through a fragrant zodiac run;
> And, as it works, the industrious bee
> Computes its time as well as we (ll.65–70)[35]

with its play on time and eternity. It is useful also to remember the long history of astronomical clocks and the excitement generated by the more prominent ones in the early modern period. One example of such interest is Sir Stephen Powle's account of the astronomical clock at Strasbourg. The great astronomical clock at Strasbourg Cathedral, one of the largest astronomical clocks in Europe, was first built in 1352 but failed to function 150 years later. A new clock for the cathedral was commissioned in 1547 but was delayed because of the Catholic controversy. Finally, the new clock, designed by Conrad Dasypodius, a professor of mathematics at Strasbourg and son of a humanist and lexicographer, and built by the Habrecht bothers, became operational in 1574. It incorporated the most advanced scientific knowledge of the time in astronomy, mathematics, and physics.[36] Sir Stephen Powle, chancery official and friend of Sir Walter Raleigh, found himself in Strasbourg in 1581 in the course of his travels in Europe. On June 20, 1581 he wrote a letter to William West, one of the clerks of chancery, and enclosed a copy of it in a letter to his father.[37] In the letter, in the course of a detailed and admiring account of this "rare devise," the Strasbourg Cathedral astronomical clock, Powle also paused to philosophize and cite Aristotle:

> Tyme is figured by the heavenly globe; for as by the one wee knowe
> the revolution of the moveable yeare, so by the other wee discerne

the distinction of all motion, for the philosophers define tyme to be *mensura motus*. Before the heavens were created there was no naturall motion, and, by that reason, there would be no *mensura motus*.[38]

The intricate details that so fascinated Powle, and the impetus to philosophize that such clocks encouraged, show the natural alignments between mechanics and metaphysics in the late sixteenth and seventeenth centuries. Milton's astronomical clock in *Paradise Lost* needs to be understood in that context.

The clarity with which, in *Paradise Lost*, Milton presents spatial expansion into infinity on the one hand, and the erosion of eternity by time on the other needs to be looked at in the context of two factors—Milton's own sense of political isolation and mid-seventeenth-century disappointment at the failure of the promised millennium. The exhilarating explorations of infinite space in the epic are a contrast to Milton's own experience of constraints and denial of ideological space. In the invocation in Book 7 he charts his descent from heaven with the help of Urania:

> Up led by thee
> Into the heaven of heavens I have presumed,
> An earthly guest, and drawn empyreal air,
> Thy tempering; with like safety guided down
> Return me to my native element...
> Half yet remains unsung, but narrower bound
> Within the visible diurnal sphere;
> Standing on earth, not rapt above the pole,
> More safe I sing with mortal voice, unchanged
> To hoarse or mute, though fallen on evil days,
> On evil days though fallen, and evil tongues;
> In darkness, and with dangers compassed round,
> And solitude. (7.12–16, 21–28)

The invocation records Milton's personal sense of claustrophobia, of a shrinkage of meaningful space. He finds himself "In darkness, and with dangers compassed round, / And solitude" (7.27–28). As narrator, he has experienced the exhilaration of open spaces in his flight up to heaven from the lowest depths of hell in the opening books of the epic, and then in the rendering of infinite space and multiple worlds within the cosmos. Now, returning to earth, his "native element," he considers himself safer in his familiar earthbound world. Yet the very fact of rejoicing at finding firm ground beneath his feet, however reassuring, has its own diabolic analogue. Such had been the sense of relief felt by Satan, too, in Book 3, as he landed on the hard outer shell of the cosmos after his journey from hell in search of the new world. The Satanic analogue provides a subtext for Milton's sense of having

> fallen on evil days,
> On evil days though fallen, and evil tongues;
> In darkness, and with dangers compassed round,
> And solitude. (7.25–28)

In the epic narrative, Satan's invasion of space had been felt by Milton as an intrusive presence. The invocation translates that into the condition of pre-Restoration Britain. The experience of defeat makes Milton conscious of his extreme solitariness, the claustrophobic awareness of being surrounded by hostile presences sharpened by his feeling of political isolation. Not surprisingly, he finds the "visible diurnal sphere" (7.22) to be "narrower bound" (7.21). Again the lines find a disturbing echo in Eve's complaint to Adam of finding the experience of being in Paradise one in which, perhaps as a result of her space flight with Satan in the dream temptation, she feels herself to be "in narrow circuit straightened" (9.323) by an enemy, which itself is a perversion of Milton's description of Paradise as "a narrow room" (4.207) in which nature's whole wealth is to be found. *Paradise Lost* reverberates with such highly charged metaphors of space.

For Milton, time is as heavily loaded with political and personal implications as space in *Paradise Lost*. In the invocation in Book 9 Milton fears that his epic might fail because of three factors:

> Higher argument
> Remains, sufficient of it self to raise
> That name, unless an age too late, or cold
> Climate, or years damp my intended wing. (9.42–45)

Time is felt here as an oppressive presence—the age of the world, with decay at its core but the millennium not yet at hand, and his own advancing years, which might jeopardize the completion of his work. This double betrayal creates a sense of belatedness for a project perhaps too long delayed in "long choosing and beginning late."

Milton's construction of space and time within the new universe of his epic draws upon the resources of metaphysics, traditional cosmology, the new astronomy, and literature. If his chaos is "formless infinite" (3.12), his cosmos is its opposite. It is a carefully constructed

mechanism within which all details are arranged in clockwork preci-
sion. And yet it is not a finite, mechanical device. It has a mathematics
that is mystical. This conversion or transcendence is achieved through
a dynamic presentation of space and a multilayered presentation of
time. Simultaneously, Milton constantly keeps within the radii of his
focus the dramatic interpersonal nuances of perceptions of space and
time. As a result, as perceptions of space and time evolve, they define
character. The roles of Satan and Raphael in the extension of cosmic
space in Milton's epic is one segment of a larger framework of simi-
larities and contrasts that draws these two characters together. The
fragmentation of time into specific hours that begins with Satan's
entry into Paradise, on the other hand, is projected through cosmic
devices that are associated with Uriel and Gabriel. Like Dee's angels,
Uriel arrives on earth and returns to the sun moving along solar rays.
These moving sunbeams mark definite hours in Paradise, the frag-
mentation of eternity into sequential time, after Satan's entry into
the cosmos. The dark cone of night is positioned immediately above
Paradise as Gabriel directs Satan's gaze toward Libra and secures his
departure from Paradise. Like the sunbeams, the moving cone of
night also marks definite hours during the critical phase of the action
in Paradise. The operation of these two devices in situations shared
by Uriel and Gabriel with Satan directs attention to the comparatively
limited and, in its way, fragmented roles that these two angels have
in the epic narrative. The relativity of his construction of space and
time in *Paradise Lost* not only has a role in defining the characters
of Satan, Adam, and Eve, it also contributes to Milton's challenging
of stereotypes in his presentation of the angels Raphael, Uriel, and
Gabriel.

CHAPTER 6

Satan and Astronomical Signs

If the configuring of space and time in *Paradise Lost* demands a contextual reading, this is even more imperative with regard to the references to variable celestial phenomena that Milton works into his text at strategic points in the epic. In depicting space, time, and celestial movement, he is concerned with the larger picture, however innovative that might be. Even the specifics of celestial movement, such as the moving sunbeams, the dark cone of night, or the various signs of the zodiac, deal with regular cosmic events. But, in *Paradise Lost*, Milton also sets up a structure of astronomical signs comprising such variable celestial phenomena as new stars and comets. It is not unusual to find references to stars and comets in an early modern text. There would be many motivating factors to explain their presence. Astrology, astronomy, navigation, and a range of other contemporary activities relied on a reading of stellar positions as well as variable celestial occurrences. That *Paradise Lost*, too, is a text with many references to such celestial phenomena is therefore not intrinsically remarkable. The special significance of these images emerges only when the specific contemporary debates are identified and related to references in the text.

The complexity of the images of space, time, and celestial movement in *Paradise Lost* is a consequence of the interweaving of tradition, new astronomy, and the cultural politics of Milton's age. While the uniqueness and vitality of the images was the product of new perceptions introduced by early modern astronomy and optics, as well as speculations about these subjects in contemporary treatises, encyclopedias, and almanacs, a greater degree of intensity was added by Milton's personal experience of defeat and remembrance of the passionate hopes of times past. This combination of factors that makes the images of space and time in the epic so powerful and compelling also generated the structure of astronomical signs in the epic.

However, although the impulses behind the creation of the space and time images and the network of astronomical signs dealing with new stars and comets were similar, in comparison with space and time images, the deciphering of the implications of astronomical signs in the poem is a much more complex activity today. This is because the contextualization of astronomical signs in *Paradise Lost* is much more specific than the space and time images and an understanding of the implications of the images demands a recovery of issues debated at the time.

In the seventeenth century, millennial hopes were first energized and then dissipated. New stars and comets of the late sixteenth and early seventeenth centuries were visible signs that acted as a catalyst for intense debate about the possibilities of the end of the world and the coming of the new millennium. As hopes for the imminence of the Second Coming faded with the failure of the Puritan revolution, the controversies and discussions centering around astronomical signs gradually evaporated. When that happened, the scientific impact of the new stars and comets remained and significantly modified astronomical thought. But the millennial issues associated with astronomical signs, so potent in their time, were erased as having no permanent impact on the history of ideas. *Paradise Lost*, written at a time when the millennial implications of new stars and comets were still fresh and vibrant, demands a recovery of that context. It is only when that lost phase of intellectual history is investigated and reconstructed that the full extent of the implications of the astronomical signs in *Paradise Lost* can be understood.

In one of his verse letters to the Countess of Bedford ("To have written then"), composed around 1609, Donne declared "We have added to the world Virginia, and sent / Two new stars lately to the firmament."[1] Editors have suggested that the reference to the "two new stars" may be to two friends who had died recently, Cecilia Bulstrode and Lady Markham. It is also likely to be a reference to the two supernovas that were the subject of intense speculation in the late sixteenth and early seventeenth centuries. One of these appeared in 1572 in the constellation Cassiopeia, the other in 1604 in the constellation Ophiucus. Taken in conjunction with the reference to Virginia, Donne's lines could be understood to refer to the two spheres of life in which the most spectacular discoveries of the early modern period took place—navigation and astronomy. The appearance of the two new stars was not only an astronomical wonder, but was also hailed as a miracle. In the excitement generated by the triumph of Protestantism and expectations of a new millennium in the seventeenth century, these two new stars were regarded as visible emblems of Christ's promised return. In another verse letter, this time to the Countess of Huntingdon ("Man to God's image"), Donne made an explicit reference to this possibility:

Who vagrant transitory comets sees,
Wonders, because they are rare; but a new star
Whose motion with the firmament agrees,
Is miracle; for, there no new things are,...
As such a star, the Magi led to view
The manger-cradled infant, God below. (Ll. 5–8; 13–14)

These two new stars of 1572 and 1604 have a crucial role to play in *Paradise Lost* not only in communicating to us Milton's position in the millennial debate of the seventeenth century but also in defining Satan's character in the epic.

In "Milton and Millenarianism," Stella Revard has examined the political and theological dimensions of the millenarian fervor of the 1640s and 1650s.[2] Milton's belief in the certainty, if not the imminence, of the millennium is apparent not only in the very open expectation of Christ's Second Coming in *Of Reformation*—"at that day when thou the Eternall and shortly-expected King shall open the Clouds to judge the several Kingdomes of the World"—but also in his early poetry. His consciousness of ends of time generates the anxieties of sonnets such as "How soon hath time" and "When I consider how my light is spent." At the same time, these anxieties are offset by the redemptive spirit enshrined in other poems of the time such as "On the Morning of Christ's Nativity" and "The Passion." As a result, his poems of the 1620s and 1630s are essentially, in a broad sense, aligned to millennial ideas because the millennium is both an end and a new beginning. Nowhere is this so explicit as in *Lycidas*, where the destruction of the corrupt by the two-handed engine leads to resurrection, immortalization, and a new world order. While Milton's early faith in the coming of the new millennium is quite explicit, the failure of millennial hopes signaled by the imminent Restoration must have had considerable impact on him. Even if he still retained faith in the millennium through the 1660s and early 1670s as Revard argues, there would inevitably have been a sequence of questionings, analyses, and formulations of the reasons for its failure in the immediate present. Such questionings are an intrinsic part of *Paradise Lost* written at a time when the Restoration was at hand. In this process of inquiry that underlies and energizes the epic, Milton uses his knowledge of the controversy surrounding the appearance of the new stars and comets, and the millennial debate revolving around their appearance, as means of diagnosis and discovery.

In 1572, a star of unusual brilliance appeared in the constellation Cassiopeia and was hailed by astronomers, astrologers, theologians, and men from many walks of life as a miracle. In the Aristotelian science of the sixteenth century,[3] the regions above the moon were thought to be unchanging with neither generation nor decay. Comets and other changeable phenomena in the sky belonged to the sublunary world. At such a time, the appearance of a new star that indubitably belonged to the celestial sphere was fraught with extraordinary significance. Today, while sophisticated instruments such as NASA's Hubble Space Telescope bring us pictures of embryonic stars, it is difficult to appreciate the enormity of the event.

The new star of 1572 was observed with great excitement by the Danish astronomer Tycho Brahe and, in Britain, by John Dee and his pupil Thomas Digges. Among his unpublished manuscripts Dee listed one with the title "De stella admiranda in Cassiopeiae Asterismo." In Dee's mind, the appearance of the new star in Cassiopeia had implications for magic and alchemy, as well as for astronomy. In his copy of Marcus Manilius's *Astronomica* (1533), Dee noted the connections between the appearance of the 1572 nova and the finding of the philosopher's stone.

> I did coniecture the blasing star in Cassiopeia appering a 1572 to signify the fynding of some great Thresor or the Philosophers stone...This I told to Mr. Ed. Dier. at the same tyme. How truly it fell out in a 1582 Martij 10 it may appere in tyme to come ad stuporem Mundi.[4]

March 10, 1582, is the date of Dee's first angel conversation with the assistance of Edward Kelly. Clearly, for Dee, the appearance of the new star was of enormous significance. Dee's excitement about the 1572 nova must have been further fueled by the fact that toward the end of the sixteenth century, a number of other astronomical signs appeared and caused considerable speculation and debate. Shortly after the appearance of the new star of 1572, a blazing comet appeared in the sky in 1577 followed by a "great conjunction" of the planets Saturn and Jupiter in 1583. Such celestial events were regarded as cataclysmic and their implications suggesting the imminent decay of the world were much discussed by those involved in prognostications. Such prognostications often combined moral, religious, and political predictions. William Lilly, astrologer and physician, who published almanacs from 1644, declared in 1654 that the new star of 1572 was a sign of divine wrath and signaled the downfall of "monarchical pomp" and "pontifical pride." When a second warning in the shape of the comet of 1618 was ignored, the result, it was said, was the Thirty Years War and the civil war in England.[5] These celestial phenomena were also closely analyzed by men of science. In 1573, Thomas Digges published a work called *Alae seu Scalae Mathematicae*, which contained a discussion of the new star in Cassiopeia.[6] The most extensive observations of the new star, however, were made by Tycho Brahe. His mathematical calculations led him to conclude that this celestial object was not a sublunary phenomenon but a new star in Cassiopeia belonging to the eighth sphere of the fixed stars. Recording his observations in *De Nova Stella* in 1574, he announced that "it is a star shining in the firmament itself— one that has never previously been seen before our time, in any age since the beginning of the world."[7] Inevitably prompted to think of the star that guided the magi, Tycho was filled with excitement as he declared that this new star was "a miracle indeed, either the greatest of all that have occurred in the whole range of nature since the beginning of the world, or one certainly that is to be classed with those attested by the Holy Oracles."[8]

Having observed that the new star shone brightly for a whole year, he wondered about its possible significance. He had no doubt that it was likely to produce "strange, great, and wonderful effects."[9] Yet he momentarily hesitated to speculate on the exact nature of these effects, declaring, like Raphael in Book 8 of *Paradise Lost*, that such speculations were beyond the range of human inquiry. The temptation to indulge in prognostications was, however, too great and almost immediately he ventured into a whole series of speculations. He suggested that "the joviall, cleere, and bright lustre" of the star "doth seeme to fore-shew a prosperous and peaceable estate of humane affaires." At the same time he detected a "Martiall fiery glittering thereof," which seemed to signify violence and trouble. With millenarian fervor Tycho declared: "By this joviall figure it seemeth to portend, a great alteration, if not an utter subversion of religion; so that those devices which by outward shewes and Pharisaicall Hypocrisie, have long time bewitched ignorant people, shall now come to their full point and end." Curiously enough, he interpreted the fact that the star shone at first with great brightness and clarity, then changed color and eventually faded away, as a paradigm of the fate of "false Planets"[10] whose modus operandi seems similar to that of false prophets in that their outward plausible appearance seduced men away from the light of truth until their eventual exposure and downfall.[11] While Tycho presents a range of prognostications regarding the 1572 nova, considering it from diverse perspectives including location, position, color, dimension, and duration, his basic predictions can be reduced to the dualism of the new star as at once a harbinger of "strange, great, and wonderful effects" and a deceitful "false Planet." This could be regarded as the germ of the Miltonic image, in *Paradise Lost*, of Satan as a new star.

Tycho concluded by fixing both a time and a place where the cataclysmic changes heralded by the 1572 nova would occur. His prediction regarding the place was as follows: "And as this Starre appeared in the highest heavens, to the full view of the whole world, so it is credible, that there shall happen a great Catastrophe and universall change throughout all the chiefe Nations of the Earth, especially those which are situated Northward from the Aequinoctiall." After an astrological computation of time, he arrived at the very specific prognostication that "it is likely that the force and influence of this Starre, will chiefly show itself in the yeare of our Lord 1632."[12]

The partial translation of *De Nova Stella* that appeared in London in 1632 contained the prediction relating to the significance of that year as indicated by the 1572 nova. The translator's own verses pointed out:

> Astrologie is but the speech of Starres,
> Which doe fore-tell vs both of Peace and Warres,
> And by this Starre great Tycho did intend
> To shew the World was coming to an end.[13]

The same year, similar prognostications of Sibyl Tiburtina, Theodore Beza, and Paracelsus were republished.[14] These predictions, focusing on 1632, marked the climax that year of the career of King Gustavus Adolphus of Sweden, great reformer and champion of Protestantism against the Catholic Counter-Reformation. It was also the year of Gustavus's death, an event that many in England found difficult to accept.

Another treatise on the 1572 nova appeared in 1632, entitled *The New Starr of the North, Shining Upon the Victorious King of Sweden*.[15] The author was Alexander Gil the Younger of St. Paul's School in London, the man with whom Milton was on terms of close friendship and to whom he sent some of his Latin poems. Gil gave a detailed account of the publication history of *De Nova Stella* and an analysis of the contents. He suggested that "if Eclipses of the two great lights, and conjunction of Planets under some portions of fixed stars have at any time, or may portend events upon earth, much more may new Starrs moulded by the hand of God in the highest heavens challenge the like propheticall language." Gil also gave an account of the career of King Gustavus Adolphus of Sweden who, because of his virtue and valor, had become the "spectacle of the Christian world" and the man whose achievements appeared to have been heralded by Tycho's nova.[16] But he was convinced that the implications of the 1572 nova were in fact likely to be much greater. He reminded his readers that "by some it was deemed to be the very same Starre, which appeared unto the Sages of the East at the birth of our Saviour, and thereupon conjectured to be the neerefore-runner of the second coming of Christ, as that was the attendant of his first coming."[17]

Meanwhile, in 1604, another new star had appeared, this time in the constellation Ophiucus. The 1604 nova was observed by Johannes Kepler who noted that "the significance of this wonderful work of God's hand far exceeds that of the star of 1572," particularly as it was accompanied by the Great Conjunction of Saturn, Jupiter, and Mars.[18] But beyond suggesting that this new star signified "something of such exalted importance that it is beyond the grasp and understanding of any man," Kepler refused to be drawn into any speculation, concluding: "Time will teach us the true and actual meaning of this star."[19]

When the 1630s initiated discussion on the millennial implications of the 1604 nova, such discussions repeatedly brought together the 1572 and the 1604 novae. One example is John Swan's popular treatise on astronomy, the *Speculum Mundi*, printed in Cambridge in 1635 and then reprinted in 1643, 1665, and 1670. Like Alexander Gil, Swan declared that the 1572 nova was a celestial phenomenon the like of which had never been seen except "at our Saviour's birth." Its appearance, he suggested, could be said to "animate distressed Christians" two months after a sad event, "the cunningly plotted Massacre of the Protestants in France."[20] Predictably, his discussions included Tycho's prognostications about 1632 and the expected reference to King Gustavus Adolphus of Sweden. But Swan hastened to bring into the orbit of debate also the other new star of extraordinary brilliance, the 1604 nova, pointing out that its appearance coincided with the discovery of the Gunpowder Plot. The implication is clear: that the new star in Ophiucus gave warning of "that damnable powder plot of the Papists."[21] Swan's conservative reading of the new stars as celestial warnings is very close to the traditional view of unusual sightings in the sky such as that of comets as signs of impending disaster. Although at times he does go a step further, regarding the new stars as bringers of comfort and hope for the distressed, Swan lacks Tycho's enthusiasm for interpreting the new stars as a covenant or assurance of the promised millennium.

In the same chapter, chapter 5, Swan refers to another celestial marvel, the comet of 1618, as belonging to the same celestial regions as the new stars. This comet was earlier examined and analyzed in great detail by John Bainbridge in *An Astronomicall Description of the late Comet.*[22] Bainbridge was a fellow of Emmanuel College, Cambridge, and later the Savilian Professor of Astronomy at Oxford, where he was a contemporary of Robert Burton. His *Astronomicall Description* is primarily concerned with the position, trajectory, and other scientific matters relating to the 1618 comet. In a detailed analysis of the location of the comet he notes that it was always in opposition to the sun and in the region of Scorpio and Libra. In the second part of *Astronomicall Description*, entitled *Morall Prognosticks or Applications of the late Comet or Blazing-Starre*, Bainbridge examines the 1618 comet as "not so much a cause of elementary alterations, as a celestiall signe of greater consequents."[23] He had already asserted that the comet was not a sublunary phenomenon but a celestial event like the appearance of the 1572 and 1604 novae. In a sustained passage of millennial faith and aspirations, he declares:

> That blessed Starre, which conducted the Magi to Christs poore, but sacred nurcery (of whose incarnation, and happinesse to mankinde thereby that Starre was an heauenly Harbenger) doth enforce me often to thinke that those many new stars and Comets, which haue beene more this last Century of the world, then in many ages before, did amongst other things signifie that glorious light of the Gospell, which hath lately illumined the whole world.
>
> About the preaching of Luther were at least five Comets in tenne yeares, after which followed the happy departure of Germany, England, and many other Northerne parts from the spirituall Babylon. This new Comet doth give us hope, that the rest of Christendome before long will follow...
>
> Yea did not that admirable new Starre in Cassiopeia 1572 and that remarkable Comet 1577 plainly from heauen remonstrate, that howsoeuer the Euangelicall Churches in *France*, and the *Low-countries* might be for a time greiuously afflicted, yet maugre Sathan, and all his hellish Furies they should at length flourish, and triumph ouer their cruell aduersaries... I am verily perswaded that the new Star which appeared so long from 1604 to Ianuary 1606 in the foot of *Serpentarius*, hauing coincidance with the great conjunction of the three superior Planets... giues us hope, that his other great promise shall shortly be accomplished... the second coming of our blessed Sauiour.[24]

This network of associations assigned to comets a position of importance in the celestial regions and linked the comet of 1618 with the new stars and millennial hopes. There was an extant tradition according to which the star that guided the Magi was actually a comet. Analyzing Marsilio Ficino's *De Stella Magorum,* which examined both the significance of the star that guided the Magi and the role of the Magi themselves as "oriental astronomers," Stephen M. Buhler points out that the ancient tradition of regarding the star the Magi followed as a comet would explain the star's curious behavior, as an ordinary star could not be expected to travel across the sky guiding them, or to appear, disappear, and reappear as that star seems to do in Matthew.[25] Such movements appear to be more in keeping with the parabolic trajectory of comets. He also highlights the fact that, as a consequence of deliberating along these lines, Ficino asserted, citing many authorities, that comets were not necessarily evil omens. If this was indeed an established tradition, it is not surprising that, in the atmosphere of millennial expectations in the seventeenth century, the 1618 comet should have been regarded as a good omen.

What emerges from the scientific and popular thought of this time is clearly this: that in the seventeenth-century debate about the advent of the millennium, the two new stars of 1572 and 1604 were seen as emblems sent to herald the great event. The millennium was after all a promised age of peace and prosperity, not a calendar event. The two new stars of 1572 and 1604, and the comet of 1618, were interpreted as celestial signs indicating the imminence of the millennium. The enthusiastic response to new stars and comets in the 1630s and the millennial speculations they inspired may be seen as the context for Milton's fabrication of the eternalizing myth in the closing section of his pastoral elegy of 1637, *Lycidas.* The resurrected Lycidas is likened to the "day-star" (l.168) or sun shining in the morning sky. He takes his place among the saints in heaven "that sing and singing in their glory move." The idea looks forward to Book 3 of *Paradise Lost* where the angels circle around God "thick as stars" (III, 61), singing hymns of praise. Lycidas's transformation into a "genius of the shore" guiding sailors lost at sea may be seen in this millennial context as his reincarnation into a star directing sailors to a safe haven.

In any event, millennial hopes in the seventeenth century centered on gifted individuals thought to be able to usher in the rule of saints. The repeated references to King Gustavus Adolphus of Sweden in discussions about the new stars and the 1618 comet point to this conviction. While the Swedish king was the center of hope in the wider European context, in the context in fact of the entire Christian world, in Britain such hopes centered first on King James I, the "terrestiall Phoebus" to whom John Bainbridge dedicated his work on the 1618 comet. James had written commendatory verses for Tycho's *De Nova Stella*, part of which was reprinted by Alexander Gil. Later, millennial hopes focused on Oliver Cromwell. Marvell's "First Anniversary," written in 1655, is an unequivocal celebration of Cromwell's prophetic destiny.

The failure of the Puritan cause signaled also the failure of millennial aspirations, and Milton's *Paradise Lost* presents a passionate questioning of the reasons for this failure. While his declared intention is "to justify the way of God to men" (1.26), his epic in fact explores the depths of loss, disorientation, and malaise. *Paradise Lost* is haunted by the fear of possible uncreation. The moment of sin, "man's first disobedience" (1.1), marks the initiation of a degenerative process affecting the entire cosmos.[26] In Book 9, Eve's excited narration to Adam of her transgression brings the first sign of decay as the roses in the garland in Adam's hand fade and drop. As Adam joins Eve in the transgression, a whole series of changes take place. The harmonious relationship between them breaks down into discord as they point accusing fingers at each other. Animals turn predatory and seek to destroy each other. The balanced position of sun and earth is altered, with nights and days becoming unequal, and eternal spring gives way to the change of seasons. These events generate a precarious sense of the beginnings of uncreation.

These cataclysmic changes are brought about by the machinations of a character who presents himself time and again in the epic as millennial hero. Satan portrays himself as the courageous leader of his troops as he energizes them with a show of faith and compassion. While he had sought the "aid" (1.38) of the rebel angels in achieving his own objective so clearly defined by Milton—"to set *himself* in glory above his peers" (1.39; italics mine)—his opening speech to Beelzebub disguises this selfish ambition by projecting it as a collective achievement:

> If he whom *mutual* league,
> *United* thoughts and counsels, *equal hope*
> And hazard in the glorious enterprise,
> Joined with me once, now misery hath joined
> In *equal* ruin. (1.87–91; Italics mine)

As he launches into his series of rousing speeches directing the devils to "Awake, arise, or be for ever fallen" (1.330), he is compared to

Amran's son (1.339), Moses, in a clear indictment of his role-playing, his assumption of a prophetic stance. Read in the context of Milton's focus on the Mosaic tradition in the invocations, the comparison underlines the falsity of Satan's assumption of inspirational leadership. Later, he portrays himself as the wise counselor of Eve to whom he apparently reveals the actions and motivations of the highest powers. He is the bold adventurer discovering new lands and new cosmic worlds like a Renaissance navigator or a Galileo looking through his telescope (*PL* 1.283–95) and is thus able to capture the imagination of readers. With his apparent leadership abilities, compassion, insight, and pioneering qualities, Satan is the archetypal millennial hero. This self-fashioning as millennial hero needs to be understood in the light of the widespread millennial aspirations that marked seventeenth-century Puritanism. Satan becomes a travesty of the kind of heroism displayed by Cromwell and King Gustavus Adolphus of Sweden.

Throughout *Paradise Lost* we are always conscious of Satan's dissembling, of the disjuncture between his real and projected selves. The many disguises he adopts are only the physical manifestations of a more pervasive condition of personality, a compulsive role-playing, which becomes intensified during his visit to the new cosmos. While Satan deceives even his followers in hell with a show of loyalty and compassion, his self-fashioning moves into a higher mode as he turns his attention to man and the new cosmos. There, in the two temptations of Eve, he presents himself as one who brings enlightenment and deliverance. To the fallen angels in hell, he had displayed courage, fortitude, compassion, and defiance, but always admitted God's superior strength and the inscrutability of divine intention. In the two temptations of Eve, he assumes the role of deliverer. In the first temptation, he is able to lift Eve up in her dream above and beyond the confined space that is Paradise, enabling her to glimpse the world from a perspective as yet unknown to the human pair. In the second temptation, he offers to guide Eve to a higher order of being, from human to goddess, claiming insight into the workings of the divine intellect. The superior knowledge and ability he claims for himself, his assumption of the role of visionary and leader, constitutes his self-fashioning into the role of prophet. This adoption of the prophetic role marks him out as the archetypal false prophet. The prophetic mode, in particular the Mosaic tradition—sacred, insightful, empowering—is at the heart of the epic's invocations, and Satan's false, cunning, deceitful assumption of the role of visionary and deliverer is a travesty of true prophecy. This self-fashioning also contributes to the series of patterned oppositions in the poem between the divine and the diabolical—the divine and devilish trinities, Christ's bright cosmic chariot and Satan's dark "car of night" (9.65), the promised return of the Messiah and Satan's projected image of himself as millennial hero.[27]

Milton depicts Satan's self-presentation as millennial hero in the new world within two framing images, the comet in Ophiucus in Books 2 and 4 and the new star in Ophiucus in Book 10. These are defining images of enormous significance in *Paradise Lost*. Their significance emerges when they are examined in the context of millennial speculations of the time regarding the new stars and the comet of 1618. The comparisons with these phenomena achieve a narrative fashioning much more complex than Satan's self-presentation alone, since they both facilitate Satan's projection of himself through these images of celestial phenomena (image as disguise) and provide an ironic commentary (through the act of comparison) on the entire millennial issue. More than once in the epic Milton compares Satan and his followers to comets and falling stars. There is, for instance, the memorable description in Book 1 of how Mulciber fell from heaven and in the evening "Dropped from the zenith like a falling star" (1.745); and in the same book Satan's flag unfurled shines "like a meteor streaming to the wind" (1.537). Comets and falling stars, however, were generally regarded as sublunary phenomena in Milton's day and while these could also have millennial implications signifying the fall of Antichrist,[28] the comparison of Satan to the new stars, which clearly belonged to the celestial sphere, is, by contrast, a deeply troubling one as it seems to connect Satan with the promised Second Coming. The region in which the Miltonic image of Satan as a comet places Satan is the same celestial region in which Bainbridge locates the 1618 comet in Ophiucus in his treatise of 1619. The millennial implications of the two framing images of Satan as the comet and the new star in Ophiucus are therefore both powerful and provocative.

As Satan confronts Death on his way out of hell in Book 2, Milton describes his awesome presence thus:

> Incensed with indignation Satan stood
> Unterrified, and like a comet burned,
> That fires the length of Ophiucus huge
> In the Arctic sky, and from his horrid hair
> Shakes pestilence and war. (2.707–11)

In his treatise, Bainbridge explains the position of the comet of 1618 in detail with the help of a planisphere, which shows the comet stretching from the equinoctial line to the north, the cometary line running parallel to Ophiucus. It seems likely that this is the comet in Milton's mind in Book 2, since he gives it a specific location that matches the location of the 1618 comet: "That fires the length of Ophiucus huge/ In the Arctic sky." In the atmosphere of discussion and debate regarding variable celestial phenomena and their millennial implications, both Milton and his readers were more than likely to be familiar not only with Bainbridge's treatise but also with references to this comet in popular encyclopedias such as Swan's *Speculum Mundi* and in almanacs such as those of William Lilly. He would have been conscious also of the tradition that regarded the star of Bethlehem as possibly a comet, and comets—particularly the comet of 1618—as not just good omens but, even more, signs of the coming millennium. In a poem that is unusually alert to both traditional cosmology and the new astronomy, Milton's orthodox view of comets as celestial phenomena bringing "pestilence and war," combined with a deliberate reference to Ophiucus, is not without a special significance. If Bainbridge had dared to hope that the comet in Ophiucus, like the two new stars, was a sign of the imminence of the Second Coming, Milton's lines are an acknowledgment that such hopes had not been fulfilled. The allusion thus provides a direct and open refutation of the millennial hopes raised both by the 1618 comet and the 1604 nova.

The image of Satan shining like an unusually brilliant comet looks forward to his appearance at the end of Book 4. Discovered by the touch of Ithuriel's spear, Satan starts up like a keg of gunpowder unexpectedly set on fire and "with sudden blaze diffused, inflames the air" (4.818). As he confronts Gabriel we see his immense stature:

> On the other side Satan alarmed
> Collecting all his might dilated stood,
> Like Teneriff or Atlas unremoved:
> His stature reached the sky. (4.985–88)

This flaming figure at the end of Book 4 stands directly below the constellation Libra at midnight in the same part of the hemisphere again as the constellation Ophiucus, which would be directly below Libra at that hour. While the image of gunpowder, which precedes the exchange between Satan, Zephon, and Gabriel, emphasizes Satan's destructive potential throughout, it also strategically reinforces Milton's earlier refutation in Book 2 of millennial aspirations heralded by the comet of 1618. Bainbridge's treatise raises such expectations linking the Ophiucus comet to the promised millennium, and

Swan's encyclopedia interprets the significance of the same comet as a providential warning, but to Milton's disillusioned mind it is neither promise nor celestial warning but the first visible sign or appearance of the agent of destruction. Seventeenth-century readers, familiar with contemporary astronomy and astrology from scientific treatises, almanacs, textbooks, and encyclopedias of the time, would not have failed to make the connection between the two passages in Books 2 and 4 and contemporary speculations about the 1618 comet.

While Satan's appearance as a comet in Ophiucus in Books 2 and 4 is a potent reminder of the failure of millennial hopes raised by the 1618 comet, a more insidious and ironic reminder comes through the Ophiucus image in Book 10. There Satan is on his way back from Paradise after having successfully corrupted Adam and Eve and thus achieved apparent success in his devious war against God. Sin and Death meet him.

> And now their way to earth they had descried,
> To Paradise first tending, when behold
> Satan in likeness of an angel bright
> Betwixt the Centaur and the Scorpion steering
> His zenith, while the sun in Aries rose:
> Disguised he came, but those his children dear
> Their parent soon discerned, though in disguise. (10.325–31)

He steers his course between the Centaur and the Scorpion, that is, in that part of the heavens where the constellation Ophiucus is to be found and in which the new star had appeared in 1604. Satan appears "in likeness of an angel bright." The likeness is not to an angel resembling a human form with wings, as such a figure would have attracted immediate attention and exposure. Satan appears instead as a new angelic star in Ophiucus. In many passages in *Paradise Lost* the angels are identified with stars, and Milton's portrayal of Satan as a star here is reinforced by Satan's position between the Centaur and the Scorpion. This startling appearance justifies the emphasis on "behold" in the passage, its sharply explosive impact indicative of both the sense of surprise in the reaction of Sin and Death and an expression of irony as the dominant feeling of the narrator's consciousness.

Indeed, Satan retains his star disguise even after he reenters Pandemonium:

> At last as from a cloud his fulgent head
> And shape star bright appeared, or brighter, clad
> With what permissive glory since his fall

Was left him, or false glitter: all amazed
At that so sudden blaze the Stygian throng
Bent their aspect, and whom they wished beheld,
Their mighty chief returned. (10.449–55)

Milton's use of "aspect" here is deliberate. It is a word whose astro-
logical significance with reference to the planets and stars was widely
known in the early modern period, and it invests the whole host of
fallen angels with a "permissive glory," which enables them to shine
like stars until their final transformation into a colony of hissing
serpents.

Within the context of seventeenth-century millennialism, the
appearance of Satan as the comet and the new star in Ophiucus
enhances our perception of him as powerful and compelling, but also
as deceitful and evil. Helen Gardener has written of a progressive
degeneration of Satan indicated through his disguises of cherub, toad,
and serpent.[29] Yet these disguises are but instances of cunning and
expediency. Satan's self-fashioning is proactive and he uses disguise
for the purpose of negotiation and control. There is a clear distinc-
tion, however, between two modes of self-fashioning that he under-
takes. There are moments when all his faculties are concentrated on
seeking, devising, and insinuating, as in his conversation with Uriel
and the two temptations of Eve, when motivation is more impor-
tant than image and apparent degradation through disguise may be
expedient. After all, as an inferior, he was likely to gain greater indul-
gence. There are other situations when his energies are concentrated
on a self-conscious projection of a public image of himself to impress
those whom he encounters before and after the Fall. In the modes of
self-fashioning through which he projects himself to an audience he
wishes to impress, whether it be Sin and Death, or Gabriel and the
angels, or the devils in Pandemonium, Satan undergoes not degrada-
tion but a reinvention of himself as celestial phenomena of millennial
value. The process involves exploitation of both Biblical myth and
history as these strategies of simulation are at once expressions of
loss, a hallucinatory attempt to recover earlier cosmic positions—as
an angel Lucifer had once been like a star in heaven—and at the same
time subtle negotiations of empowerment. They are mimetic acts that
skillfully manipulate the texture of beliefs associated with celestial
phenomena that energized the millennial aspirations of this century.

In depicting Satan's self-presentation as millennial star or comet,
Milton is able to focus attention on the millennial debate of the
seventeenth century, not to subvert millennialism itself but implicitly

to criticize those who misread the signs. In his state of despair and disillusionment at the failure of the Puritan cause, Milton looks back at those earlier celestial signs and their interpretations and, in a process of diagnosis and discovery, sees those earlier interpretations as misreadings. His own version of those celestial signs as being linked with Satan rather than the Second Coming is almost a regressive step in astronomical terms, reverting to the earlier view of celestial changes as bad omens. Aware of the debates and discussions that swirled around the appearance of variable celestial phenomena in the early modern period, this is a considered position that Milton adopts. He now sees these celestial phenomena as diabolical manipulations of cosmic signs. The cosmic signs that lit up the sky for almost a hundred years were not signs of hope but were deceitful illusions.

The identification of Satan with the new stars thus provides for the millennial hopes of the century Milton's personal ironic commentary. It is a fierce indictment of the false hopes raised of the immediate advent of the promised millennium and the misreadings of celestial signs that fueled such hopes. Moreover, seventeenth-century millennialism had become inextricably connected with achievements in intellectual inquiry, as the millennium was expected not only to restore the rule of the saints, leading to the Second Coming of Christ, but also to recover, for man, the encyclopedic knowledge and power over nature that Adam had enjoyed in paradise before the Fall. In the circumstances, Milton's passionately felt sense of betrayal of millennial hopes could not have been more eloquently expressed than by using a landmark event of the new astronomy as the text for the expression of his sense of failure.

Alertness to astronomical debates of the early modern period not only deepens our understanding of the political subtext of this great epic and Milton's own position in the cultural politics of his time, it also sharpens our perception of the poetic strategies Milton employs in defining Satan's character. The new astronomy was a field in which some of the greatest, and permanently meaningful, advancements in human knowledge took place. These astronomical discoveries also aroused speculation and debate among astrologers, almanac writers, and alchemists as well. Milton takes materials relating to the discovery of new stars by two of the greatest astronomers of the time, Tycho Brahe and Kepler, and discussions of the 1618 comet, to construct an incisive and intelligent expose of Satan. It is a construction that utilizes the findings of the new astronomy to create two striking images of Satan, one as the 1618 comet and the other as the 1604 new star in Ophiucus, reminding his readers of the immense range of discussion and debate from the 1570s to the 1640s and beyond in which these variable celestial occurrences were seen as either signs of the imminent Second Coming or as providential warnings pointing to some catastrophic event such as the Gunpowder Plot. By aligning these celestial signs with Satan, Milton subverts the millennial possibilities of these signs and challenges the many prognostications that were made. In its way then, Milton's utilization of variable celestial phenomena in his portrayal of Satan's character is part of the larger pattern of excitement and questioning, of simultaneous appropriation and challenging, of varied resources, both scientific and nonscientific, that characterizes this great epic poem. The new stars and comets are of course only part of the story. Milton continues to engage with other details of the new astronomy—among them telescopes and sunspots—in defining the role of Satan in *Paradise Lost*.

CHAPTER 7

Milton's Angels and Celestial Motion

The incorporation of details of variable celestial phenomena in the portrayal of Satan in *Paradise Lost* reveals a complex process at work. It suggests that Milton consistently places Satan in the fallen world, aligning him with cosmic events—the appearance of new stars and comets—that cannot belong to the prelapsarian state. Such images defining Satan's character that rely upon postlapsarian celestial details act as a means of collapsing the vital divide between the unfallen and the fallen worlds, projecting the Satanic presence as a perpetual threat. Satan thinks that he appropriates these variable cosmic phenomena, the new stars and comets, as modes of self-fashioning, disguises through which he wishes to demonstrate both his power and his astronomical acumen. But, for the reader, once these are contextualized, the cosmic details are seen to be in fact a powerful narrative device through which Satan's true self is revealed. This becomes another instance of his evil intentions recoiling back on himself.

Milton's good angels, moving through a prelapsarian cosmos, are not associated with such specific, debated, variable cosmic phenomena, but their individual roles with regard to regular celestial movement, represented with care and precision by the epic poet, are important for an understanding of the critical differences between the major angels. Equally important is their knowledge about the new cosmos and their mode of configuring space and time. Just as the striking images of Satan as the comet and the new star in Ophiucus define his character, the involvement of Milton's good angels with celestial movement help define their personalities. This is because, as Joad Raymond suggests, there can be no doubt about Milton's decision to make angels creatures, not merely instruments of narrative but beings who live independently of the specific duties that God assigns them.[1]

Milton's angels are characters in the epic poem and their engagement with the astronomical details of the new cosmos is one of the means of revealing the subtle differences between the angels. While the most astronomically sophisticated of Milton's angels is Raphael, who both contributes to the dynamics of space in the epic and communicates scientific knowledge to Adam and Eve, the two angels stationed by God within the cosmos, Uriel and Gabriel, have their own role in directing attention to celestial movement in the new universe. The function of these two angels with regard to utilization of knowledge about the cosmic details of Milton's universe reveals complex motivations at work. The incentives for their actions are multilayered, and not as transparent as suggested by Angelica Duran for whom Milton's angels participate in an important pedagogical exercise, sharing responsibility for imparting knowledge to Adam and Eve.[2] About Uriel, Gabriel, Raphael, and Michael she says, "The four archangels blaze onto the learning environment of *Paradise Lost* endued with qualities to help them in a collaborative effort of knowledge reconnaissance and combat."[3] Communicating knowledge is only part of the story, particularly for Uriel and Gabriel. Once their actual role in the new cosmos is examined, and their engagement with astronomical details is analyzed, what emerges is the curious situation of angelic exploitation of celestial movement, rather than dissemination of knowledge.

Unlike Satan, and unlike Adam and Eve, Milton's archangels are not dazzled by the new cosmos and show different levels of interest in the workings of the new universe. They were present at the creation of this world and Uriel and Raphael give their own accounts and analyses of creation, which are sophisticated and challenging, incorporating mid-seventeenth-century vitalist theories.[4] As Raphael explains to Adam later, he was not present on the sixth day of creation when man was created ("I that day was absent" [8.229]) as God had sent him with others on a special mission to check that the gates of hell were securely shut. Therefore, by implication, he was present on all other days. Yet cosmic details still fascinate him, and as he journeys through the cosmos toward Paradise in Book 5, he examines the stars as he flies past them and his speculative glance configures them as "worlds." The details of the new cosmos also fascinate Satan when he first lands on the hard outer shell and looks down through the aperture examining the new world. Unlike Raphael and Satan, however, cosmic details are not examined by Uriel and Gabriel with any apparent interest. Presumably since these angels were present at creation, they possess a greater depth of knowledge about the mechanism of the cosmos than either Satan or Adam and Eve. Uriel, indeed, lays stress on the fact that he was a witness to the creation of the cosmos: "I saw when at his word the formless mass, / This world's material mould, came to a heap" (3.708–709). Light appeared followed by the creation of sun, stars, planets, and earth. However, Uriel and Gabriel's utilization of this knowledge creates a curious narrative of negotiation and empowerment.

The first instance of this is in Book 4 when Uriel descends from the sun to the earth to warn Gabriel about the entry of some evil spirit into Paradise. "Thither came Uriel, gliding through the even / On a sun beam, swift as a shooting star" (4.555–56). Having completed his conversation with Gabriel, Uriel returns:

> Uriel to his charge
> Returned on that bright beam, whose point now raised
> Bore him slope downward to the sun now fallen
> Beneath the Azores. (4.589–92)

John Dee believed that angels traveled along light rays from the supercelestial to the natural world and, as a prelude to his angel conversations, Dee used his "showstone" to capture and magnify light rays.[5] In *Paradise Lost*, Milton avoids such combinations of occult philosophy and optical theory. Uriel's journey at this point is conducted within the natural world and Milton's other angels cover the vast distances between Heaven and Paradise by means of direct flight through air. Raphael's great wings "winnow(s) the buxom air" (5.270) as he flies from Heaven through the cosmos toward Paradise. Michael is attired as a man and a warrior, not as a winged seraph, and we do not see his transit from Heaven to earth. In the urgency of the situation in Book 11, there is no leisure for a detailed account of space travel. Michael, accompanied by the cherubim, is simply seen alighting in Paradise from a sky of jasper. His mode of travel is unspecified.

Uriel covers a much shorter distance than either Raphael or Michael, from the sun to Paradise, within the cosmos, and he achieves this with the help of light rays. Uriel's journey gliding down sunbeams to reach Paradise and to return from Paradise to the sun might seem, at first sight, at best, childlike innocent enjoyment. But seen within the matrix of angelic manipulation of celestial movement, Uriel's cosmic play emerges as more than benign science fiction. It is a statement of his attempt to demonstrate his complete mastery over the mechanism of the new universe, which enables him to utilize celestial movement for his own particular space travels. And yet, when one looks closely at the episode, troubling questions surface at once. Having noted the unholy passions that disfigured Satan's face, Uriel has detected the presence of an evil spirit within the universe. Satan, disguised as a cherub, had spoken to Uriel "at hight of noon" (4.564) and, on being guided toward Paradise, had reached his destination with great speed. The sun was still "high in his meridian tower" (4.30) when Satan, standing on earth within sight of Eden, imagining himself undetected, allowed his evil identity to be revealed through the "passions foul" (4.571) on his face. But Uriel waits till sunset before commencing his journey. Once he has knowledge of the entry of an evil spirit, it is his urgent duty to warn Gabriel who is in charge of Paradise. In point of fact he waits until "the setting sun / Slowly descended" (4.540–41) before journeying to Paradise. The journey itself is accomplished with enormous speed—Uriel travels "swift as a shooting star" (4.556). But there is the delay in setting out, which seems to be prompted by nothing other than the desire to deploy celestial phenomena, in this case, the moving sunbeams. Either, as Empson suggests,[6] Uriel is looking for a safe means of space travel—at the risk of endangering the safety of Paradise and Adam and Eve—or he finds his knowledge of celestial movement so satisfying that he cannot resist the opportunity of demonstrating his complete mastery over the workings of the universe. In the event, precious time is lost and, instead of establishing control, Uriel is trapped by his own fascination with celestial movement.

While Uriel's utilization of celestial movement seems almost irresponsibly self-indulgent, Gabriel's use of such phenomena is fraught with anxiety. His use of celestial movement is fortuitous, but it is presented as a mode of empowerment. At the end of Book 4, as Gabriel and Satan confront each other, tension is generated by the prospect of a stupendous battle. But, after warlike speeches are exchanged by the two adversaries in true epic fashion, the situation is unexpectedly defused by a celestial occurrence.

> The eternal to prevent such horrid fray
> Hung forth in heaven his golden scales, yet seen
> Betwixt Astrea and the Scorpion sign,
> Wherein all things created first he weighed,
> The pendulous round earth with balanced air
> In counterpoise, now ponders all events,
> Battles and realms: in these he put two weights
> The sequel each of parting and of fight;
> The latter quick up flew, and kicked the beam. (4.996–1004)

Gabriel, seeing this, apparently deciphers it as a sign that Satan will lose. He tells Satan:

> for proof look up,
> And read thy lot in yon celestial sign
> Where thou art weighed, and shown how light, how weak,
> If thou resist. The fiend looked up and knew
> His mounted scale aloft: nor more; but fled
> Murmuring, and with him fled the shades of night. (4.1010-15)

There is a difficulty in explaining these lines as Milton clearly indicates specific divine intention—"the eternal *to prevent such horrid fray* / Hung forth in heaven his golden scales" (italics mine). Yet the occurrence referred to is a regular celestial phenomenon. In Milton's universe, since the sun is fixed in Aries, Libra or the scales would be at the zenith at midnight. At the exact hour of midnight the two arms of the scales would always be evenly balanced. With the movement of time, as Libra moved, one arm of the scales would dip and be lower than the other. This was a celestial phenomenon Gabriel must have seen every night. And yet, at this point, he manipulates this natural regular celestial movement to serve his own ends. His interpretation of the position of Libra as a sign of Satan's imminent defeat achieves his immediate objective, that of banishing Satan from Paradise. And in the process prevents a confrontation in which victory could have gone either way. For Gabriel, celestial movement thus provides a mode of empowerment in which he presumes his superior knowledge of the mechanism of the universe will help him avert a crisis.

It is also perhaps significant that the two regular celestial phenomena that are used for the marking of definite hours in Paradise, the moving sunbeams and the circling cone of night, are the precise astronomical details that are associated with Uriel and Gabriel. While Uriel utilizes the moving sunbeams as a means of transit, Gabriel's investigations into the presence of an evil spirit in Paradise are curiously guided by the positioning of the cone of night. If Uriel arrived shortly before sunset, that is, following the structure of Milton's cosmos, shortly before six o'clock in the evening, and left shortly after six, it is surely surprising that Gabriel waits until it is nine o'clock at night before marshalling his forces, giving commands, and beginning the search for Satan.

> Now had night measured with her shadowy cone
> Half way up hill this vast sublunar vault,
> And from their ivory port the cherubim

> Forth issuing at the accustomed hour stood armed
> To their night watches in warlike parade,
> When Gabriel to his next in power thus spake. (4.776–81)

As Alastair Fowler points out, the cone of night would be "Half way up hill" at nine o'clock.[7] If Uriel is guilty of waiting for the sunbeams to be at the appropriate angle before setting forth to warn Gabriel, Gabriel is similarly guilty of wasting precious hours before setting out, with his band of angels, in search of Satan. Are we to surmise that, as archangels, Uriel and Gabriel move at a measured pace, as haste would be unbecoming of them? Or is it that Gabriel has to wait for Adam and Eve to be safely ensconced in their bower before setting forth? Do guardian angels need to hide from those they are appointed to protect? Or are we to understand that Adam and Eve are so fragile in Gabriel's understanding that they cannot be exposed to the reality of an evil spirit's presence in Paradise? In the event, Gabriel's delay is as critical as Uriel's and allows Satan adequate time to begin the first temptation. Gabriel's investigations into the presence of an evil spirit in Paradise are conducted between two positions of the cone of night, its position "half way up hill" (4.777) at nine o'clock and its position at the zenith at midnight. This marking of exact time is part of the fragmentation of time into specific hours that happens after Satan's landing on earth, and Satan could be said to have brought with him his own tragic version of *carpe diem*. Turning aside in envy from Adam and Eve, he says, "Live while ye may, / Yet happy pair; enjoy, till I return, / Short pleasures, for long woes are to succeed" (4.533–35). Between Satan's entry into Paradise and the second temptation of Eve, there is the precise marking of exact hours by means of the moving sunbeams and the cone of night. Satan brings with him a consciousness of the passing of time, and, with it, a deep sense of mutability and tragic end. While no such desire for termination, or insinuation of transience and loss, can be imputed to the angels Uriel and Gabriel, their fascination with the instruments that mark the passing of time and contribute to a feeling of tension and loss cannot be inadvertent. In an epic poem that constantly directs attention to character and motive, the least one can say is that, apart from revealing their sense of mastery over cosmic details, Uriel and Gabriel's appropriation of celestial phenomena that mark the fragmentation of time into definite hours directs attention to the comparatively limited and, in its way, fragmented roles that these two angels have in the epic narrative. Even Duran, who assigns to Uriel and Gabriel the role of "good teachers," recognizes the limited contribution of each, suggesting that while Uriel and Gabriel collaborate as good teachers and good researchers, their knowledge remains static and limited while Satan is discovered to have "improved / In meditated fraud and malice" (9.54–55).[8] Indeed, Uriel presumably feels that he has performed his duty once he has warned Gabriel and assumes he has no further role to play. Gabriel, who had confined his vigilance to the gates of Paradise and thus failed to keep the garden under adequate surveillance, acknowledges the possibility of intrusion by some evil spirit and takes it as his task to seek out the intruder whose presence in Paradise had been detected by the sharp-sighted Uriel. Once confronted by Satan, he utilizes his knowledge of the movement of Libra to avoid a direct fight. After Satan's expulsion from Paradise at the end of Book 4, neither Uriel nor Gabriel is seen to take any further interest in Satan's whereabouts or his possible reentry into Paradise. Their roles end at the end of Book 4 leading to an uneasy feeling that the whole mechanism of an angelic guard for the human pair in Paradise is nothing but an elaborate charade. Later, after the Fall, they return to heaven to be absolved of all blame. Divested of leadership, with no direct reference to Uriel and Gabriel, they are now a confused group—described as "the angelic guards" (10.18)—left speechless ("mute" [10.18]) and wondering how Satan had managed to reenter Paradise. There can be no doubt that Milton exposes the limited power of these two archangels as both prove incapable of the tasks assigned to them—Uriel, as "regent of the sun" (3.690), should have been more alert and energetic, and Gabriel, "chief of the angelic guards" (4.550), should have been better able to keep Paradise secure. For his part, Satan, intent on completing his evil mission, masters the working of the great cone of night and uses it for his temporarily successful seven day journey in space (9.63–66). He then conducts his second, and successful, temptation of Eve. But, at the end of it all, he is vanquished. The dynamic celestial phenomena, the moving sunbeams and the cone of night, the two instruments used to introduce a sense of fragmentation and finality, in which Satan, Uriel, and Gabriel have a shared interest, seem to draw these three together into a network of futility.

For all Gabriel's presumption of superiority in their confrontation at the end of Book 4, Satan is in no way deficient in knowledge about the cosmic details of the new universe. Unlike Uriel, Gabriel, and Raphael, he has no prior knowledge about the mechanism of the new universe. As he "looks down with wonder at the sudden view / Of all this world at once" (3.542–43) on his arrival at the new universe, he is amazed and fascinated by it. His excitement and fascination are matched by his enormous self-confidence as he flies through the pure air of this cosmos without any hesitation (3.555–64). In no time at all he masters the workings of this universe. This becomes apparent in the complete control over celestial movement he demonstrates during his seven-day journey between the first and second temptations.[9]

At the end of Book 4, Gabriel points to the raised arm of Libra as a visible indication of Satan's imminent defeat and Satan flees from Paradise. He reenters Paradise at midnight seven days later. He spends the interim period in a journey that provides proof of his knowledge about celestial movement. Indeed, he in fact participates in that movement and uses his knowledge of celestial motion as a means of empowerment and superiority over the angels.

> Thence full of anguish driven,
> The space of seven continued nights he rode
> With darkness, thrice the equinoctial line
> He circled, four times crossed the car of Night
> From pole to pole, traversing each colure;
> On the eighth returned. (9.62–67)

As Satan flies up from Paradise at midnight he flies into the dark cone of night. At midnight, the cone would have been directly above Paradise. For the first three days he hides within this dark cone, circling within it inside the hard outer shell of the universe, making the dark cone his dark cosmic chariot. This is the one part of the universe where the sun's rays do not enter and he would not be detected a second time by Uriel. For the remaining four days of the week of uncreation, planning the fall of man, he decides to vary his journey while at the same time remaining within the umbral region, and thus remaining undetected. This variation during his space travels takes him along the colures, the two great circles of the universe, which, according to their astronomical definition, intersect at the celestial poles, one passing through the equinoctial points and the other through the solstitial points. As Fowler pointed out, there were no equinoctial or solstitial points in the prelapsarian universe as, in Milton's model of the cosmos, the path of the celestial equator and the ecliptic were the same—or all points could be regarded as equinoctial points.[10] There could be no distinct colures associated with the equinoctial and solstitial points. It is possible to rely on this strict definition of "colure" and suggest that here, again, as in the passages associating Satan with variable celestial phenomena, Milton shows Satan inhabiting a fallen world. But it is also possible to approach this description of Satan's journey keeping in mind the simplicity and harmony of Milton's cosmos, omitting the references to the equinoxes and solstices in standard definitions of colures, and simply regarding the two colures as two great circles intersecting at the celestial poles. In terms of this simplified definition, Satan's movement along the colures would secure four specific crossings of the umbral cone or car of night along the colures and justify Milton's very specific detail "four times crossed the car of Night / From pole to pole, traversing each colure" (9.65–66). Satan then would have spent the second part of his travels not within the cone but near it and still within the darkest segment of the cosmos. It is remarkable with how much sophistication and intelligence Satan adapts himself to the details of this new cosmos. For Uriel and Gabriel, celestial movement was an objective reality to be utilized on its own terms and in its own time. During his seven-day orbit in space, Satan also relies on celestial movement as objective reality, but his clever and appropriate utilization of these details, and the variations in his own movements that he is able to work out within the given parameters, is a mark of his achievement and shows great imagination and control. In this context, one clarification needs to be made. The view expressed by Gabor Ittzes that Satan traverses the earth during this seven-day journey is based on a misunderstanding of the nature of colures, which Ittzes imagines to be terrestrial rather than celestial.[11] A brief look at elementary textbooks of astronomy with which Milton and his contemporaries would have been familiar, such as Sacrobosco's *De Sphaera*, would clarify this. Sacrobosco states clearly that the colures pass through the "poles of the universe,"[12] conscious that the colures are celestial circles. Ittzes's difficulty arises out of trying to fit in Satan's astronomical journey with the geographical one described a few lines later (9.75–91). On this point, Sherry Lutz Zivley is surely right in suggesting that that is a separate journey, a "narrow search" (9.83) orbiting the earth looking for a creature within which Satan could hide himself.[13]

Of the four angels who have a major role to play in Milton's epic— Uriel, Gabriel, Raphael, and Michael—the maximum space is given to Raphael, an indication that this angel has multiple functions to perform. One of these is Raphael's role in communicating his understanding of complex areas of knowledge such as vitalist theories of creation, higher alchemy, and the finer points of the new astronomy, thereby registering Milton's own advanced thinking on these subjects. At the same time, through Raphael's agency, these subjects are made functional in the epic, contributing to the subtle negotiations that structure this remarkable poem.

In Book 5, Raphael is described as "the sociable spirit" (5.221) and as he flies down toward Paradise with his "gorgeous wings" (5.250) all the birds of Paradise look with curiosity at this radiant winged angel who seems to resemble that fabulous bird, the phoenix. The phoenix image, both in a positive and in an inverted and negative form, recurs in Milton's poetry—notably in *Samson Agonistes*—but the classic use of the phoenix myth in Milton's poetry is in Book 5 of *Paradise Lost* where Raphael, flying from heaven to Paradise, is regarded by the birds of Paradise as a phoenix.

> To all the fowls he seems
> A phoenix, gazed by all, as that sole bird
> When to enshrine his relics in the sun's
> Bright temple, to Aegyptian Thebes he flies. (*PL*, 5.271–74)

Raphael is likened to a phoenix for a number of reasons. While there was a long tradition of regarding the phoenix as a symbol of Christ, the bird was also proverbially understood to be an emblem of a faithful friend. It is therefore not only for his glorious winged shape, but also for his role as friend to Adam and Eve that Raphael is likened to a phoenix. Additionally, with the reference to the story of the phoenix enshrining its relics in the temple, the resurrection motif is introduced to synchronize with Raphael's role as not only the "admonisher" sent by God but also the messenger of hope. God's express instructions to him are to spend half a day conversing with Adam "as friend with friend" (5.229), advise him of his happy state and his free will, and warn him about the danger posed by Satan. Those are the specific instructions given to him. And Raphael does perform his tasks. The question is, what else does he do? Having been given the assignment of conversing with Adam as friend with friend, Raphael utilizes these wide terms of reference to go beyond the agenda set down by God and to introduce Adam to a vast range of ideas from early modern thought, including creation theory, the philosophy of alchemy, and new astronomy. Adam's intellectual curiosity is no doubt encouraged and, as a "Divine instructor" (5.546), this must be satisfying for Raphael. But it also almost challenges divine authority as Raphael ventures far beyond the terms of references set down by God.

It is therefore not surprising that Kent R. Lehnhof should find Raphael's role in *Paradise Lost* to be "perplexing on several points."[14] However, his proposition that Raphael's role is "sinister, perhaps even satanic"[15] is open to debate, particularly because it can be argued that Milton, in fact, sets up Raphael and Satan as a set of contraries. In *Paradise Lost*, it has long been recognized, Milton constructs sets of antitheses—among them, the divine Trinity and the infernal triad of Satan, Sin, and Death, the automatic doors of Heaven that glide open effortlessly and the rusty, creaky gates of Hell, the bright cosmic chariot in which the Son rides out to create this cosmos in the middle of chaos and the dark "car of Night" (9.65) within which Satan spends seven days and nights of darkness devising his plans for uncreation. Raphael and Satan form another set of contraries, one of whose major functions is to demonstrate the positive and negative values of challenging forms of knowledge of the early modern period. Raphael's understanding of the new astronomy and higher alchemy is wide-ranging and intelligent, but Satan's ventures into the world of the new astronomy is limited and his attitude to alchemy manipulative and distorted. Karen Edwards, in her essay on "Inspiration and Melancholy in *Samson Agonistes*,"[16] describes Satan as a failed phoenix unable to reinvent himself—a description that supports the reading of Satan and Raphael as a set of contraries. Satan is certainly a gifted astronomer able to master the workings of the new cosmos in a very short time, and the assurance with which he makes his way through the celestial spaces of the cosmos matches the assurance of Raphael's voyage within the cosmos. Satan shares with Raphael, again, an enquiring mind that speculates on the possibility of multiple worlds. But, beyond that, Satan's astronomical knowledge is limited and his imagination much more conventional, like that of Uriel and Gabriel. Raphael's understanding of astronomy is much more sophisticated. Moreover, Satan's astronomical knowledge is utilized by him solely to seek empowerment for himself, while Raphael has no such selfish agenda and is intent on sharing his knowledge with Adam and Eve. So, too, with alchemy. While the devils have no particular interest in alchemy, Satan does utilize the basic principles of transmutational alchemy in his arguments in the temptation scene, but this is only to subvert alchemy for his own evil ends. Raphael, on the other hand, has a clear understanding of philosophical alchemy, which he attempts to share with Adam and Eve for their benefit. Raphael communicates to Adam the secrets of higher alchemy, and knowledge about vitalist theory of creation and the new astronomy. Uriel and Raphael's vitalist accounts of creation have been discussed earlier and the importance of alchemy in *Paradise Lost* will be considered in a later chapter. But in the entire range of knowledge that Raphael communicates to Adam and Eve, the most complex and fascinating are his provocative suggestions about celestial motion.

The dialogue on astronomy between Raphael and Adam at the beginning of Book 8 has been much discussed. As far back as the 1930s, Grant McColley[17] had analyzed the texts that made up the famous Ross-Wilkins controversy of the 1640s,[18] believing that these were the works that provided the materials for Raphael's warning to Adam, while, more recently, Marjara[19] has examined the scientific basis of many of the ideas advanced by Raphael. In Book 8, Adam asks Raphael for an explanation of the "disproportion" of so many great stars and planets circling through "spaces incomprehensible" in "restless revolution" at enormous speed round this "punctual spot," the "sedentary earth" (8.15–32). Raphael's long reply, bristling with clauses and qualifications, is in part a commendation of Adam's desire to understand the cosmos and thereby admire the Creator, and in part a warning to Adam not to make too many conjectures like the "quaint opinions wide" (8.78) of astronomers that prompt divine laughter. But, if McColley and others thought that Raphael is truly admonishing Adam and forbidding astronomical speculations, nothing can be further from the truth.

Raphael begins first by defining his own position regarding celestial movement. In an account that needs to be read in the context of the early modern controversy regarding alternative cosmological models, he begins from an Aristotelio-Ptolemaic position, attributing the "speed almost spiritual" (8.110) of celestial bodies, as observed by Adam, to divine omnipotence. He then questions the authenticity of this astronomical system even as he dissociates himself from assuming any position at all (8.114–18) in the cosmological debate. With remarkable agility he steers his way through affirmation ("Admitting motion" [8.115]) and denial ("Not that I so affirm" [8.117]) to reach a position of intellectual detachment. The account of celestial motion that follows may be understood at first as Tychonic as Raphael describes the dance of the stars and planets around the sun, and then Copernican as he suggests the possibility of a moving earth. The result is twofold. First, it allows Milton, as the epic poet, to record his own awareness of the cosmological debates of his time and to maintain his consistent position of openness to the viability of any one of the available cosmological models. Second, within the dramatic structure of the poem, Raphael's endorsement of this position of inclusiveness is a mark of the angel's sincerity and superior intelligence that acknowledges the possibility of a divinely ordered mechanism whose complexity and sophistication may be beyond even angelic comprehension. Also, unlike Uriel or Gabriel, Raphael has no personal agenda in dealing with celestial motion.

As he proceeds, Raphael goes on to raise a number of hypothetical questions:

> What if the sun
> Be centre to the world, and other stars
> By his attractive virtue and their own
> Incited, dance about him various rounds?
> Their wandering course now high, now low, then hid,
> Progressive, retrograde, or standing still,
> In six thou seest, and what if seventh to these
> The planet earth, so steadfast though she seem,
> Insensibly three different motions move? ... (8.122–30)

Adam must have been bewildered by this series of questions introducing, with a hypothetical "what if," a range of celestial movements beyond his wildest imagination. As the angel puts forward the possibility of heliocentricity, he does so with a glance at another area of debate in new astronomy, the magnetic properties of the sun. As in earlier passages in *Paradise Lost*, Milton brings in here the notion of cosmic dance and the magnetic power—the "attractive virtue"—of the sun that directs the movement of the stars and planets. William Gilbert's work on magnetism had sought to provide material in support of the Copernican system, and in the course of that work he had speculated on the sun's magnetic power in generating planetary motion. Kepler extended this idea of a magnetic sun. However, the philosopher and physician Robert Fludd, and the astronomer in whom Milton had an avid interest, Galileo, both rejected this magnetic theory.[20] Raphael puts forward the possibility of the sun's magnetic function again as a possibility, not a certainty. As with heliocentricity, Raphael sees his role as that of a sophisticated, intelligent, dispassionate instructor, opening Adam's mind to an array of possibilities, rather than directing his belief.[21]

The Copernican revolution had initiated a sense of rootlessness and uncertainty by locating the earth high up among the planets, giving it motion, and assigning its former central position to the sun. As Donne, echoing popular sentiment, complained in the following familiar lines:

> As new philosophy arrests the sun,
>   And bids the passive earth about it run,
> So we have dulled our mind, it hath no ends;
>   Only the body's busy, and pretends.[22]

For Adam, the most bewildering and radical suggestion must have been that of the earth's motion. The three different motions Raphael refers to are those attributed by Copernicus to the earth, namely, diurnal rotation, annual orbital revolution around the sun, and a "third motion" or "motion in declination" in which the axis of the earth describes the surface of a cone in about a year moving in a direction opposite to that of the earth's center.[23] This third motion was dismissed by Tycho Brahe but still often discussed and disputed in Milton's time. Bacon, as is well-known, rejected Copernicanism and, with it, the belief in a moving earth. When Raphael puts forward his suggestion that the apparently stationary earth "insensibly three different motions move" (8.130), he appears to be instructing Adam on one of the finer points of the new astronomy thereby revealing Milton's own familiarity with the subject. Of critical importance here, though, is Raphael's use of the provocative form of interrogation, "what if." It is a subtle means of opening up Adam's mind to undreamt of astronomical possibilities. At the same time, it holds its position as a question, enabling Raphael to voice Milton's own questioning stance on this subject. As with many occasions when Milton foregrounds Aristotelio-Ptolemaic, Tychonic and Copernican cosmology as contested sites, without deciding in favor of any one, here, too, he makes the angel Raphael put forward the notion of the three possible motions of the earth as a strong probability, but not as the truth.

If the earth is thus released into space as a moving planet, Raphael suggests, may it not be possible that the earth, as it turns, releases the light it has received from the sun and transmits it toward the moon? Here he appears to be referring to another debated issue of the times relating to the new astronomy, the concept of "secondary light." As Eileen Reeves explains, this was a term long used in optics and in painting "to describe the faint illumination that occurs when a bright light, falling on a certain kind of surface, is reflected to and scattered over a second surface."[24] This was taken up in the seventeenth century in support of the Copernican hypothesis. Galileo argued that the moving earth reflects the light of the sun on to the moon, and this "secondary light" was a clear proof of heliocentricity. Reeves draws attention to the lines

> What if that light
> Sent from her through the wide transpicuous air,
> To the terrestrial moon be as a star
> Enlightening her by day, as she by night
> This earth? (8.140–44)

to suggest that "John Milton, among the most brilliant of Galileo's interpreters, had the angel Raphael present the question of terrestrial reflection and the inhabited planets as the inescapable conclusion drawn by all who saw the cosmos as heliocentric."[25] Milton was not the only literary figure to have put forward this argument. So did Burton in a familiar passage:

If the earth move, it is a planet, and shines to them in the moon, and to the other planetary inhabitants, as the moon and they do to us upon the earth: but shine she doth, as Galileo, Kepler, and others prove, and then *per consequens*, the rest of the planets are inhabited, as well as the moon.[26]

But for Milton this knowledge is important not only for its intellectual content and radical position but also as an imaginative stimulus. The image of light sent from the earth "through the wide transpicuous air" utilizes the Latin root of "transpicuous," a word that the OED defines as "pervious to vision" or "that can be seen through," derived from the root meaning of the Latin *specere*, to look. It enables Milton to set up an image of light waves radiating out through infinite space, integrating into it, in an age that saw considerable developments in optics, a projection of unimpeded vision, of clarity. It is an image rich in visual suggestiveness, incorporating both a consciousness of space and a sense of dynamism. In its way, Raphael's image structures and focuses celestial movement in terms of the movement of light and provides an analogue for movements in space of the angels. The movement of light was to be a focal point of Newtonian science late in the seventeenth century, but throughout this century through the work of Kepler, Galileo, and others, the movement of light continued to be at the center of interest. The assurance of this visual image of "secondary light" in Raphael's speech, the ease of transmission across vast spaces within the cosmos, contrasts also with the bewilderment and awe felt by Adam and Eve with regard to celestial movement.

In a natural transition from the depiction of the earth radiating light to the moon, Raphael moves to the suggestion of a plurality of worlds. In the brief space of a few lines he appears to be suggesting to Adam that perhaps the earth moves, perhaps the cosmos is heliocentric, perhaps the earth, like other planets, reflects light from its surface, perhaps therefore there is no difference between the earth and other planets, that perhaps the other planets, and the moon, may be inhabited, that perhaps there may be a plurality of worlds. While the notion of the plurality of worlds was still a potentially volatile and controversial subject, it does find acceptance in *Paradise Lost* and Raphael in fact utilizes it to make one of his major contributions in the field of new knowledge in the epic, establishing, early in *Paradise Lost* in his voyage from heaven to Paradise, the consciousness of an infinite universe.

The movement of the angels and of Satan in space within the cosmos has a further defining quality. Speed of light as a unit of measurement is never specifically mentioned in *Paradise Lost*, although Milton does relate degrees of incorporeality with concomitant speed. When Uriel makes his journey from the sun to the earth, he travels directly, in a straight line, down a sunbeam, at enormous speed, "swift as a shooting star" (4.556). When Raphael makes his way to Paradise soon after, his flight is assured and steady. "Down thither prone in flight / He speeds, and through the vast ethereal sky / Sails between worlds and worlds, with steady wing" (5.266–68). In fact, the image of Raphael sailing through the air conveys a greater sense of control than that of Uriel gliding down sunbeams. Raphael's flight is "prone" or a downward plunge, and therefore direct. Satan, however, descending to the sun from his position at the aperture of the hard outer shell, moves "through the pure marble air his oblique way" (3.564) among innumerable stars. Perhaps, as Marjara suggests, this is "because of his villainous nature, which makes him incapable of doing anything straight."[27] And as he leaves the sun and makes his way to earth, he flies "in many an airy wheel" (3.741). Satan's devious "oblique" movement and "airy wheels," in comparison with the direct trajectory of Uriel and Raphael, suggest another possible explanation. Satan's circuitous movements follow the pattern of concentric spheres of the older astronomy that Milton carefully avoids in his depiction of the cosmos, limiting it to a single reference in the context of the Paradise of Fools (3.481–83), while the direct space flights of the good angels are in keeping with the vast unconfined spaces, liberated from the notion of solid spheres, of the new astronomy. In spite of his cunning and quick comprehension skills, Satan's limitations are conveyed through these contrasting movements. With exceptional alertness, Milton uses movements in space to define character.

At the end of Raphael's speech, Adam, suitably chastised and impressed, agrees to abjure "wandering thoughts, and notions vain" (8.187). Raphael uses celestial motion to assert the superiority of angelic intelligence over human. But he also plants in Adam's mind the seeds of speculation on subjects related to the new astronomy.

Overall, Raphael's handling of celestial movement in his discussions with Adam, like the assurance of the earlier image of his flight, sailing between "worlds and worlds" (5.268), establishes his superiority over the other angels regarding space, time, and celestial movement in *Paradise Lost*. It also establishes his suitability for the role of not only "divine / Historian" (8.6–7) but also "divine interpreter" (7.72), mediating between God and man, striking the right balance between faith in divinity and scientific curiosity.

Raphael has a significant role in Milton's strategies for meaningful integration of knowledge about the new science, in particular astronomy and alchemy, into *Paradise Lost*. For the other angels— Uriel and Gabriel—the cosmic details that matter are celestial movements rooted in the older astronomy. Raphael's understanding of the cosmos, incorporating details from the new astronomy, has much greater depth and vitality. Milton's Gabriel, positioned on the earth, shows no interest in space, time, or celestial movement except at the moment when he apparently waits for the cone of night to mark nine o'clock and the one occasion when he draws Satan's attention to the moving sign of Libra. Uriel, stationed at the sun, has a more enquiring mind, raising vitalist questions about creation, pointing to a shining earth, and revealing a fascination with moving sunbeams. Raphael's mind, as revealed through his conversations, ranges over many areas of enquiry—traditional knowledge, new astronomy, vitalism, and alchemy. He is thus able to open up the whole field of knowledge, simultaneously instructing, suggesting, and challenging.

The last of the angelic visitors to Paradise, Michael, has his own unique role to play with regard to celestial phenomena. Although his assigned task as instructor in the closing books is limited specifically to giving Adam an account of human history, including the story of redemption through Christ, his discourse is also directed to a closure of cosmic speculations. The visions of the future extending to the Day of Judgment, and the promise of a new earth and new heaven, allow Adam to achieve a fresh perspective in which the anxieties of the fragmentation of time are resolved and Adam's earlier sense of eternity is restored.

> He ended; and thus Adam last replied.
> How soon hath thy prediction, seer blest,
> Measured this transient world, the race of time,
> Till time stand fixed: beyond is all abyss,
> Eternity, whose end no eye can reach. (11.552–56)

While Michael thus redirects Adam's perception of time, he also instructs Adam on knowledge about space and the celestial regions. In words that almost echo some of Raphael's in Book 8, he says

> This having learned, thou hast attained the sum
> Of wisdom; hope no higher, though all the stars
> Thou knew'st by name, and all the ethereal powers,
> All secrets of the deep, all nature's works,
> Or works of God in heaven, air, earth, or sea...(12.575–79)

With the promise of "A paradise within thee, happier far" (12.587), Adam is being asked to turn away from the exciting cosmic speculations to which he had been introduced by Raphael before the Fall. And yet, in another instance of the many challenges and subversions that are constantly set up in Milton's handling of cosmic details, Michael's suggestion of "all the secrets of the deep" relating to heaven, air, earth, or sea reminds us of Raphael's warning to Adam regarding the "secrets to be scanned" (8.74) in the "fabric of the heavens" (8.76) that God has concealed from man, a warning that in fact encourages Adam to investigate more than it persuades him to refrain. Michael's words, too, open many doors into nature's works and the works of God, but, unlike Raphael, Michael, in spite of his role of "teacher" (11.450) and "celestial guide" (11.785), does not dwell on these secrets in any detail.

The final image of Michael we are left with is connected with variable cosmic phenomena. Michael had been advised by God to take with him his choice of "flaming warriors" (11.101) from among the cherubim. Accompanied by them, Michael had made his "swift descent" (11.127) and "Down from a sky of jasper lighted now / In Paradise, and on a hill made alt, / A glorious apparition" (11.209–11) appeared to Adam like a "blazing cloud" (11.229) that veils the hill. Now, at the end of his conversation with Adam, the cherubim descend like meteors and the sword of God blazes like a bright comet. These flaming celestial apparitions immediately bring to mind the new stars, comets, and other variable celestial phenomena that are used so effectively to define Satan's character. A deliberate contrast seems to be intended. Satan had utilized these celestial signs as modes of self-fashioning and thus provided the narrator with the means for ironic commentary on the millennial hopes of the seventeenth century. The celestial signs in Books 11 and 12 are representations rather than disguises. The cherubim's movement, "gliding meteorous" (12.629), suggests luminosity as well as a quality of being intangible and therefore pervasive. The representation is one that combines indefiniteness with pervasiveness and thus makes the cherubim represent what might be described as a total takeover of Paradise. As Adam and Eve look back toward Paradise in the closing lines of the epic, the figure of Michael has receded beyond their range of vision. Only the meteor-like cherubim, now with a terrifying and forbidding aspect, and the flaming comet-like sword of God, are seen as an overpowering presence. This flaming sword of God that "blazed / Fierce as a comet" (12.633–34) scorching the air with its heat shuts out Adam and Eve forever from Paradise. While Michael's words in Book 12 gently urge Adam not to read the stars, these fierce celestial signs achieve their own means of closure, shutting out speculations about the meaning of such signs and establishing these signs as unmistakable divine warnings. Milton's final word on the millennial debate surrounding variable celestial phenomena in the seventeenth century is that these were not promises but warnings. It is a fact that the variable celestial phenomena in this final scene do not incorporate allusions to specific celestial locations, such as Cassiopeia or Ophiucus, and are therefore not the controversial sightings debated in the seventeenth century. They are less specific, rooted in Genesis, and belong to the eschatological role assigned to comets and similar cosmic phenomena in the early modern period. However, since *Paradise Lost* utilizes the specific millennial debates relating to new stars and comets in exposing Satan's self-fashioning, the references to variable celestial in these closing scenes reflect back on those issues. The celestial signs of the final book of the epic have an apocalyptic intensity and show once again the power and impact that celestial phenomena had on Milton's imagination. In the process, they also define the character of the angel Michael as direct, intelligent, incisive, powerful, and compelling.

There are other named angels who appear in *Paradise Lost*—Abdiel, Ithuriel, Zephon, Uzziel, and Zophiel. But they are restricted to playing cameo roles and have no direct contribution either in helping us to understand the characters of Adam and Eve or in the matter of controversial representations of science, alchemy, and magic. Robert West had concluded that Milton's angels are never "controlled" by the science of angelology. His sources are much more eclectic and his "angels are always poetic fiction before they are angelology."[28] More recently, Joad Raymond has designated them as independent "creatures."[29] As individual characters, their roles have been understood in a pedagogical context. While Angelica Durran sees them as pre- and postlapsarian teachers, Anna K. Nardo argues that the good angels make up "a subplot of angelic education"[30] that expands the vision of *Paradise Lost* beyond its focus on Satan, Adam, and Eve.[31] Indeed, Uriel, Gabriel, Raphael, and Michael are a blend of tradition and imagination who emerge as dramatic characters. The significant hesitations that mark the delayed responses of Uriel and Gabriel at a time when urgent action seems to be needed raise uneasy questions about their motivation and sincerity. Raphael's intellectually stimulating conversation is conducted over an extended period of time and incorporates an informed and scientifically detached attitude to knowledge. This pedagogic role is blended with grace and friendship. He is quintessentially the "sociable spirit." Michael is firm but compassionate in his difficult role of rehabilitating Adam and Eve in the fallen world. In *Paradise Lost*, these subtle differences between the angels, the fallibility of Uriel and Gabriel, the communicative tact of the multifaceted Raphael, and the incisive power of Michael are conveyed through Milton's engagement with the vital intellectual ferment of the seventeenth century including the debated areas of science and popular belief.

CHAPTER 8

The Galileo Question

Milton's angels and the enigmatic figures Chaos and Night are characters within the epic narrative. They are the supporting cast for the dramatic confrontation between Adam and Eve and Satan. Galileo is not. Yet he is the only contemporary to be named in *Paradise Lost*. What compelled Milton to single out one individual for special mention in his epic is a question that has been much debated, and answers have been sought through an examination of Galileo's achievements, contemporary reputation, and the persecution that he suffered. All three passages in the epic where the astronomer is directly mentioned refer to the telescope. For the seventeenth century, the telescope was one of the great inventions, enabling a precise examination of the cosmos while at the same time enhancing the mystery of the universe. Rolf Willach suggests that astronomical discoveries through the telescope in the seventeenth century "came in two big waves," the first in 1610–11, with the discoveries of Galileo, Harriot, Scheiner, Fabricius, and others, and a second, more pronounced and of longer duration, associated with the discoveries of Schyrl de Rheita, Baptista Hodierna, and Christian Huygens.[1] This second wave naturally aroused fresh interest in the initial telescopic discoveries of Galileo and Harriot. Milton's own interest in the telescope may have become sharper and more focused after his visit to Galileo, although doubts have been raised about the authenticity of that visit. The references to the telescope in Milton's early poems are scientifically less precise than those in *Paradise Lost*. "Time's long prospective glass" in *At A Vacation Exercise*[2] is ambiguous at best, its ability to look into the future suggesting that it could be a crystal ball, although that would be a globe rather than a long glass. If it is a telescope, it is likely to be a poetic emblem, drawing upon emblem books "where such allegorizations of scientific instruments were not uncommon."[3] In *Paradise Lost*, with Galileo's name specifically mentioned, the reference is to the telescope as a scientific instrument, which had opened up new vistas of knowledge and generated enormous excitement in the seventeenth century. However, Milton's genuine interest in intellectual enquiry, and his regard for Galileo as a figure representing the spirit of scientific discovery, may not provide a complete answer to the presence of Galileo in the epic. The other suggestion that has been made is that Milton looked upon Galileo as "a martyr to the cause of intellectual freedom."[4] Both for his pioneering role in intellectual enquiry and as someone who suffered in the cause of truth, Galileo is well qualified to deserve the distinction of being the only living person to be mentioned in Milton's epic. But is that an adequate explanation to account for his presence in *Paradise Lost*?

It can be argued that over and above such canonization of Galileo as intellectual and martyr, there are, in fact, unexpected textual parallels between Galileo's early writings and Milton's epic poem, that there are ideas, images, and attitudes in *Paradise Lost* that are a reflection of the life and writings of the astronomer. This may have been in the form of an intellectual resource, helping Milton shape his epic poem. It may equally have been a recognition of similarities in perception and attitude that prompted the poet to take the unusual step of singling out one contemporary for direct mention in *Paradise Lost*. Identification of such similarities, which are distinct from the public recognition of Galileo as scientific pioneer and as martyr in the cause of truth, would help us view some of Milton's poetic strategies in *Paradise Lost* from a fresh perspective. This investigative journey can begin from Milton's visit to Galileo. By 1638, around the time Milton perhaps visited him, Galileo had become blind, a condition that was to afflict the epic poet by the time he wrote *Paradise Lost*. While this shared disability must have imparted a special poignancy to Milton's personal response to Galileo,[5] the astronomer's blindness would have seemed particularly tragic to all those who knew of him because of the critical importance of eyesight for his work. It was Galileo's observations through the telescope that contributed significantly to the development of science. Mathematical analyses, experiments, and theory all contributed to his great scientific achievements, but the discoveries he announced in print, in the first two decades of the seventeenth century, relied, to a great extent, on observations through the telescope. Appropriately, each of the three passages in *Paradise Lost* where Galileo is directly mentioned shows the astronomer engaged in looking through his optic glass. If the Galileo passages foreground the importance of sight for the astronomer, one needs to acknowledge at the same time that a strong reliance on visual perspective is one of the distinguishing features of *Paradise Lost*. As a poetical work, Milton's epic is remarkable for its visual intensity. The poet configures both external data, including space and time within the cosmos, as well as states of mind, through visual perspective. Space is constructed through the visual perspectives of Raphael, Satan, Adam and Eve, and the mechanism for the configuring of time, the moving sunbeams and the cone of night, rely on sight. Again, Uriel's detection of the evil passions in Satan as revealed through the changing expressions on his face is only possible because of the angel's powerful eyesight. Another example of the importance of sight for the epic narrative is Eve's telescopic view of the earth in her dream temptation, which subtly alters her personality. Just as the dynamism of the epic's physical universe, expanding space and the movement of time in the cosmos, is configured through visual images, critical events that change the course of the epic's action rely on sight. Dramatically significant moments in the epic reveal a strong visual imagination. Moreover, the image of the eye, with multiple layers of meaning, is invested with critical importance in the poem. Within a work in which the visual dimension is of such importance, the iconic figure of Galileo provides an identifiable symbolic focus.

Milton's suggested meeting with Galileo has been received with some skepticism.[6] In the *Areopagetica*, while drawing attention to the danger of a censured press, he mentions his meeting with the imprisoned astronomer: "There it was that I found and visited the famous *Galileo* grown old, a prisoner to the Inquisition, for thinking in Astronomy otherwise than the Franciscan and Dominican licensers thought."[7] On the basis of this evidence it is thought that Milton met Galileo during his Italian journey, 1638–39. While no other external evidence is available, Frank B. Young is right to note that Milton's cosmology in the poems written before his Italian journey is much more medieval while in *Paradise Lost* he incorporates Galileo's major discoveries including the moon's topography (7.375–78), moon spots (1.287–91; 5.419–20; 8.145–48), sunspots (3.588–90), the composition of the Milky Way (7.577–81), and the four moons of Jupiter (8.148–51) Galileo discovered.[8] While in Florence, Milton frequented two private academies, the Svogliati and the Apatisti, and made many friends, with some of whom he was to continue to correspond for many years. Among the people he came to know well were the astronomer's son, Vincenzo Galilei, and Carlo Dati, a former pupil of Galileo's. Either could have arranged a meeting between Milton and Galileo.[9] Still, other than the brief mention in *Areopagetica*, no conclusive external evidence exists about a possible meeting between the two. If no such meeting at all took place, it must be all the more significant that Milton needed to invent such a meeting. While the specific context in which Galileo is mentioned in *Areopagetica* in 1644 relates to political oppression and the need for intellectual freedom, the Galileo who appears later in the epic poem is portrayed rather differently.

Galileo, in *Paradise Lost*, has a complex role to play and the implications of the brief allusions need to be examined within the larger fabric of the poem. At the heart of Milton's great epic is a consciousness of analogy as the nearest one could approach to truth. "How shall I relate" (5.564), asks the angel, except by "likening" (5.573). Meanings and definitions are constantly elided, endlessly deferred, negotiated through similes and other metaphorical devices. Statements limit and confine. Analogy extends meaning in a suggestive exploration. All three Galileo passages in *Paradise Lost* are similes—adjusting, focusing, suggesting—sharing in the conscious coalition of defining with indefiniteness that reflects Galileo's attitude and marks Milton's poem. The acknowledgment of doubts, uncertainty, and illusion was an integral part of Galileo's understanding of the cosmos and the powers of science. In *Paradise Lost*, a work that privileges ambiguity and engages in viewing the traditional oppositions of time and eternity, a finite world and infinite space, unchanging virtue and spiritual ascent as simultaneously possible, Galileo is an emblematic figure, combining great scientific achievement with a conscious acknowledgment of uncertainty. This is perhaps the real reason for the presence of Galileo in Milton's epic.

Meanwhile, Galileo has a more consciously literary role, too, inspiring specific images and perspectives in Milton's poem. For this reason, unlike the biographical reference in the prose work, the Galileo passages in *Paradise Lost* demand a more critical attention to the astronomer's work, and to at least two specific texts. In his epic poem, Milton makes precise references to Galileo's observations of the surface of the moon and the details of sunspots. This should help us identify the most likely sources. Scholarly discussions about Milton and Galileo have focused attention primarily on Galileo's *Dialogue of the Two Chief Systems of the World* as the important and controversial text Milton would have been familiar with.[10] It is true that many of the issues debated in *Dialogue* are reflected in *Paradise Lost*, but in concentrating on that work, and on Galileo's fate at the Inquisition, very little attention has been paid to the *Sidereus Nuncius* or *The Starry Messenger*, published in 1610, the little book into which Galileo poured all his excitement about his new discoveries with the telescope, in particular about the surface of the moon. The *Sidereus Nuncius* caught the imagination of readers across Europe and Britain. Donne made a witty allusion to it in *Ignatius his Conclave* in 1611, the year after the publication of Galileo's work, and the popularity of Galileo's volume continued for many years. It was so well known that there can be little doubt about Milton's acquaintance with this book. It is to this book that we should turn as the immediate source of the Galileo passages in Books 1 and 5 of *Paradise Lost*. Three years after the *Sidereus*, in 1613, Galileo published his *Letters on Sunspots*. The existence of sunspots was not a new discovery, but much debate was generated by telescopic observations of sunspots in the seventeenth century. This was principally on two counts. First, there was the question of priority in telescopic observation of sunspots. Second, a controversy arose regarding the composition of sunspots. The first publication of this time on sunspots[11] was a booklet printed in the summer of 1611 by Johann Fabricius of Wittenberg. In the autumn of that year, letters on sunspots were exchanged between Father Christopher Scheiner, a Jesuit professor and amateur scientist, and Galileo, later published as Galileo's *Letters on Sunspots* (1613). Sunspots were also observed independently by the English astronomer Thomas Harriot. Galileo's observations on sunspots had many implications, including providing evidence in support of the Copernican system. But one of the major issues debated was between Scheiner's belief in sunspots being either stars or a planet moving across the face of the sun and Galileo's discovery that sunspots not only appeared and disappeared, they also changed shape, unlike stars and planets. Galileo believed sunspots to be made of some "fluid substance," "situated upon or very close to the sun,"[12] and compared them with clouds. Again, there may not be external evidence of Milton's knowledge of the *Letters on Sunspots*, but the work generated so much controversy that it became widely known. This work provides the context for the Galileo passage in Book 3.

Galileo's *Sidereus Nuncius* is relevant to our understanding of *Paradise Lost* in two specific ways. First, there are direct references in Milton's epic to some of the discoveries announced in Galileo's book. One of these is clearly Galileo's findings regarding the surface of the moon. The uneven surface of the moon is one of the first findings Galileo announces in the *Sidereus*: "The moon is not robed in a smooth and polished surface but is in fact rough and uneven, covered everywhere, just like the earth's surface, with huge prominences, deep valleys, and chasms."[13] This knowledge about the uneven surface of the moon, the presence of ridges and valleys, is woven into the

Galileo images in Books 1 and 5 of *Paradise Lost*. In the first place it provides, in Book 1, an analogy for Satan's battered shield. But this absorbing interest in Galileo's discovery that the surface of the moon is not smooth and even has an added significance in its relevance to Milton's presentation of Paradise. In Book 5, Raphael looking through the aperture in the hard outer shell of the cosmos is compared with Galileo examining the moon through his telescope. There was an extensive debate in the early modern period, recorded in treatises such as Peter Heylyn's *Cosmographie*,[14] about the topography of Paradise. As a region of perfection, Paradise was believed to be a flat landscape, not admitting the imperfection of hills and valleys. This is the view incorporated into terms of praise in country house poems such as Marvell's *Upon Appleton House* where the Fairfax estate is compared with Paradise

> A leveled space, as smooth and plain
> As cloths for Lely stretched to stain.
> The world when first created sure
> Was such a table rase and pure.[15]

Milton's Paradise is radically different, admitting a *concordia discors* of hills and valleys on its surface. Galileo's telescopic discovery of the moon's surface is a mirror image of this aspect of the topography of Milton's imagined Paradise. Similarly, Galileo's explanation of the composition of the Milky Way toward the end of *Sidereus Nuncius* is reflected in Milton's description of the starry pavement of heaven (7.577–81). Such passages make the *Sidereus* one of the important sources to consult for an analysis of allusions to the astronomer.

Second, apart from these direct references, what is intriguing is that there are also a number of similarities between *Sidereus Nuncius* and *Paradise Lost*, which are instances of parallel representations. In Galileo's record of his scientific findings there are modes of discovery and impact that are reflected in Milton's poetic strategies. It is possible to suggest that Milton may have found in Galileo's book echoes of some of his own independent images and poetic devices. Galileo's little book reveals strong emotion, above all astonishment and wonder, inspired by his discoveries. Often this is a result of a sense of direct encounter generated by looking through a telescope. There is also the shock of the sudden experience of immense magnitude that such observations revealed. Similar projections of amazement and sudden encounter with immense magnitude are also a feature of *Paradise Lost*. The greatest impact that Galileo records early in

Sidereus Nuncius is this sense of shock, amazement, and wonder at the magnificent spectacle of the moon, seen through the telescope, magnified many times and seeming to be very close.

> It is a very beautiful thing, and most gratifying to the sight, to behold the body of the moon, distant from us almost sixty earthly radii, as if it were no further away than two such measures—so that its diameter appears almost thirty times larger, its surface nearly nine hundred times, and its volume twenty-seven thousand times as large as when viewed with the naked eye.[16]

The sense of encounter such an experience generates, the sudden and unexpected change of dimension, is awe-inspiring and breathtaking. This is reflected in a narrative device Milton repeatedly uses in *Paradise Lost*. Such similarities may be incidental, but they reveal shared sensibilities. The most striking instance is in Book 4 of *Paradise Lost*. When Ithuriel's spear touches Satan, sitting at Eve's ear disguised as a toad engaged in the dream temptation, he starts up, returning to his own immense stature. The sight is awe-inspiring and "back stept those two fair angels half amazed" (4.820). A few lines later, although no direct reference to Galileo may be intended, as Gabriel and the other angels arrive, the whole scene is presented through lunar images reminding us of the *Sidereus*. Satan "waxing more in rage" (4.969) is a lunar image complemented by that of the crescent moon formation adopted by the good angels: "While thus he spake, the angelic squadron bright / Turned fiery red, sharpening in mooned horns / Their phalanx, and began to hem him round" (4.977–79). This is suggestive of a confrontation between the full moon and the new moon. It is possible to urge that these lunar images in the context of great and unexpected enlargement might have been inspired by Milton's reading of *Sidereus Nuncius*, which speculates at length both on the magnified size of the moon seen through the telescope as well as on the different phases of the moon. This sense of unexpected enormous size or magnitude is also an essential part of our first encounter with Satan. In Book 1, his "mighty stature" (1.222) is made memorable through the Leviathan simile, which is then followed by the comparison of Satan's spear with a Norwegian pine and his shield with the moon seen through the telescope—the first of the direct references to Galileo. The good angels, however, do not surprise Adam and Eve with their height or size. When Raphael arrives as "a seraph winged" (5.277), he is a "glorious shape" (4.309), but there is no suggestion of unexpected magnified dimensions. And

Michael appears "as man / Clad to meet man" (11.239–40). Raphael
and Michael intend to communicate with and teach Adam and Eve,
and a barrier of dissimilarity would not have served their purpose. But
at dramatically challenging moments in the poem the shock of unex-
pected magnitude is a poetic strategy Milton follows. And then there
are also Raphael's consistent reminders that his narrative of the war in
heaven is conducted by setting forth great things by small. The com-
parison of great and small, of the unexpected and the familiar, not
only contributes to a sublime vision and grand style, it also enhances
the dramatic quality of Milton's epic. Sometimes changes in visual
perspective in the epic, as in the stars/worlds images, are intended for
a specific effect, the creation of infinite space within a finite cosmos
in its hard outer shell. In a more general way, they also create the
strategy of surprise, which is an important device in Milton's poem.
Similarly, wonder and a feeling of intense surprise permeate Galileo's
Sidereus Nuncius from the excited opening lines of the book[17]:

> Great indeed are the things which in this brief treatise I propose for
> observation and consideration by all students of nature...the entirely
> unexpected and novel character of these things...to the closing lines:
>   Time prevents my proceeding further, but the gentle reader may
> expect more soon.[18]

In a remarkable passage in the *Sidereus*, this characteristic intense
surprise generated by visual experience inspires an unexpected visual
image. This is in the course of Galileo's account of the dark spots
he observed on the moon when the moon was approaching its first
quarter. His poetical image transforms his description of the smaller
moon spots.

> The blackish portion of each spot is turned toward the source of the
> sun's radiance, while a bright rim surrounds the spot on the side away
> from the sun in the direction of the shadowy region of the moon. This
> part of the moon's surface, where it is spotted as the tail of a peacock
> is sprinkled with azure eyes...[19]

The pastoral beauty of a sight that might well have belonged to Milton's
Paradise redeems as well as clarifies the deeply troubling discovery of
blemishes on the moon. The unfolding analogy moves from the prob-
lematic celestial phenomenon, the spotted moon, through its likeness
to a peacock's tail, to the outer limits of "azure eyes," an image that
entices as much as it enlightens. Displaying visual imagination worthy

of a "Tuscan artist" (1.288), Galileo's image is almost a metaphysical conceit and transforms the imperfection of "spots" into "eyes." "Eyes" confers empowerment and sublimity.

In *Paradise Lost*, "eyes" has complex layers of meaning derived from science, including optics, as well as philosophy and alchemy. There are memorable images in *Paradise Lost* that invite comparison with Galileo's analogy of the spotted moon with a peacock's tail studded with eyes. Above all, there is the image of "the chariot of paternal deity" (6.750) accompanied by four "cherubic shapes" (6.753) for whom "wings were set with eyes, with eyes the wheels" (6.755) and that of the cherubim who accompany Michael to Paradise—"all their shape / Spangled with eyes" (11.129–30). Milton draws upon the *Timaeus* and the prophetic books of the Bible for these images, and there is no reason to look upon the Galileo passage as another likely source. But that passage, with its suggestion of empowerment and sublimity, the analogy of "eyes" used as a transformative device, might have struck Milton as a remarkable parallel in a scientific text.

The Galileo passages in *Paradise Lost* do not directly use the term "telescope," only its variants—"optic glass" (1.288), "glazed optic tube" (3.590), and "the glass / Of Galileo" (5.261–62). It is in Book 4 of *Paradise Regained* that the scientific term "telescope" appears. The context is a moment of clearly perceptible heightening of tension. Satan has been finding it increasingly difficult to tempt Jesus. His impatience translates into an attempt to utilize advanced technical skills in the hope that this might help him achieve his ends. The first of these involves a reference to the telescope: "By what strange parallax or optic skill / Of vision multiplied through air, or glass / Of telescope, were curious to inquire" (4.40–42). A few lines later, he refers to the unique "airy microscope."

> Many a fair edifice besides, more like
> Houses of gods (so well I have disposed
> My airy microscope) thou mayst behold
> Outside and inside both. (4.55–58)

Telescopes and microscopes were both seventeenth-century inventions. The phrases that accompany the reference to the telescope in *Paradise Regained*—"strange parallax" and "optic skill"—configure the telescope in ways quite unlike the telescope in *Paradise Lost*. "Optic skill" suggests intriguing possibilities of meaning—its range of references could include Keplerian and post-Keplerian scientific theories of light and vision as well as the magical optics of

Dee's showstone. In astronomy, "parallax," the OED tells us, means "apparent displacement, or difference in the apparent position, of an object, caused by actual change (or difference) of position of the point of observation." Parallaxes have been known since ancient times in relation to the observation of planets, sun, and stars. While Ptolemy's *Almagest* recorded the parallax of planets, Hipparchus, in the second century BC, made calculations of solar parallax and the debate about the Copernican system in the sixteenth century involved discussions about stellar parallax. Galileo's investigations into sunspots also involved speculations about parallax. Parallax, involving error and displacement, was a familiar concept and it had entered the vocabulary of poetry long before Milton. The OED quotes the Elizabethan poet Samuel Daniel's lines "Undeceived with the Paralax Of a mistaking eye of passion" as an early instance of the literary use of "parallax." The alignment of the telescope of *Paradise Regained* with "optic skill" and "parallax" identifies the instrument with illusion and error. *Paradise Lost* uses a more consciously literary and less technical term for telescope. Like the references to perspective glasses in Donne and Vaughan, the Galileo passages in *Paradise Lost* capture the sense of wonder, rather than skill. Unlike *Paradise Regained*, *Paradise Lost* associates the telescope not with error but with uncertainty. After all, the telescope in *Paradise Regained* is a tool in Satan's hands. In *Paradise Lost*, on the other hand, it is an instrument that tracks Satan, first his shield and later Satan himself as sunspot.

The sunspot passage, however, is much more than a very modern scientific image drawing upon recent telescopic discoveries. It is intriguing to note that the description of the alchemical properties of the sun in Book 3 follow immediately after the reference to Galileo and sunspots. Milton's reference to sunspots, it could be suggested, belongs both to the world of astronomy as well as alchemy, its effectiveness the result of the convergence of these two areas. This might be true also of Marvell's *The Last Instructions to a Painter* (1667)[20]:

> So his bold tube, man to the sun applied
> And spots unknown to the bright star descried,
> Showed they obscure him, while too near they please
> And seem his courtiers, are but his disease.
> Through optic trunk the planet seemed to hear,
> And hurls them off e'er since in his career.
> And you, Great Sir, that with him empire share,
> Sun of our world, as he the Charles is there,
> Blame not the Muse that brought those spots to sight,
> Which in your splendour hid, corrode your light. (949–58)

J. E. Weiss and N. O. Weiss, in a note on Marvell's sunspot reference,[21] gave a statistical account of the incidence of sunspots in the seventeenth century as well as the acute shortage of sunspots since 1645, which came to be known as the Maunder Minimum. The precision of Marvell's sunspot reference, they argued, points to his informed knowledge about the phenomenon. In an age when it was standard poetic convention to compare the monarch with the sun, Marvell's poem, they suggested, "asserts his loyalty to the king (lines 961–4), but his daring image reflects the unrest felt by the country party in the House of Commons" regarding a king they saw as being governed by lust, women, and rogues. The rarity of observed sunspots after 1645, and their total absence between 1655 and 1660, was followed by the appearance of a large spot observed by Boyle in 1660. While Marvell's poem includes this precise astronomical reference, there can be no doubt that, as a poet who incorporates a range of alchemical allusions in his poetry,[22] he also intended to suggest the alchemical connotation of "spot" as blemish or impurity, "the unclean matter or earthiness of the Stone which has to be washed and purified in the philosophical fire."[23] Astronomy and alchemy come together in Marvell's poem as they do, again, in *Paradise Lost*. Satan is both a sunspot, like the ones observed by Galileo, and an impurity and impediment to sublimity that needs to be removed.

However, apart from the suggestion of blemish, "spot" could also be used with quite the opposite connotation. Amy Boesky, taking a close look at Milton's sunspots, draws attention to the ambivalent usage of "spot" in the seventeenth century when the word, although predominantly signifying blemish, either physical or moral, could also indicate a cosmetic beauty spot or patch applied either to conceal a blemish or simply to enhance beauty.[24] There is a further significance of "spot" in *Paradise Lost*. It is also used to determine perspective. Satan, a huge figure compared to the Leviathan as he lies on the burning surface of Hell, now disguised as a young cherub, looks no bigger than a spot as he lands on the sun. There are other spots of varying dimensions in the epic. That part of Paradise specially tended to by Eve where the serpent finds her is a spot ("spot more delicious" [9.439]), as is the whole of Paradise pointed out by Uriel ("That spot to which I point is Paradise" [3.733]). Again, to Adam's speculative mind, the entire earth is no bigger than a spot in the universe ("this Earth a spot, a grain" (8.17) and "this opacous Earth, this punctual spot" [8.23]). "Spot," then, is another Miltonic strategy for simultaneous magnification and reduction. The ambiguities of "spot" not only create varying visual perspectives, it succeeds also, in conjunction with the implication of "spot," as blemish, in creating a matrix of irony with strong moral connotations.

There are three passages in *Paradise Lost* that refer specifically to Galileo. As a basic premise it has to be said that all three Galileo passages, like the other Galileo allusions throughout the epic, including the reference to secondary light, incorporate details that are signs of Milton's acquaintance with new and controversial findings of the new astronomy. All three specific Galileo passages refer to the telescope and Lara Dodds suggests that "for Milton the telescope is a marker of his century's reexamination of human ways of knowing."[25] In the three passages, Galileo's observations with the telescope can be regarded almost as emblematic representations of the new vistas revealed by early modern science. On closer analysis, however, two further inescapable points emerge. First, that the specifics within the Galileo passages in *Paradise Lost* share space with the language of alchemy and Renaissance philosophy as the network of references to "eyes," the sun, and "spot" in *Paradise Lost* show. Second, while the three Galileo passages focus on new discoveries, each of them balances clarity of vision with the possibility of illusion and uncertainty.

As Galileo records in *Sidereus Nuncius*, his observations through his telescope revealed the fact that the moon's surface is not smooth but is marked with mountains and valleys. This is the material out of which the first and the third of the Galileo images in *Paradise Lost* are constructed. The first provides the analogy for Satan's massive shield.

> He scarce hath ceased when the superior fiend
> Was moving toward the shore; his ponderous shield
> Ethereal temper, massy, large, and round,
> Behind him cast; the broad circumference
> Hung on his shoulders like the moon, whose orb
> Through optic glass the Tuscan artist views
> At evening from the top of Fesole,
> Or in Valdarno, to descry new lands,
> Rivers or mountains in her spotty globe. (1.283–91)

The second defines the superiority of angelic eyesight. Raphael, looking at the earth from the gates of heaven,

> However small he sees,
> Not unconform to other shining globes,
> Earth and the garden of God, with cedars crowned
> Above all hills. As when by night the glass

> Of Galileo, less assured, observes
> Imagined lands and regions in the moon:
> Or pilot from amidst the Cyclades
> Delos or Samos first appearing kens
> A cloudy spot. (5.258–66)

Both passages invoke the image of the Galileo of *Sidereus Nuncius* looking at the moon through his telescope. In the first, the "Tuscan artist"[26] examines what appears to him to be rivers and mountains on the surface of the moon. Not only are we, as readers, invited to consider Satan's shield, presumably dented and marked through his martial encounters, to be as large as the moon, but also the Galileo reference invites also to think of the magnified moon described in *Sidereus*. In the second, it is Raphael who is actually examining the topography of the earth from a distance, but this activity is compared to that of Galileo examining the moon's surface. However indirectly, we are being initiated into some of Galileo's major findings—the size of the moon, the uneven nature of the moon's surface, the earth as a "shining" globe, in other words, radiating secondary light, and the phenomenon of moonspots. If Milton incorporates the controversial findings of the new astronomy in these two passages, the same is also true of the sunspot passage: "There lands the fiend, a spot like which perhaps / Astronomer in the sun's lucent orb / Through his glazed optic tube yet never saw" (3.588–90). Satan, in his cherub disguise, had indeed landed on the surface of the sun to conduct his dialogue with Uriel. If, then, Milton goes on to compare him with a sunspot, he is contributing to Galileo's view that sunspots were situated upon or very close to the sun and were not independent star or planet-like objects momentarily floating across the face of the sun. Galileo had noted that sunspots changed shape and had compared them with clouds. For Satan, with his devious habit of changing shape through his various disguises, sunspot is an appropriate analogy and indicates Milton's endorsement of Galileo's findings.

The unevenness of the moon's surface had led Galileo to ask an intriguing question in the *Sidereus Nuncius*. Given the fact that there are so many mountains and valleys on the moon's surface, how is it possible for the outer boundary of the moon to look smooth and give the effect of a circular outline? Should not the edges look uneven? There are two explanations that he puts forward.[27] First, that there are multiple mountain ranges, densely packed, along the moon's circumference, so that the eye, viewing them from afar, is unable to distinguish them and sees only a regular and unbroken line. Second, he suggests, wrapped around the moon is a globe of some substance denser than the aether, subtly altering the actual appearance of the moon. What Galileo suggests, in other words, is that telescopic observations may be subject to optical illusions. This same admission of uncertainty in astronomical matters is also to be found in the *Letters On Sunspots*. In the "Third Letter on Sunspots," for example, Galileo writes:

> In my opinion we need not entirely give up contemplating things because they are very remote from us...The substances composing the earth and the moon seem to me to be equally unknown, as do those of our elemental clouds and of sunspots...I know no more about the true essences of earth or fire than about those of the moon or sun, for that knowledge is withheld us, and is not to be understood until we reach the state of blessedness.[28]

The Galileo passages in *Paradise Lost* convey this sense of uncertainty, through the tentative "to descry," "less assured," and "yet never." "To descry," Donald Friedman points out, "both traditionally and contemporaneously with Milton, carried more strongly than 'to see from a distance' the connotations of revealing or betraying."[29] Such connotations further undermine belief in scientific certainty. In all three passages, Galileo's findings are conditional, uncertain, suggesting instead a dissolving of speculative boundaries and the opening up of imaginative possibilities.

Amy Boesky locates a similar suggestion of uncertainty in Milton's use of the word "spot."[30] "Five times in *Paradise Lost* the word *spot* is associated with optic lenses, astronomical investigations, and the risks of curiosity and of certitude, and in each instance the word is associated both with uncertainty and with temptation." Each one of the Galileo references is associated with the word "spot" and Boesky feels that this may be intended to indicate the limitations of the astronomer's vision in comparison with the vision of the poet. She suggests that what is at stake here is the question of certainty and uncertainty. Galileo, in *Paradise Lost*, "represents not merely the power to see, but the ambiguities that such power elicits."[31] Examining the Galileo passages in *Paradise Lost*, it is this perception of limitation that Angelica Durran also emphasizes. She identifies "the image of Galileo" as "an insufficient model for pedagogy and science."[32] Unlike the perception of "inadequacy" in Durran's model that privileges angelic pedagogy over the limitations of natural philosophy, Judith Herz sees uncertainty as positive and enriching and as a quality that connects Galileo with the epic poet.[33] The question that Eve first raises in Paradise about the function of the moon and stars, repeated by Adam to Raphael, reflected in Michael's words at the end, is a question that is continually deferred rather than answered. Herz calls it "the Galileo question," which reflects the "tension between certainty and doubt" that is also essential to Milton's own artistic practice. Moreover, she suggests, "Clearly Galileo's discoveries provided a source of expanded imaginative possibilities in their opening of the poem's space, but, even more crucially, they offered a means for the human actors in the poem to define their identity as a function of their search for ways to understand their universe." Similarly, Maura Brady has suggested that the Galileo passages in *Paradise Lost* show the limitations and imperfections of the telescope, but its "occlusions" are not intended to shun enquiry. "Rather, they are offered as a challenge to the reader to accept limited perspective and confusion as necessary conditions of the search for knowledge, and make of them something useful."[34] Science becomes a model not of closure, but of that which is contestable and contested.

It can be argued that there is an intertextuality or allusiveness, at least a matrix of shared imaginative space, between Galileo's early texts and Milton's epic poem, but it is this widely held perception of uncertainty that the Galileo passages in *Paradise Lost* convey that is perhaps the real reason for the inclusion of references to this particular astronomer in the epic poem. One can imagine Milton reading Galileo's *Sidereus Nuncius* and the *Letters on Sunspots* and discovering, in the middle of the astronomer's excited account of his telescopic discoveries, this curious, albeit scientific, conclusion to which Galileo arrived, that however much clarity of vision might be achieved, there is always the possibility of illusion and uncertainty. This position of philosophic uncertainty that Galileo adopted accorded well with Milton's own position of inclusiveness and his belief in the need to accept the possible validity of conflicting intellectual positions. For Milton, Galileo is not only the preeminent scientist of his day and a martyr in the cause of intellectual freedom. He is an inspiring example of a combination of outstanding scientific achievement and the capacity to believe in doubts and uncertainty as positive and enabling.

As the only set of references to a contemporary, the Galileo passages make their own contribution to the defining of character. One of the critical aspects of character that separates Adam from Eve is Adam's capacity for doubts and uncertainty, which contrasts with Eve's confidence. Adam reveals his capacity for doubt over a wide range of subjects. His interpretation of Eve's dream temptation reveals a mature recognition of unknown modes of thought that the human mind is capable of, which might "misjoin" (5.111) words and thoughts to produce unexpected results. Later, in his conversation with Raphael, one set of uncertainties banished as a result of the angel's narration of Satan's rebellion, the war in heaven, and the expulsion of the rebel angels ("Adam soon repealed / The doubts that in his heart arose" [7.59–60]), Adam admits that all his doubts have not been cleared ("yet something of doubt remains" [8.13]). This time his doubts are about the cosmos, and he asks Raphael to resolve them. In reply, even as Raphael seeks to provide Adam with answers to "that which thee to doubt it moved" (8.116), he commends a questioning mind ("To ask or search I blame thee not" [8.66]). In the epic, the paradigm for such doubts and questions, such sensitive hesitations, cannot be the angels or Satan, or Chaos and Night. What better model could the human world provide than one of the intellectual giants of the contemporary world who accepted the capacity to believe in doubts and uncertainties as both inevitable and stimulating.

Adam, Eve, and the "Virtuous Touch" of Alchemy

In *Paradise Lost*, Milton has the difficult task of defining the characters of Adam, the "first of men" (4.408), and the "first of women Eve" (4.409), not as a static tableaux, but as evolving figures. Both as individuals and within their relationship, the representation of Adam and Eve in the epic is remarkable for its depth and complexity. Within the very brief time span of the narrative, we notice both individual characteristics that distinguish Adam and Eve as well as subtle changes in their character as the epic proceeds. This nuanced portrayal of the changes that take place in Adam and Eve constitutes the true dramatic core of *Paradise Lost*. There is no change that we encounter, or indeed expect, in Satan and the good angels, only a series of revelations, sometimes unexpected. It is only in Adam and Eve that there are significant changes in character.

Change itself was a much debated subject in the seventeenth century. Both the possibility of change and the consequences of change were questioned in a range of intellectual spheres that engaged the early modern mind. The principle of change was debated in astronomy where the very notion appeared to run counter to the belief in the perfection of the ethereal ("unchanging") celestial spheres. The subject also became a divisive doctrine in Christianity. The climate of revolution, however, in the seventeenth century brought in its own compulsions for change even as the new astronomy dismantled the notion of the unchanging heavens and magic and alchemy made powerful projections of change as renovation.

Paradise Lost as epic urges us to consider change as positive and enriching. On a cosmic scale there is the suggestive possibility of change as the matter of chaos waits for God to create more worlds, multiple cosmoses. The dark illimitable ocean of chaos might indeed change into a vibrant region of many worlds. Within the opaque shell of this cosmos, the stars may be worlds and God might have intended to make "every star perhaps a world / Of destined habitation" (7.621–22). This surmise on the part of the angels projects a world picture totally unexpected within the Christian framework. These radical cosmic possibilities suggested within the epic configure surprise as intrinsic to change even as change is seen as enriching, and not as a sign of decay. That there should be a change in the characters of the first humans is therefore not necessarily a mark of corruption but might, indeed, be richly rewarding. This is the lesson that God's messenger, Raphael, attempts to convey to Adam and Eve through his exposition on alchemy. But change is not necessarily linear, tending toward good or evil. It may be multifaceted, the result of many compulsions, and its manifestations are therefore likely to be unexpected and dramatic. It is this basic premise that explains the complexities in Milton's portrayal of Adam and Eve.

It is not surprising that, in *Paradise Lost*, Raphael, as God's messenger, should take alchemy as the frame of reference for an exploration of internal change. In Milton's time it was understood that the higher reaches of alchemy and hermetic magic were concerned with renovation and redemption. Base and corrupt levels of alchemy and magic, involving practices of deception and ambition, were far removed from what was understood as true alchemy. Milton, after all, is writing in an age when the alchemical tradition flourished from John Dee to Robert Fludd and the achievements of alchemy and English contributions to it were highlighted by Arthur Dee and Elias Ashmole. John Dee's experiments in magic and alchemy, with the assistance of Edward Kelly, may have been ridiculed by Meric Casaubon on the ground of angel summoning, but Dee also earned the unstinted admiration of others, such as the antiquary Elias Ashmole. In 1652 Ashmole published his great *Theatrum Chemicum Britannicum*[1] to draw attention to English achievements in alchemy. In seventeenth-century England the true successor of John Dee was the physician, philosopher, and alchemist Robert Fludd. Fludd was familiar with the Rosicrucian texts, the *Fama Fraternitatis* (1614) and the *Confessio* (1615), which glorified Paracelsus and held the view that knowledge of the secrets of medicine revealed the secrets of the microcosm and that this in turn would also unlock the door to the secrets of the macrocosm. The Rosicrucians appealed to all true scholars to publish their work. This appeal led to what Frances Yates described as a period of Rosicrucian "furor" during the years 1614–24.[2] However, the propositions put forward by the Rosicrucians were much debated and there was a sharp attack on the mystical basis of Rosicrucian natural philosophy by the German iatrochemist Andreas Libavius. Fludd's first publication, the *Apologia* (1616), was a reply to Libavius and may have been inspired partly by his acquaintance with the German mystical alchemist Michael Maier who translated into Latin the most famous of the English alchemical works, Thomas Norton's *Ordinall of Alchemy*. As Allen G. Debus pointed out, "for Fludd alchemy was potentially a well of deep truth. Like Paracelsus he believed that this science was a key to the Creation itself.[3] In his attempt to probe the secrets of the universe, Fludd relied not only on Paracelsus and the Rosicrucians, but also on the Hermetic texts, quoting often from the *Pymander* and the *Asclepius*. Like John Dee, whose hieroglyphic monad was for Fludd the most powerful method of analysis, Fludd's philosophy combined magic and alchemy. His views changed little over the years and his posthumously published *Mosaicall Philosophy* (1638) expressed the same views about magic, alchemy, and the harmony of the universe that are to be found in his earlier work. While Fludd himself engaged in debate about Rosicrucianism, his own work was bitterly attacked by Kepler and Marin Mersenne. Perhaps the controversies raised by Fludd were part of the reason for the continued interest in magic and alchemy in the seventeenth century. In any event, as Debus observes,

> It is significant that Fludd's work continued to be a subject of debate at a time when one might have expected interest in Renaissance natural magic and Hermeticism to have been in deep decline. In reality the 1650s witnessed the publication of more alchemical works in England than had ever appeared previously...The English version of Fludd's *Mosaicall Philosophy* appeared as late as 1659.[4]

Although he did believe in transmutational alchemy, Fludd's mystical alchemy was motivated not by the desire to turn base metal into gold but by the conviction that alchemy and magic would reveal the essential harmony of the universe. The many publications on alchemy that appeared in the first half of the seventeenth century and the controversies that swirled around Fludd and the Rosicrucians are a clear indication of the fact that interest in alchemy was part of the general intellectual climate of the time. The literature of the time provides a reflection of this and alchemy has a major presence in the poetry of Donne, Marvell, and other metaphysical poets. It may be of interest to note that Thomas Vaughan, brother of Henry Vaughan, was a practicing alchemist.

Milton's scientific contemporaries, from Boyle[5] to Newton,[6] also held alchemy in very high regard. In the history of science, alchemy[7] has traditionally been understood to be the precursor of chemistry. Increasingly, however, it has come to be recognized as a parallel discipline. In popular perception today, alchemy is associated with the dubious art of turning base metal into gold, but in its early phases, in the work of Paracelsus and his followers, alchemy was largely, though not entirely, connected with medicine, with the program of healing. The scientific revolution in chemistry occurred much later than the revolution in astronomy and other sciences. At the time of the formation of the Royal Society, although Robert Boyle's *The Sceptical Chymist* (1661) proposed a new corpuscular theory of a single prime matter that brought to an end the three element theory that had prevailed in alchemy since Paracelsus, scientists, including Boyle, and later Newton, continued to have an abiding interest in alchemy. Many scientists, philosophers, intellectuals, and educationists who were enthusiastic about alchemy were members of the "Invisible College," an informal gathering of Anglo-Irish intellectuals patronized by Robert Boyle's sister, Lady Ranelagh.[8] The Invisible College can perhaps be seen as the precursor of the Royal Society. The group included, apart from Lady Ranelagh and Samuel Hartlib, Robert Boyle and the chemist Thomas Henshaw. Through Henshaw, Thomas Vaughan, twin brother of the poet Henry Vaughan and a reputed alchemist, probably came into contact with the Invisible College.[9] Another acquaintance of Hartlib's, the chemist Robert Child, attempted to form a "chymical club."[10] The Invisible College, and perhaps also groups such as the "chymical club," took alchemy one step beyond the alchemical pursuits of earlier groups such as the Raleigh circle and the Sidney circle. Alchemy had always been a secretive art and utmost secrecy characterized the alchemical experiments of earlier groups. Paracelsus himself had projected alchemy as a secret art. But the 1640s and the 1650s saw the beginnings of a change in perception with a greater degree of sharing of knowledge and openness about the subject. In fact, the entire Rosicrucian program of research and publications—a project that Robert Fludd supported—should be regarded not only as an effort to secure wider acceptability for the subject but also as an attempt to move alchemy from secret laboratories to a forum for open discussion. This step toward greater transparency would have been welcomed by the likes of John Milton.

It is important to note that Milton clearly legitimizes alchemy. When he speaks of the alchemical procedure as a possibility not to be wondered at:

> If by fire
> Of sooty coal the empiric alchemist
> Can turn, or holds it possible to turn
> Metals of drossiest ore to perfect gold
> As from the mine (5.439–43)

the reference comes in a context in which Raphael is explaining angelic digestion. The theme is the process of turning of "corporeal to incorporeal" (5.413), achieving an ascent or sublimation. Through the range of elements from earth to fire, the grosser feeds the purer. The moon's unassimilated collection of vapors and the sun's purer reception of exhalations transformed into light demonstrate the range of possible change from imperfect to perfect. The most appropriate model for such alchemical change is angelic digestion that transforms corporeal nourishment to incorporeal spirit. Like "sublimation," a term used as a synonym for distillation, "digestion" is also a technical term in alchemy meaning the process of separating pure from impure through the application of heat.[11] In *Paradise Lost*, set within the story of transformation throughout the cosmos and in the angelic world is the comparison of this process to the procedures of the empiric alchemist turning baser metals into gold. The very comparison imparts legitimacy to the alchemical procedure. The analogy between angelic nourishment and alchemical processes establishes a pattern of digestion and sublimation as a legitimate and desired procedure. This is the paradigm of change that Raphael communicates to Adam and Eve. The degrees of change outlined in Raphael's discourse serve also as a narrative device for the mapping of changes in the character of Adam and Eve. Read within the framework Raphael sets up, the Fall of man is a hideous parody of the alchemical process. When Satan urges Eve to eat the fruit suggesting that her action will achieve an ascent from human to divine, his arguments in the temptation scene are a travesty of higher alchemy. Eve's acceptance of it is based on her hope for possible sublimation. However, the ultimate result of the eating of the fruit for both Adam and Eve is the reverse. Instead of the process of turning from corporeal to incorporeal, human to divine, the eating of the fruit leads to distempers and greater imperfection. Raphael's discourse on angelic digestion can be said to clarify the very basis of transmutational alchemy although Adam and Eve fail to appreciate the significance of the basic premise of obedience to God that Raphael lays down as the foundation of redemptive alchemy.

In the climactic temptation scene in *Paradise Lost*, as Eve eats the fruit, she is driven not only by her ambition of sublimating herself into a goddess. Her action is also one of open rebellion, perhaps the result of the first temptation, which encouraged tendencies always latent in her. The self-absorption she displays in her own account of her creation is the vulnerable point in her character that is exploited by Satan in the two temptations. In the scene of the Fall, as she contemplates her next course of action, her reference to God as "our great forbidder, safe with all his spies" (9.815) shows that at this point she regards angels as intrusive. Perhaps she resents the injunctions put forward by Raphael, which prompt Adam to persuade her not to go out alone. She certainly wishes to rebel against Adam's dominance. Her initial decision not to disclose to Adam that she has eaten the forbidden fruit to render herself "more equal" (9.823) is extremely revealing. If these are revolutionary thoughts, one needs to remember that, in the atmosphere of widespread interest in alchemy in the seventeenth century, alchemy was appropriated also into revolutionary discourse. Milton inverts the rhetoric of revolutionary alchemy and uses alchemy in *Paradise Lost* not as a paradigm of revolution but as the means of identifying false revolution across the wider span of the epic narrative.

There was an ideological divide in the seventeenth century between the role of alchemy in royalist activities, alchemy in revolutionary discourse, and alchemy as a philosophical discipline. In spite of some inevitable overlapping, these three strands can be identified and separated. Alchemy was very much a royalist preoccupation. The alchemist's possible access to enormous wealth naturally appealed to monarchy. During the reign of Queen Elizabeth, for example, the rumor spread that Dee and Kelly, during their stay in Prague, were turning base metal into gold and efforts were made through Sir Edward Dyer to persuade Dee to return and continue this practice in England so that money could be raised for the navy.[12] Arthur Dee, John Dee's son, himself deeply immersed in alchemy and the author of *Fasciculus chemicus* (1631), one of the most important sources of the history of alchemy, was appointed physician-in-ordinary to Charles I on his return to England from the court of Tsar Mikhail Romanov at Moscow. Alchemy continued to flourish with the return of monarchy at the Restoration. Buckingham's interest in alchemy has been made memorable through Dryden's ridicule of Zimri in *Absalom and Achitophel*: "But, in the course of one revolving Moon, / Was

Chymist, Fidler, States-Man, and Buffoon."[13] Charles II himself, it is reputed, was a practicing alchemist.

The politics of *Paradise Lost* may well have led Milton to present alchemy and wealth generation as a devilish activity, but any such suggestion is notably absent from the text. It is true that gold itself is systematically downgraded in this Puritan epic. While Raphael warns Adam that "great / or bright infers not excellence" (8.90–91), Satan in his serpent form has a "burnished neck of verdant gold" (9.501) and the forbidden fruit take on an attractive red and gold color in the temptation scene. Gold thereby becomes the color of deception, entrapment, and ruin. Interestingly, though, the transmutation of base metals into gold is not an activity undertaken by the devils. The devils do not see themselves as accomplished alchemists as they might well have done had Milton chosen to present alchemy as a questionable activity. Nowhere in *Paradise Lost*, in fact, does Milton treat alchemy with the degree of contempt that one finds in Chaucer or Ben Jonson. The devils are industrious miners digging for gold but they do not undertake what might have been for them an easier option, the transmutation of base metal into gold. Instead, Mammon and his associates dig out "ribs of gold" (2. 690) from beneath the surface of Hell. They are also accomplished architects. Their great achievement is the construction of Pandemonium. But transmutational alchemy is beyond the range of their activities. The ironic vision that integrates demonic activity into the network of astronomical signs does not establish a Jonsonian model of the avaricious devilish alchemist. This straightforward, almost expected, traditional literary response to alchemy is absent because Milton had a deeper understanding of the complexities of alchemy and *Paradise Lost* achieves a richer and nuanced negotiation of this volatile subject.

Alchemy was in fact an integral part of revolutionary discourse and the Levellers and Diggers had their own version of the value of alchemy. As P. M. Rattansi points out, "Paracelsus became a live issue during the Puritan revolution."[14] Paracelsus's chemical therapy was integrated into the mid-seventeenth-century framework of ideas about man, nature, and God. His elevation of "illumination" above reason had a strong appeal in the atmosphere of revolution and John Webster, chaplain in the Parliamentary army, proposed the introduction of Hermetic and Paracelsian texts into the university education system. In a scathing attack on Webster, Thomas Hall, pastor of King's Norton, declared that Webster's advocacy showed that he belonged to the "Familiasticall-Levelling-Magical temper."[15] Hall's attack recognizes the presence of Paracelsian thought in contemporary radical discourse. A specific example of the way in which Paracelsian alchemy was in fact integrated into revolutionary discourse can be seen in the writings of Gerrard Winstanley, a Digger or true Leveller, a believer in progress. As David Mulder has persuasively argued, Winstanley shared the traditional belief in cosmic correspondence.[16] He believed that any change in the affairs of men in society would have the possibility of inducing cataclysmic changes in the universe. Change and revolution were therefore fraught with anxiety. Yet change in the form of progress and social justice was necessary and imperative. How was this contradiction to be resolved? The answer was to be found in alchemy. In a conviction that John Rogers has appropriately described as "the peculiarly passive voice of the political activist,"[17] Winstanley urged a belief not in human agency but in the divine. God was an alchemist and the change brought about by the igniting of the divine spirit within man could not but be beneficial. In traditional alchemy, "sophic" sulfur or the masculine principle and "sophic" mercury or the feminine principle are placed within the vessel called the "Philosopher's Egg" together with a "secret fire" or "sophic salt" and the vessel hermetically sealed then heated. Eventually this process leads to the creation of the androgynous Philosopher's Stone having the power to transmute base metals into gold. For Winstanley, this triad of sulfur, mercury, and salt was represented by Original Sin, the four elements, and the spirit of God.[18] The alchemical process thus provided a model for change or revolution involving different cosmic levels. One specific image used repeatedly by Winstanley is the image of fire. In *Truth Lifting, Works* Winstanley declares "This is the Kingdome of God within man...This is the fire, that shall dry and burne up all the drosse of man's worke , and turne all things into his owne nature." In *Saints Paradise* he explains "this fire is the father himself, into whom, when any creature fals, he burns up the drosse in the creature." Fire, heat, and burning—fundamental concepts in alchemy—are integrated with their alchemical connotations into the metaphoric structure of revolutionary discourse. God's spirit, for Winstanley, is a consuming fire that burns up all the dross to reveal the inner being. Jacob Boehme was later to describe God as the "divine tincture" that "ignited the fire that had become dark within the essence of the soul."[19]

Once Raphael imparts to Adam and Eve his lesson in true alchemy, there are early signs of a positive result. At the end of their midday meal, corporeal nourishment leads to a sharpened intellect—"sudden mind arose / In Adam" (5.452–53)—and he proceeds to question

Raphael. Encouraged, the angel clarifies the fundamentals of true
alchemy whereby body can turn to spirit.

> From these corporal nutriments perhaps
> Your bodies may at last turn all to spirit,
> Improved by tract of time, and winged ascend
> Ethereal, as we, or may at choice
> Here or in heavenly paradises dwell;
> If ye be found obedient. (5.496–501)

It is this final caveat—"if ye be found obedient"—that Adam and Eve
defy. This is the "foul revolt" (1.33) that the epic narrates. In the epic,
alchemy, a potent subject in revolutionary discourse, is the means of
uncovering false rebellion. The story begins with the alchemy of Hell
in the opening books. The first impact on the reader's mind as the
narrative unfolds is that of an intensity of change and debasement.
The rebel angels have been hurled down into the burning region
of Hell, which "as one great furnace flamed" (1.62). The *Hermetic
Museum* describes the metaphysical alchemical furnace as one that
purges man of all impurities "and there arises a new man created after
God in righteousness and true holiness."[20] In one of the poem's many
demonic inversions of things divine, the alchemy of Hell does not
remove impurities to reveal inner worth. Its process is the converse.
It removes the false angelic exterior to reveal the evil within. This is
a fire that does not consume—as indeed it cannot as the fallen angels
are immortal. But it is corrosive. It transforms them, exposing their
baseness. Satan's first words in Hell are an acknowledgment of this
change as, turning to Beelzebub, he says, "If thou beest he; but O how
fallen! How changed" (1.84). The furnace of Hell is fed with "ever-
burning sulphur unconsumed" (1.69). In the sulfur-mercury theory
of the generation of metals, the principle of sulfur was masculine and
provided the form of metals, while the principle of mercury was femi-
nine and provided the matter. But there is no "chemical wedding"
in Milton's Hell, nothing productive is achieved. Only sulfur in its
most primitive violent form feeds the flames. "Sublimed with mineral
fury" (1.235), the divinely created alchemical furnace of Hell alters
the appearance of the fallen angels revealing their inherent baseness.
Although Satan declares that "this empyreal substance cannot fail"
(1.117), he is conscious of "this dire change" (1.625) and the word
"ruin" occurs repeatedly.

However, Milton not only inverts traditional alchemy when he
presents the change brought about by alchemy in Hell as an exposure

of degradation rather than an achievement of sublimation, he also inverts revolutionary discourse. The effectiveness of the alchemy of Hell is reinforced by its relation to the revolutionary context. *Paradise Lost* inverts the Digger ideology of alchemical revolution as a divinely inspired fiery liberating force destroying accumulated social evils to reveal an inner core of value. The fallen angels who burn in the fiery furnace of Hell are themselves participants in a revolution, but a revolution without a cause. The fires of Hell in the opening books of *Paradise Lost* therefore consume their false show of zeal to reveal the evil within. The process is one of exposure rather than of liberation. As with the astronomical images, Milton's experience of defeat dictates the use of alchemy, turning the Digger ideology of the alchemy of revolution on its head. For the devils revolting against God, the divine fire is directed at the participants of a false revolution, burning and removing their deceptive zealous exterior, rather than acting as a liberating force facilitating true revolution. This defining of false revolution through alchemical fire is later extended to the story of the fall of Adam and Eve. Adam and Eve's transgression is a "foul revolt" (1.33) and not true revolution. In the temptation scene in Book 9, Eve's disobedience of two figures of authority, first Adam who tries to prevent her from separating from him and then God who had forbidden her to touch or taste the fruit, is prompted by her desire to assume a role that does not belong to her. Her apparent assumption of equality with Adam is without foundation. Her desire to be rendered "more equal" (9.823) and her easy acceptance of Satan's depiction of her as "a goddess among gods" (9.547) are both based upon false premises. So actions that might seem to her to be revolutionary and restorative of gender justice are, in fact, within the framework of the epic, indefensible. It is not surprising therefore that images of fire should resurface in Book 9. Just before the Fall, Eve is described as carrying tools not fashioned in a furnace—"guiltless of fire" (9.392). However, just after the Fall, as Adam joins Eve in the transgression, "in lust they burn" (9.1015). The deliberate disassociation of fire from Eve moments before the Fall is now reversed. It has long been noticed that light and darkness forms one of the basic metaphoric patterns that runs through *Paradise Lost*.[21] Light in its many forms, either as physical light or as inner illumination, provides a set of positive connotations signifying virtue, knowledge, enlightenment, and other related attributes. Although fire can also be a source of light, and indeed was so to primitive man, from the beginning Milton directs our attention to its discrepant status in the epic. The fires of Hell do not give light but project a consciousness of "darkness visible" (1.63) and this negative image of fire is continued into the scene of the Fall. This status of fire as corrosive is an inverted alchemical image. It is in the two closing visionary books of the epic that the metaphoric function of fire changes dramatically. Here biblical images from Genesis and Exodus predominate together with the apocalyptic vision of the final conflagration from the book of Revelations. This final vision may also be taken as an analogy of the true alchemical process.

In *Paradise Lost*, one of the key lessons in alchemical change is projected through the narrative of angelic digestion, a physiological procedure. Another is constructed through a demonstration of the corrosive agency of fire. A further perspective on alchemy is provided by alchemical images of light. D. C. Allen[22] has identified the light metaphysic of the Pseudo-Dionysius, which can be traced back to Origen as one of the sources of Milton's presentation of a descent into darkness and ascent to light and its incorporation of the doctrine of double vision. Milton would indeed have inherited a rich tradition of light metaphysics from Plato and the Neoplatonists, from Pseudo-Dionysius, St. Augustine, Dante, and Ficino. While the complex fabric of the passages on light in *Paradise Lost* points to the interweaving of many strands, one of the dominant threads is the alchemy of light, which leads up to the critical presentation of the "arch-chemic sun" (3.609).

Light had always been of importance in Paracelsian as well as Hermetic thought. Whether it be in the "doctrine of signatures" fundamental to Paracelsian medicine or in Hermetic astral magic, light from the celestial bodies, the sun, moon, stars, and planets, was of central importance in the whole of the Paracelsian and Hermetic tradition. But if one were to isolate a philosophy of light that focuses on the divine radiance at the moment of creation and the special significance of the sun, this should be explored in particular in the line of thought that extends through Ficino's solar magic, Giordano Bruno's expositions on the centrality of the sun, Dee's alchemy of light, and, finally, in the seventeenth century, in the great importance given to light and the sun in the philosophy of Heinrich Khunrath, Jacob Boehme, and Robert Fludd. Milton would have had access to most of these works in the eclectic library of Dr. Nathan Paget[23] and he used these varied resources to create his own exposition of the alchemy of light.

The mystery of creation is at the heart of all alchemical enquiry and it is hardly surprising that light, the first creation of God, should be at the center of alchemical interest. Where this investigation proceeds in alchemy, two things happen at once. The alchemist seeks to understand the secrets of creation by unraveling the mystery of the divine creation of the cosmos. Simultaneously, understanding gives the alchemist the key to creation, which will enable him to perfect his own art. Knowledge leads to empowerment. This line of thought can be seen clearly in the two alchemical writers Milton and his seventeenth-century contemporaries would have been familiar with—Jacob Boehme and Robert Fludd.

In *The Aurora* (1612), Boehme sees light as enlightenment. Like William Blake two centuries later,[24] Boehme's philosophy is based more on mystical experience than on intellectual speculation. The two key biblical texts he relies on are the first chapter of Genesis and the interpretation of it in John. In *The Aurora* he describes his liberation from the "gates of Hell" into the presence of God in a moment of inspired vision as a Resurrection and says:

> In this Light my Spirit suddenly saw through all, and *in* and *by* all the Creatures, even in Herbs and Grass, it knew God, who he is, and how he is, and what his Will is: And suddenly in that Light my Will was set on by a mighty *Impulse*, to describe *the Being of God*.[25]

Boehme sees a great radiation outward from God and the greatest role in creation is played by sound—the Word of God—and by light, God's first creation. Light is not one of the seven primal powers and counterpowers of Boehme's philosophy but is generated by them collectively. This light is reflected in the Son, the sun, the receptacle of light, and the soul and spirit of man. Boehme expresses deep anxiety about the inadequacy of language to communicate his visionary experience. Robert Fludd, too, was conscious of the limitations of language and the profusion of diagrams in his published philosophical works, which produces a Blakean composite art in which text and illustration need to be "read" simultaneously, is one way of overcoming this felt inadequacy.

An examination of the textual and visual representation of the beginning of light in Fludd reveals a three-stage development that Alexander Roob describes as an alchemical process: "For the Paracelsian Robert Fludd, the divine act of creation took on concrete and visible form as an alchemical process, in which God, as a spagyrist, divided primal, dark chaos, the *Prima Materia*, into the three divine, primary elements of light, darkness and spiritual waters."[26] The initial phase, not chaos but the original darkness, represented as a uniformly black square, is followed by the appearance of light as a shining bright wheel in the middle of darkness. While commenting on these illustrations Roob quotes from the *Zohar*: "When the secret of secrets wished to reveal himself, he began to produce a point of light. Before that point of light broke through and became apparent, the infinite (en soph) was entirely hidden and radiated no light." The description of the radiating finger of light in the *Zohar* is very similar to the diagrammatic representation of a vertical projection of divine light toward the sun in another familiar illustration in Fludd.[27] The diagram shows God placing his tabernacle in the sun in the middle of the ethereal or planetary world. As Szulakowska points out,

> Fludd explains the descent of the Tetragrammaton in the form of divine light to create the material light of nature in a cabbalistic exegesis of the *Book of Genesis*...On this cabbalistic foundation Fludd accounts for the qualities of the sun which is unique in being the father of light, the tabernacle of Christ, the Word and Apollo.[28]

Fludd accepts the visible sun as the mystic body of Christ. Two other illustrations are relevant in this context, both from the second volume of *Utriusque Cosmi Maioris scilicet Minoris* (1619), the discussion on the microcosm. In the first,[29] the illustration forms three horizontal planes. Figure one at the center of the upper plane of the illustration depicts the Trinity as an eye in which the white represents God, the iris the Son, and the pupil the Spirit. This may, in fact, be compared with the figurative representation of the Creator in Boehme's philosophy. In Boehme's vision of creation, the eternal silence with which the universe began—the *Ungrund*, the pure unmanifest aspect of God—is likened to an eye,[30] which sees itself. Hidden within the eye is the entirety of creation in unmanifest form. To return to Fludd's diagram, the figure at the center of the middle panel is that of the Sun with a human face, surrounded by radiating fingers of light with a circle of densely packed dark lines beyond it. Godwin explains this as another depiction of the Trinity in a form of convergence—God at the center, the Son as light in the inner ring, and the Spirit as heat or energy as the outer ring. The third section at the bottom of the illustration, depicting a dynamic structure of cloud, thunder, and lightning, continues the same theme. While the illustration depicts Fludd's concept of the Trinity through the three recognizable Renaissance magical spheres—supercelestial, celestial, and natural—the motif of the eye with which the illustration begins and which is reinterpreted in the middle and lower planes is particularly relevant for *Paradise Lost*. In another illustration in the same work,[31] clouds part to reveal the Tetragrammaton as an eye in the middle of a circle of radiance. A conical shaft of light from the divine vision comes cascading down to the kneeling figure of King David sitting on a rock below. The Hebrew words inscribed in that shaft of light invoke the Trinity. These and other related illustrations show the network of associations in Fludd between God, the Son, light, the sun, the eye, and inspiration. In this network the sun holds an important intermediate position between the divine and the mundane worlds. The dynamism of Fludd's philosophy is strongly related to its alchemical content. If Christ is the sun in this phase of Fludd's work, in his later works, the *Clavis Philosophia* (1633) and the *Philosophia Moysaica* (1638), Christ, Fludd states, is the philosopher's stone.[32] It is against the background of this network of associations defining the role of Christ and the status of the sun in terms of higher alchemy that one needs to take a fresh look at light and the sun in *Paradise Lost*.

The invocation to light in Book 3 begins by directing attention to different strands of the metaphysics of light. Light is "holy light," the dwelling of God, uncreated, co-eternal, the effluence or emanation of the divine essence. Light is also the "offspring of heaven first-born," the Son. In this intricately constructed invocation, the different connotations of light are carefully distinguished. "Hail, holy Light, offspring of heaven first-born, / *Or* of the eternal co-eternal beam" (3.1–2; italics mine). Light as the Son or first-born offspring of heaven is distinguished from the divine radiance, "the eternal co-eternal beam," by the firmly placed "or" at the beginning of line 2. A similar "or" at the beginning of line 7 ("*Or* hear'st thou rather pure ethereal stream" [3.7; italics mine]) identifies the third form of light, God's first cosmic creation at the beginning of Genesis, the first appearance of physical light before the creation of the sun. The opening phrase "Hail, holy light" (3.1) is simultaneously divine light and light in its composite form as divine radiance, the Son, and the first created physical light. Significantly, in Book 3, Milton begins by invoking the Son, then turns to invoke divine light before finally invoking physical light. As the invocation finally proceeds to register the poet's blindness and to seek inner illumination, the plea for spiritual enlightenment is figured through the image of "eyes" implanted in the mind. This need for the implanting of "eyes" deserves scrutiny. Sight or eye contact is of utmost importance in Heaven. We are told, in Book 3, not only that God "bent his eye" (3.58) to survey the created world, the cosmos, but also that the angels "from his *sight* received / Beatitude past utterance" (3.61–62; italics mine). Similarly, the "lordly eye" (3.578) of the sun dispenses light to the cosmos while keeping "distance due" (3.578) from other celestial bodies. Later, in Book 5, Adam and Eve, in their morning prayers, will address the sun as "Thou sun, of this great world both eye and soul" (5.171).

Viewed in this context, the implanting of "eyes" in the poet's mind signifies not only the imparting of inspiration and spiritual enlightenment but also a conferring of authority and empowerment. These layers of meaning that alchemical philosophy invested in the sun that would have been recognized by a seventeenth-century "fit audience" provide a framework to explain the significance and centrality of the sun in Milton's epic. While the importance of "eyes" is a recognizable component of earlier philosophy, especially Ficino, the train of connection between God, the Son, the sun, and light in the context of "eyes" in the invocation in Book 3 is strongly reminiscent of the visual representation of Fludd's philosophy.

The sun, which holds a dominant position in the poetry of Donne, has a crucial role to play in *Paradise Lost*. It is the brightest celestial body and the only one, apart from the earth, to which God has assigned one of the archangels as regent. It is the heavenly body that attracts Satan most and toward which he feels the greatest envy. It is also the one cosmic object that causes anguish in Satan and releases the floodgates of soul-searching in him. It is, again, the celestial body that Satan fears and from which he hides during the seven-day voyage between the two temptations. Other celestial objects, the stars and comets, are, for Satan, objects of wonder or materials to be appropriated for self-construction. Sailing through space within the new cosmos, he is struck by the immensity of the stars, which "seemed other worlds" (3.566), but they still remain outside his psychodynamic field. Later, specific stars and comets are appropriated by him as forms of self-representation. The sun is the one object within the universe that he can neither dominate and appropriate nor remain unaffected by. It initiates in him a definite chemistry of reactions. For Adam and Eve, again, the sun has a special significance though vastly different from the significance it has for Satan. It is the one celestial object that they regard as of highest authority second only to God ("Acknowledge him thy greater" [5.172]) and again the one from which they hide after the Fall. For the angels, the sun has no special appeal. They are conscious of its importance. In Raphael's account of creation in Book 7, the sun sojourns in a "cloudy tabernacle" (7.248) until God

> Of light by far the greater part he took,
> Transplanted from her cloudy shrine, and placed
> In the sun's orb, made porous to receive
> And drink the liquid light, firm to retain
> Her gathered beams, great palace now of light. (7.359–63)

While Raphael thus acknowledges the sun's position of importance, it has no emotional relevance for him. For Uriel, it provides a means of easy transport and for Gabriel a mechanism for noting the passage of time. For the good angels, with direct access to the radiance of God and the Son, the sun has no special significance. For Satan, and for Adam and Eve in a different way, the sun exudes a definite chemistry, which affects their emotions and their thinking.

That the sun should have such chemical or alchemical role to play in *Paradise Lost* can be surmised from Milton's early presentation of the sun as the philosopher's stone. In a passage in which alchemical references are deeply embedded, Milton describes the sun thus:

> The place he found beyond expression bright,
> Compared with aught on earth, metal or stone;
> Not all parts like, but all alike informed
> With radiant light, as glowing iron with fire;
> If metal, part seemed gold, part silver clear;
> If stone, carbuncle most or chrysolite,
> Ruby or topaz, to the twelve that shone
> In Aaron's breastplate, and a stone besides
> Imagined rather oft than elsewhere seen,
> That stone, or like to that which here below
> Philosophers in vain so long have sought,
> In vain, though by their powerful art they bind
> Volatile Hermes, and call up unbound
> In various shapes old Proteus from the sea,
> Drained through a limbeck to his native form.
> What wonder then if fields and regions here
> Breathe forth elixir pure, and rivers run
> Potable gold, when with one virtuous touch
> The arch-chemic sun so far from us remote
> Produces with terrestrial humour mixed
> Here in the dark so many precious things
> Of colour glorious and effect so rare? (3.591–612)

Alastair Fowler has commented on the numerological and alchemical implications of the passage, drawing attention to the stones, the stages in the magnum opus, the forms of mercury, and other significant alchemical references.[33] Apart from the incorporation of references to Hermes, limbeck, elixir, and other familiar alchemical details, the passage as a whole focuses on red as the dominant color and red or rubedo was the final stage of the opus alchymicum. The sun is both the true and perfected philosopher's stone and the accomplished alchemist ("arch-chemic") who, with his "virtuous" touch, can effect transformations of the highest order.

In *Paradise Lost* the role of the sun as philosopher's stone should be examined in the context of Milton's presentation of God as divine alchemist. God prepares the alchemical furnace of Hell to expose and reveal the inherent baseness of the fallen angels. For man, he sends his angels, first Raphael to communicate the basis of transmutational alchemy and then Michael to initiate Adam and Eve into the stages followed by the alchemical adept, so that change can be understood as renovation. The sun in *Paradise Lost* performs a further extension of these procedures. While the fires of Hell had scorched and corroded the outward physical beauty of the fallen angels, the sun is God's touchstone and reaches into Satan's heart to expose the negative emotions of hatred, jealousy, and despair within him. For the epic poet, this same stone has a healing touch, shining upon him, reaching into his spirit, planting "eyes" within, elevating and sublimating him to the role of a true prophet so that he can "see and tell / Of things invisible to mortal sight" (3.54–55). For Adam and Eve and the world they inhabit, the sun's "potent ray" (4.673) imparts creative energy and fosters growth. The alchemy of light in *Paradise Lost*, and the projection of the sun as an "arch-chemic" (3.609), is a cosmic version of the physiological paradigm of change through which Raphael connects the actions of the "empiric alchemist" (5.440) with angelic digestion, the turning of "corporeal to incorporeal" (5.413).

The closing books of *Paradise Lost* incorporate a philosophical view of alchemy, appropriating a familiar network of alchemical ideas into the narrative of healing and redemption. One of Michael's functions as messenger is to complete the lessons in alchemy that Raphael had introduced. It is important to remember, in this context, that, in the Jewish Cabala, Mercury was often identified with Raphael and sometimes with Michael.[34] The figure of Mercury/Hermes is central to alchemy and, in philosophical terms, symbolized transmutation. Of the many functions attributed to him, Mercury also performed the function of mediating at the chemical wedding of Sol and Luna. When Milton, in *Paradise Lost*, Book 3 (3.602–605), refers to the binding of volatile Hermes in the context of the philosopher's stone, he is referring to a lower form than that of the divine Mercury. The visiting angels, Raphael and Michael, in their role as Mercury, perform the functions of mediation between God and man and that of showing the way forward toward change and renovation.

In Book 5, Raphael's discourse establishes the basis of transmutational alchemy just as later, in Book 8, he initiates Adam into the exciting world of the new astronomy. In the closing books of *Paradise Lost*, Michael conducts a process of purification, with definite alchemical resonances, for Adam and Eve, before revealing to Adam the unfolding drama of human history as a process of change leading to eventual redemption. Purification and redemption were, in principle, the ultimate aim of all alchemy. Michael administers medicine to Eve's eyes ("I have drenched her eyes" [11.367]) to induce a sleep in which God can instruct her through dreams ("For God is also in sleep, and dreams advise" [12.611]). As a prelude to Adam's vision of key episodes of human history, Michael applies to Adam's eyes two herbs with opposite properties, euphrasy signifying joy and rue signifying melancholy (11.414–15). Three drops are then instilled from the "well of life" (11.416). These penetrate beyond the senses "even to the inmost seat of mental sight" (11.418). Adam closes his eyes, sinks down, and his spirits become "entranced" (11.420). He is then gently "raised" (11.422) by Michael and led forward to see the visions of the future. This entire sequence (11.414–22) is a complex interweaving of alchemical processes. The opposite natures of euphrasy and rue match the basic oppositions of sulfur and mercury, Sol and Luna, and other such binaries in alchemy. Moreover, embedded in the text are references that might be interpreted as concepts signifying ablution, sublimation, resurrection, and other alchemical processes. Such references would not be considered unusual in a Christian epic. As Gareth Roberts points out, "Alchemical discourse was also suffused with the language of Christianity...Images of death and resurrection...were central to Christian doctrine and also to the mystery religions, both of which provided cultural contexts for the earliest alchemical texts.[35] The resurrection motif can be found in such early writers of the Christian era as Zosimos of Panopolis (*ca.* third century AD) and Johannes Fabricius[36] has examined in detail the prevalence of this motif in medieval alchemical writers. The cleansing of Adam's eyes followed by his "raising" by Michael enacts the alchemical process of purification and resurrection. In *Paradise Lost*, the angelic visitors are Adam's intellectual and spiritual guides. Their familiarity with the higher forms of alchemy confers dignity and value on this controversial subject.

Milton's attitude to alchemy was generated by the belief that alchemy was not only a laboratory procedure but also a philosophical discipline. This was indeed a traditional division and one that John Dee understood well. As Deborah Harkness points out, "spiritual alchemy was a more complex and philosophical process wherein the ascent of the matter toward the philosophers' stone was a material reflection of the spiritual and intellectual ascent of the alchemist toward God."[37] Dee felt that his conversations with angels gave him access to knowledge about "true" alchemy, higher than the alchemy he had practiced. As Harkness suggests, "alchemical motifs, ideas, and parables in the angel conversations, therefore, are analogous to, but not strictly derivative from, the alchemy Dee had been practicing."[38] Through parables, in the course of spirited theatrical exchanges, the angels instructed Dee in Adam's alchemy. It is amazing to what extent the conversations of Adam with Raphael and Michael perform functions similar to Dee's much-debated conversations with angels. While Raphael instructs Adam in the process of "digestion" and "sublimation," both terms in use in alchemy, Michael initiates Adam into a millennial view of alchemy looking forward in human history to the promised redemption. This is not to suggest that Dee's conversations with angels provided a model that Milton worked into his epic poem. Rather, Dee's conversations constitute an unexpected analogue and help us as readers to structure Milton's angelic conversations in our own reading.

The dramatic tension that is generated by Milton's presentation of Adam and Eve in *Paradise Lost* is in large measure due to the fact that while change as renovation, through its alchemical analogy, is urged as desirable, what transpires is change of a different kind. Alchemy projects change as linear, in Raphael's terms from corporeal to incorporeal, or from body up to spirit ("Your bodies may at last turn all to spirit, / Improved by tract of time, and winged ascend" [5.497–98]). The changes that take place in Adam and Eve are much more complex, multifaceted. Adam's immediate response to Raphael's discourse on alchemy is to move from corporeal to intellectual. At the end of an enjoyable midday meal with Raphael, Adam questions the angel on a variety of issues—the war in heaven, the life of the angels, the workings of the cosmos. If, as Campbell and Corns suggest, "Adam, after as before the fall, engages both affectionately and intellectually with Eve,"[39] it is significant that these are questions he never discusses with Eve. Yet, as he tells Raphael, these issues were questions in his mind even before the angel's visit. The fact is that Adam never regards Eve as his intellectual equal. On no point, except the domestic matter of selecting fruits and juices for Raphael, does he ever consult Eve. He sees his own role as that of Eve's guide offering answers to her questions. He is content to remain kind, but, in his own assessment, superior. This feeling of completeness—one might even suggest complacency—is jolted momentarily when Eve recounts to him her experience of the dream temptation. Adam puts up a brave front explaining deep psychology to Eve, telling her about imagination and "mimic fancy" (5.110), which "misjoining shapes, / Wild work produces oft" (5.111–12). He suggests that their conversation about cosmic movement the previous evening may have been distorted into this dream. Yet he is conscious that there is much more to this dream than the contents of that conversation in Paradise. He admits as much—"but with strange addition" (5.116)—but quickly glosses over this lacunae in his own understanding. Eve's dream might have reminded Adam of his own dream experiences. In the first of these he had been "raised, / And over fields and waters, as in air / Smooth sliding without step" (8.300–302) led up to the garden of Paradise. In the second, he saw the creation of Eve. Eve's dream temptation might have struck Adam as a distortion of his own first dream experience, but that connection, so tantalizingly suggested to the reader, is never made by Adam. He reserves his account of his own dream experiences for his conversation with Raphael. It is significant that he does not discuss his dream with Eve or Eve's dream with Raphael. While Adam shares with Raphael his many anxieties regarding the cosmos, as well as the story of his own creation and that of Eve, it is curious that, in spite of the angel's warning about possible threat from the enemy, he does not give Raphael an account of Eve's dream temptation. Apart from this one inhibition, when Adam has his man-to-man talk with the angel Raphael, he feels free to disclose his doubts and ask searching questions. Sometimes these are questions first posed by Eve to which, he is aware, he was not able to give fully satisfactory answers, such as Eve's questions about diurnal movement. Raphael's answers satisfy Adam's curiosity, but they also perplex and open up unexpected intellectual fields. It is perhaps fitting that, at this point, Eve having left them to attend to her flowers, Adam feels impelled to tell Raphael "my story" (8.205), his account of his own and Eve's creation, the details of which were not known to the angel. At the end of their conversation, Raphael leaves Paradise with the injunction that Adam should value "self esteem" (8.572), love and obey God, and "take heed lest passion sway / Thy judgment" (8.635–36). Milton's portrayal of Adam that includes the account of his creation and that of Eve reveals significant changes in his character. He appears initially as both superior and confident, his manly grace matched by his intellect. In his first few moments after creation, he looks around him, gives names to all the objects of nature, and deduces the existence of a divine creator. He is remarkably forthright, too, as he asks for a companion in Paradise for, as he points out, "among unequals what society" (8.383). As time passes, he reveals his growing intellectual strength, engaging in conversation with Raphael on difficult subjects. He is unfailingly tender and passionate in his relationship with Eve. He is sensitive, too, to his own position within the new universe and uncomfortable with the vast spaces within the cosmos and with the enormous velocities of celestial bodies. The first impression of Adam as confident, majestic, almost godlike is enriched by the suggestion of a questioning mind, admitting uncertainties, and his acknowledgment of anxiety. These are positive changes, but they are accompanied by revelations of vulnerability that surface in his relationship with Eve, in particular in his need to maintain a position of superiority. This is exposed when he tries to gloss over his failures—his inability to explain Eve's dream or satisfactorily answer her questions about the stars and planets. He does not admit that his own understanding is limited and pretends to a greater self-assurance than he actually possesses. But if these imperfections make Adam less of a man, they enhance his appeal as an epic character. They prepare us also for the utter confusion in Adam at the beginning of Book 9 when Eve puts forward her proposal to separate, as well as for the inevitability, emotional engagement, and dignity with which he arrives at his decision to join Eve in her transgression.

Milton's Eve is an innocent, submissive, companionable figure, but she unquestionably has a mind of her own. In her conversation with Adam in Book 4, as she narrates to him the story of her own creation, she does not hesitate to dwell on her initial rejection of him. Her account of this episode reveals her vanity, but it also shows her honesty. Nor does she hesitate to ask Adam the difficult question as to why the moon and stars shine at night when all are asleep. Honesty, sincerity, and intelligence combine with unsurpassed beauty to create the perfect companion for Adam. If her realization "how beauty is excelled by manly grace / And wisdom, which alone is truly fair" (4.490–91) marks a growing maturity, her distress when she wakes from her dream temptation proves her continued innocence. Yet, there are subtle changes of a different kind that take place in Eve. It is curious that Eve leaves Adam and Raphael (8.40) precisely at the moment when Adam puts to Raphael the question she herself had put to him about diurnal movement. It is surely to be expected that she will want to know what answer the angel gives rather than wait for Adam to explain all later. This was her question. Is she no longer interested in the explanation? Has her dream temptation given her some of the answers? At the beginning of Book 9, Eve, who had till now spoken only when she was spoken to, for the first time, much to Adam's discomfiture, begins a conversation and indeed announces her decision to separate and work alone. When Adam reminds her of the angel's warning about an enemy who seeks their ruin, she replies

> That such an enemy we have, who seeks
> Our ruin, both by thee informed I learn,
> And from the parting angel overheard
> As in a shady nook I stood behind,
> Just then returned at shut of evening flowers. (9.274–78)

This is a surprising statement. Eve may not have eavesdropped, but she had not divulged to Adam before this moment that she had overheard part of his conversation with Raphael. As a prelude to the imminent scene of temptation and fall, Eve's words reveal a change in her personality. The sudden revelation that Eve has so far concealed from Adam the fact that she had overheard his conversation with Raphael foreshadows her desire, after her eating of the forbidden fruit, to keep that knowledge to herself to render herself "more equal" (9.823). With Eve, as with Adam, Milton carefully charts changes in character that make their actions in the critical scene of the Fall convincing.

Fallibility is as much a condition of angels as of man. The errors of Uriel and Gabriel are as much indications of imperfections in their character as the result of Satan's cunning and power. Adam and Eve fall because of weaknesses not inherent but acquired. Milton shows them evolving as characters who develop imperfections, which are then exploited by Satan. Raphael's prescribed alchemical ascent from "body up to spirit" (5.478) does not work although, after the Fall, Michael is able to instruct the human pair and bring in changes that inspire them to achieve a "paradise within" (12.587). The "virtuous touch" (3.608) of true alchemy prefigured by the "arch-chemic sun" (3.609) finds a more powerful expression through the agency of God's messenger, Michael.

In *Paradise Lost*, Milton appropriates the discourse generated by a pervasive seventeenth-century interest in alchemy to construct an allusive framework that helps define character. Alchemy was not only a dominant intellectual field, it was complex and varied. It provided the means to indicate exposure and degradation as well as sublimation. It was also a potentially challenging subject in which aspiration and rate of failure was higher than the level of success. This made it the appropriate filter through which the story of the Fall of man could be projected.

Conclusion

To ask or search I blame thee not, for heaven
Is as the book of God before thee set,
Wherein to read his wondrous works, and learn
His seasons, hours, or days, or months, or years:
This to attain, whether heaven move or earth,
Imports not, if thou reckon right, the rest
From man or angel the great architect
Did wisely to conceal, and not divulge
His secrets to be scanned by them who ought
Rather admire. (8.66–75)

Raphael warns Adam not to try to scan the secrets of the universe, but that injunction is part of one of the most provocative speeches in *Paradise Lost* that encourages Adam to investigate more than it injuncts him to refrain. As such, it is also implicitly an invitation to Milton's readers to follow Adam's example and uncover the contextual references to scientific, alchemical, and magical resources that lie embedded in the text. The recovery of vital contextual data shows Milton's incorporation of ideas and images drawn from urgently debated fields of new astronomy, optics, and vitalism, as well as hermetic and cabalistic magic, and alchemy. Once these are retrieved, they reveal the new and unusual ways in which *Paradise Lost* creates a unique cosmos and engages with construction of character. Although the epic spans the vast spaces of hell, chaos, heaven, and cosmos, the focal point of the poem is Milton's cosmos where the Fall of man takes place, where Satan has to contend with Uriel and Gabriel, and Raphael and Michael instruct Adam and Eve before and after the Fall. The structure of this imaginary cosmos, and the construction of space, time, and celestial movement within it, including regular and variable celestial phenomena, have a direct bearing on the unfolding of the epic action and rely upon traditional cosmology, new astronomy, optics, alchemy, and prognostications. Moreover, much that is compelling and unusual about Milton's characters—the fallibility of his angels, the sharper intellectual power of the morally indefensible Satan and his just defeat, the ambiguity of Chaos and the significance of Night, above all, the unexpected complexities in the characters of Adam and Eve—is conveyed through a discourse that draws upon images, ideas, and words generated from the vital intellectual ferment of the new science, magic, and alchemy. Understanding this context adds significantly to knowledge and understanding of Milton's achievement in *Paradise Lost.*

The range of interests Milton draws upon is varied, and *Paradise Lost* relies substantially on two seventeenth-century figures who belong to the opposite extremes of the century's intellectual spectrum—Robert Fludd and Galileo. Fludd was a physician and Paracelsian, a hermeticist, cabalist, and believer in the philosophy of alchemy. Milton's version of chaos and Night in his epic has unmistakable roots in the first part of Fludd's *History of the Macrocosm and Microcosm* (1617). The clarity and intensity of Fludd's visual representation of the original darkness and chaos provided the inspiration and the materials for Milton's allegory of Chaos and Night. The powerful visual impact of Fludd's illustration of the original darkness can be said to have its contrary in the diagram of the infinite Copernican sphere by John Dee's pupil Thomas Digges, and this diagram, with its countless stars spilling over the margins of the page, in an appendix to an almanac, was probably one of the major sources of inspiration for Milton's imaginative exploration of infinite space in *Paradise Lost.* If Fludd can be said to have made specific contributions to Milton's epic, so, too, did Galileo. Sunspots, moonspots, the earth's secondary light, and the consciousness of space that Galileo's telescopic observations revealed enliven and vitalize Milton's presentation of his cosmos and contribute defining images for Milton's presentation of Satan. Additionally, alchemy, hermeticism, and cabalism, through sources such as Dee, Bruno, and Fludd, contribute as much as the new science of Digges and Galileo to the imaginative exploration of light and the complex nature of Milton's sun. Cabalism also contributes to Milton's configuring of his own role as epic poet and alchemy is a key factor in our understanding of the changes that take place in Adam and Eve. Optics is another subject that seems to have fired Milton's imagination, creating an exhilarating play of rays of light within the cosmos and inspiring significant incorporation of visual trajectory as a means of establishing spatial expansion. The impact of such diverse intellectual fields not only creates a text that is challenging, but also directs attention to the intensity of Milton's visual imagination.

Reading *Paradise Lost* in this context reveals two important features. First, there is a remarkable degree of inclusiveness in Milton's attitude to early modern science as well as to a range of ideas from alchemy and magic. This is not to suggest that he was eclectic in his beliefs but that he was genuinely open to multiple, even conflicting, possibilities. Milton displays a very modern scientific ability to consider the possible validity of conflicting intellectual positions and a refusal to be swept along by the impassioned arguments of the time in favor of one of many debated issues. This is in fact a conscious decision that strengthens the fabric of the epic. It does Milton injustice to believe that he either lacked the courage to take up a position in these various debates, or that we misunderstand him when we think him undecided and, if we look closely enough, we will see the manner in which he triumphs over uncertainty reaching some grand magisterial position. Instead, we should examine the ambiguities and uncertainties as intended and as part of Milton's narrative strategies. Second, embedded in *Paradise Lost* is a radical questioning of traditional notions of authority, these subtle negotiations often conducted through the new astronomy, vitalism, as well as alchemy.

Recognition of Milton's achievement in *Paradise Lost* demands that we ask ourselves what special qualities account for the continuing relevance, vitality, and resilience of his epic poem. Its continuing appeal across cultures must mean that there is more to this great work than a powerful rendering of Christian values. An assessment of the special strengths of the epic needs to direct attention to the intellectual inclusiveness and openness that the narrative privileges, its imaginative configuration of the different regions where the action takes place, its nuanced exploration of character and motivation, and the complexity of Milton's own intellectual journey through pre- and postlapsarian worlds and in the invocations. That there are contested issues relating to these aspects of Milton's epic has always been understood and acknowledged. Understanding of the specificities involved in these debates can be reached through a process of retrieval of contextual data, which will further enhance our appreciation of the intellectual content of *Paradise Lost* and Milton's poetic craftsmanship. However, the contested positions that have been allowed to coexist in the epic poem have been the cause of some critical discomfort. Peter C. Herman's survey of traditional Milton criticism that always yielded a stable Milton shows Milton scholarship's recurring need to engage with the tropes of resolution of conflict, consistency and unity, imaginative transcendence, and reconciliation, as strategies through which the Miltonic text achieves stability.[1] Herman himself sees Milton as "a poet of deep incertitude," a condition that, he feels, "results in large part from the failure of the English Revolution."[2] While Herman's reading clears the air and rescues Milton from the burden of certitude, the contextual reading I have attempted in this book suggests that we need to go further than political ideology. "It is out of the turmoil of not knowing what to affirm in the wake of the Revolution's failure that Milton creates some of his finest poetry"[3] is only part of the story. The intellectual ferment that allowed the vibrancy of conflicting intellectual positions of the new astronomy, astrology and prognostications, vitalism and alchemy, and magic and mechanics, throughout the seventeenth century, urged that the best minds, including Milton and Newton, should be open to multiple possibilities. This is not confusion, but the capacity to recognize the possible validity of conflicting intellectual positions. *Paradise Lost* continues to enchant readers as it incorporates this enriching uncertainty into the experience of the epic.

One of these uncertainties is in the cosmic alternatives Milton puts forward in Books 4 (ll. 592–95) and 10 (ll. 668–73), admitting the possibility of a geocentric or heliocentric universe, which has been much derided as evidence of his evasion and refusal to chose between the Aristotelio-Ptolemaic, Copernican, and Tychonic systems. The truth is that it indeed "imports not" (8.71) whether the sun moves or the earth. Milton configures astronomy in his epic not in encyclopedic terms as decisive knowledge but as complex possibilities that can be directed toward the needs of the epic narrative. Milton's cosmos is apparently Ptolemaic in having a stationary earth at the center with Paradise always facing heaven. But it is Copernican in its projection of infinite space and Tychonic in its rejection of solid spheres. Moving between the various cosmic models, *Paradise Lost* constructs the notion of infinity within an apparently earth-centered cosmos enclosed within the outer boundary of an opaque shell. This suggestion of infinite space is achieved, primarily, through his exploration of multiple worlds. Plurality of worlds was both an exhilarating cosmic possibility and a controversial issue, which is integrated into the texture of the epic to create this sense of infinitely expanding space. In *Paradise Lost*, this complex amalgam of a comforting finite boundary and vertiginous infinite space is, in turn, one of the deliberate ambiguities Milton uses to reveal unexpected aspects of the character of Adam and Eve.

The debates that vitalize *Paradise Lost* not only accommodate controversies within a specific area, such as astronomy, but also cut across different intellectual fields. To take an example, the invocations chart Milton's epic aspirations through its initial surge to great heights to a more tempered, mature position. This journey of aspiration is narrated through two different cosmologies. One of these is the intertwined cabalistic fabric that weaves together Bruno's cosmological narrative of Mosaic empowerment with Fludd's version of cabalism that focuses more on the question of cosmic origins. Composing his "adventurous song" (1.13) of "things unattempted yet in prose or rhyme" (1.16) that looks back to the beginnings of creation, discourses of empowerment and of cosmic origins are both relevant. The other governing image is generated by the cosmic spaces opened up by the telescope, which enables the poet to envisage his own imagined cosmic journey into the depths of hell, through the boundless regions of chaos into heaven, and then down through the aperture and interstellar spaces to earth and Paradise. In depicting the ambitious range of his own epic aspirations and its subsequent tempering, the imagined dismounting from Pegasus in the invocation in Book 7, with its Brunian cabalistic implications, is as relevant a paradigm as safe landing on earth after a series of space travels. The downward descent "to my native element" (7.16) is as much a dismounting "from this flying steed" (7.17) as a return from a journey through space to find himself "Standing on earth, not rapt above the pole" (7.23). Cabalism and the new astronomy are parallel resources that Milton unhesitatingly draws upon for images and ideas in an age in which such intertexture of science and occult philosophy would have been perfectly acceptable. In the epic's final invocation Milton draws in ideas generated by radical vitalist theories of creation to question the relation of empowerment to creativity. With remarkable intellectual inclusiveness, Milton is able to hold together models of ascent and descent and questions of empowerment from widely diverse fields of magic and science to strengthen the epic invocations.

Another complex interweaving of different fields generates the powerful image of Milton's sun. In the narrative structure of *Paradise Lost*, the sun occupies a position of eminence. It is the only celestial object to which God has assigned one of the major archangels as regent. It has a powerful attraction for Satan as well as for Adam and Eve, and has a decisive role to play in the cosmic structure in maintaining eternal spring and equality of days and nights in Paradise. It is also a key to character in the epic. It reveals unexpected weaknesses in Uriel who, as regent of the sun, and in spite of being specially gifted as the sharpest sighted angel, allows his great fascination with the moving sunbeams to delay action and expose an unexpected failure of responsibility. The sun provokes Satan into a speech of soul searching that reveals his evil intentions and, later, inspires reactions of guilt and flight from the fallen Adam and Eve. In representing these and many other functions that the sun performs in the epic poem, Milton configures the sun through varied resources. Drawing upon the discourse of alchemy, Milton designates the sun as an "arch-chemic" (3.609) as well as the much sought after philosopher's stone (3.600). It is also a celestial object examined by the astronomer through his telescope and Satan, landing on the sun, is like a sunspot. Just as the invocations draw upon varied fields, here, too, alchemy and the new astronomy reinforce each other in positioning the sun as a symbol of dominance. Both the touchstone and the telescope were instruments of revelation, inspiring much debate and speculation in the seventeenth century. They are the appropriate tools, incorporated as images, that establish the critical role played by the sun in *Paradise Lost*. Here, as elsewhere, Milton does not hesitate to bring together ideas and images from the divergent fields of alchemy and the new astronomy.

If this inclusiveness and foregrounding of uncertainty breaks the mould of traditional expectations of a majestic and decisive Milton, a similar radical approach marks his privileging of change and questioning of authority within the cosmos. *Paradise Lost* is, by all accounts, a work that is invested with a clear sense of hierarchical order. As Raphael explains to Adam, in words that combine Platonic philosophy with alchemical thought

> O Adam, one almighty is, from whom
> All things proceed, and up to him return,
> If not depraved from good, created all
> Such to perfection, one first matter all,
> Indued with various forms, various degrees
> Of substance, and in things that live, of life;
> But more refined, more spirituous, and pure,
> As nearer to him placed or nearer tending. (5.469–76)

These gradations include inequality of the sexes as in the unequal hierarchical status of Adam and Eve

> Not equal, as their sex not equal seemed;
> For contemplation he and valour formed,
> For softness she and sweet attractive grace,
> He for God only, she for God in him. (4.296–99)

Strict observance of systems of command is impressed from the beginning through the reverberating "disobedience" of the epic's first line—"Of man's first disobedience." Yet the poem guides us persuasively to consider the possibility of doubts, the lengths to which curiosity might be legitimately extended, and the consequences of realignment of hierarchical positions. Questioning authority is not itself considered questionable. It is after all in hell that authority is never questioned. None of the devils question Satan's authority, either directly or indirectly. He remains supremely in command even as he voices his own resistance to what is, to him, the unacceptable authority of God. It is true that in heaven, the consequences of questioning of authority are cataclysmic—the rebellion and fall of a third of the angels in heaven. As a place of perfection, Milton's heaven does not admit the possibility of change. But in Paradise, the situation is quite different. Raphael arrives as God's messenger entrusted with the task of cautioning Adam and Eve. Having been given the assignment of conversing with Adam as friend with friend, he utilizes these wider terms of reference to go beyond the agenda set down by God to introduce Adam to the secrets of alchemy and the new astronomy. The discourse on alchemy urges Adam and Eve to seek change as a process of sublimation. Besides, the incorporation of material from these two debated fields—areas of knowledge far beyond anything within Adam's intellectual reach—is Raphael's way of opening Adam's mind, encouraging him to ask questions, raise doubts. Doubt, rather than certainty, is a mark of Adam's superior intellect and, although he claims to abjure "perplexing thoughts" (8.183), it is precisely such thoughts and the questions they give rise to that enliven the conversation with Raphael in the middle books of the epic. If "God hath bid dwell far off all anxious cares" (8.185) and warned him "not to know at large of things remote" (8.191), this is a command Adam clearly circumvents, asking questions about the war in heaven, the creation of the world, and the structure of the cosmos.

With Milton's Eve, questioning of authority takes a new direction with the integration of problems of gender. Initially she had declared to Adam "My author and disposer, what thou bid'st / Unargued I obey; so God ordains, / God is thy law, thou mine" (4.65–67), but this submissive position is soon set aside. From the beginning Eve displays uneasy signs of being too concerned with her own self. Following her narcissistic account of her own creation, she questions Adam about the celestial objects they see in the night sky. Her questions about diurnal movement in Book 4 are similar to those Adam asks Raphael in Book 8, but there is a significant difference. Eve questions the need for moonlight and starlight when they are asleep, by implication suggesting that the celestial objects exist for them. "But wherefore all night long shine these, for whom / This glorious sight, when sleep hath shut all eyes?" (4.657–58). When he asks Raphael the same question about celestial movement, what perplexes Adam is disproportion in the cosmos, where "so many nobler bodies" (8.28) move in "restless revolution" (8.31) around the insignificant earth. The difference in perspective is an index of character, Eve clearly self-involved unlike Adam whose question is mathematical and philosophical. It is this flaw in Eve's character that Satan exploits in the dream-temptation, suggesting "heaven wakes with all his eyes, / Whom to behold but thee, nature's desire" (5.44–45). Her dream-temptation is also the cause of a radical repositioning within her mind as it gives Eve access, however imperfectly, to a level of experience with which Adam is clearly unacquainted. As Lara Dodds suggests,

> Eve gets an astronomical view of the Earth. In this scene, knowledge of the stars and the privileged view of the Earth provided by a distant perspective (associated in the poem with the view provided by the telescope) draw Eve (temporarily this time) into a story in which her narrative diverges from that of the earthbound Adam…Eve's astronomical vision offers her other worlds and other stories that disrupt her position in the hierarchy of Milton's Paradise.[4]

Paradise Lost gives us several telescopic sightings of the earth. Uriel, from his position in space as regent of the sun, had pointed out the earth to Satan disguised as a cherub—"That spot to which I point is Paradise, / Adam's abode, those lofty shades his bower" (3.733–34). In Book 5, Raphael looks down from the gates of heaven through the aperture in the opaque shell, that is, down the length of the golden chain and through interstellar spaces, toward "Earth and the garden of God, with cedars crowned" (5.260). And in her dream-temptation Eve flies up to the clouds and sees "The earth outstretched immense, a prospect wide / And various" (5.88–89). The astronomical experience Eve shares with angels cannot but have an impact on her character. As time goes by, Eve changes. The submissive Eve who had declared her obedience to Adam, becomes a self-contained character who no longer needs to hear Raphael's explanation of diurnal movement and keeps to herself the fact that she overheard the angel's warning, without sharing it with Adam. Eventually, she goes on to question Adam's authority in Book 9, insisting on her need to separate from him, find her own space, and firmly and unhesitatingly makes sure she wins the debate. Astronomy becomes the discourse through which Milton presents Eve's repositioning of herself, the motivations for her questioning of authority.

While compelling reasons are provided for Eve's questioning of the established gender equation, her desire for a superior status does, however, bring in sinister echoes. The possibility of such radical repositioning of authority is prefigured in *Paradise Lost* in the allegory of Chaos and Night. Night is the female partner of Chaos, but she subverts the gender equation of the epic in being unquestionably more powerful than Chaos. However, unlike Eve, Night has immense destructive potential, which is consistently related to her status of being uncreated and never to what might be seen as an unnatural usurpation of power. Moreover, Milton's Eve, "mother of mankind, whose fruitful womb / Shall fill the world" (5.388–89), is the exact antithesis of Night as an "abortive gulf" (2.441). Nevertheless, the uneasy suggestion remains and reflects ominously on Eve's sudden self-assertion.

Questioning of authority begins with Milton's portrayal of the angels as characters. Fallibility, in *Paradise Lost*, is not confined to the human protagonists. The angels Uriel and Gabriel are fallible, their weaknesses revealed through their irresponsible delay in taking action against Satan's intrusion, a delay that is triggered by their fascination with astronomical details. But their error is not sin. They do not disobey divine commands. Their errors show a lapse in judgment and a degree of self-involvement. This makes Uriel and Gabriel the uncertain angels, although they are guardians entrusted with the security of the sun and Paradise. While within the cosmos, they appear as unsure and vulnerable as Adam and Eve, though there is never any direct interaction between them and the human pair. These angels do not question authority, but fail in their role as figures of authority. The other two angels, Raphael and Michael, are teachers and instructors, clearly exalted beings. But Adam's candid questions to Raphael about angelic sex, and the tone in which he offers to tell Raphael "my story, which perhaps thou hast not heard" (8.205), register a reorientation of human attitudes to angels. Of the four archangels who operate within the cosmos, Michael appears last, after the Fall, and is treated with utmost respect and awe. By this time, Adam and Eve no longer enjoy the comfort level with angels they did at the time of Raphael's visit. The actions of Uriel and Gabriel within the cosmos raise questions about their sincerity and authority even as Raphael's discourse on alchemy and astronomy goes beyond God's instructions and tests the limits of divine command. Meanwhile, the time span between Satan's entry into the cosmos and the Fall is a period of flux that allows the human pair to evolve as characters. The narrative of Eve's growing assurance and repositioning of herself as Adam's equal coincides with the time span during which the motivations of angels are questioned. This entire pattern seems to suggest that what might seem subversion of authority at various points in the epic is, in fact, a repositioning that is suggested as possible in a prelapsarian world. As Adam's "other half" (4.488), Eve might assume a position of equality, while angels and man may be friends and equals. Raphael's initial discourse on alchemy suggests such realignments as possible. "Your bodies may at last turn all to spirit, / Improved by tract of time, and winged ascend / Ethereal, as we" (5.497–99). The imagined prelapsarian cosmos of *Paradise Lost* is the crucible within which these reorientations could have taken place. This vision of the possibilities that had been opened up within the prelapsarian cosmos deepens the tragedy of the Fall. Once the Fall takes place, rigid lines of authority are drawn up, angels become admonishers and not friends, woman becomes the weaker sex not man's equal. Change and fluidity, explorations of difference, that had begun, are abruptly terminated by the Fall.

Questioning of authority takes a different, more tentative form in the epic invocations. The final invocation in Book 9 provocatively suggests that the subject matter of the poem is exalted enough to inspire an epic poem without assistance from a divine muse—"higher argument...sufficient of itself to raise / that name" (9.42–44)—a vitalist autogenerative creativity. But that claim is soon tempered with the admission of a higher source of inspiration that appears like a benediction and dictates to the poet in his sleep. The parallel to this is in the account of the dark materials of chaos, inherently good prime matter, which are in their "pregnant causes mixed" (2.913), admitting the vitalist possibility of multiple cosmoses being generated by chaos. But here again the poem makes it clear that such autogeneration of cosmoses does not in fact take place. Instead, chaos waits submissively for God to create more worlds. Angels may be fallible like humans, but divine authority is never challenged. Milton's position in the vitalist debate is quite clear. Although he admits self-generative continuity as a process to be possible, such activity must be preceded by a divine first cause.

The central stage where the main action takes place is the cosmos, the universe within its hard outer shell. In defining the cosmos—its creation, its structure, the modalities of space and time within it, the depiction of variable celestial phenomena including new stars, comets, and sunspots—Milton undertakes a complex intellectual journey, moving between different time zones, the imagined prelapsarian world and the early modern world. The skill with which this is done shows his alertness to the finer points of cosmological distinction between pre- and postlapsarian worlds. The prelapsarian or imagined cosmos of *Paradise* Lost is a unique structure some of whose materials may be traced to postlapsarian theories and discoveries. But as an idealized construct it enjoys a status of perfection and of wonder. It is neither Ptolemaic, nor Copernican, nor Tychonic. In creating a reorientation of compass points and merging the planes of the ecliptic and the celestial equator, Milton is able to create a unique cosmos that cannot be identified directly with postlapsarian models. The perfection of the imagined cosmos is quite unlike anything early modern astronomy discovered and reflects the simplicity and harmony of the prelapsarian condition. Cosmological events that belonged to the postlapsarian situation or the early modern world and are integrated into the narrative framework of the epic include references to the new stars and comets and to Galileo's observations with his telescope. The chain of allusions to the new stars and comets relate to Milton's presentation of Satan. Millenarian debates encouraged by these variable celestial phenomena in the seventeenth century are utilized by Milton in *Paradise Lost* to frame specific images that provide significant insights into Satan's character. The contextual framework of these references exposes the errors and false hopes generated by contemporary speculations related to observation of new stars and comets. These findings were, however, scientifically correct and the names of the great astronomers Tycho Brahe and Kepler are associated with the discovery of these variable cosmic phenomena. Fallibility belonged to the millenarian speculations encouraged by the scientific findings, although even Tycho indulged in such speculations. The other postlapsarian astronomical details Milton incorporates into his epic are associated with Galileo, the only contemporary mentioned by name in *Paradise Lost.* Two of the three Galileo references also relate to Satan. Galileo's telescopic observations of the moon provide the image for Satan's shield and later Satan himself is compared to a sunspot like the ones observed by Galileo. The intermediate reference is uniquely dismissive of human ability. Raphael's telescopic identification of Paradise seen from the gates of heaven through the aperture in the opaque shell is pronounced as being superior to Galileo's "less assured" (5.262) examination of the moon through his telescope. Postlapsarian details function not as the means of defining the cosmos, but as ways of exposing Satan's pretensions and human limitations.

The critical events of *Paradise Lost* take place within a visually and intellectually exhilarating landscape. The imagined spaces of heaven, hell, chaos, and cosmos—each progressively conceptually more complex—have their own contribution to make in the process of defining character. Milton's heaven is like a virtual domain, without the specificities of known regions, so that Raphael wonders how he should "unfold / The secrets of another world" (5.568–69) to Adam. Yet it shares in some of the characteristics of Milton's cosmos. There is the same absence of specificity—the walls of heaven adorned with opal towers and battlements are of "undetermined square or round" (2.1048). If heaven as space is indefinable, time certainly exists, but as virtual time. "For time, though in eternity, applied / To motion, measures all things durable / By present, past, and future" (5.580–82). Heaven has its days and nights, "our evening and our morn" (5.628) for "change delectable" (5.629). As Raphael explains,

> There is a cave
> Within the mount of God, fast by his throne,
> Where light and darkness in perpetual round
> Lodge and dislodge by turns, which makes through heaven
> Grateful vicissitude, like day and night. (6.4–8)

Plato's *Timaeus* linked time with cosmic movement and Milton, conscious that the narrative demands breaking up of eternity into units of days, has the difficult task of constructing time in the ineffable regions of heaven. Unlike Paradise, there is no pressure of specific hours here but sequentiality is not lost as days are created through alternation of light and darkness. Radiant heaven is represented with reference to an array of precious and semiprecious stones. It has "opal towers" (2.1049), battlements "of living sapphire" (2.1050), and the bright pavement of heaven shines "like a sea of jasper" (3.363). This bejeweled heaven reminds us of the New Jerusalem of *Revelations*,[5] but reminds us also of the sun adorned with jewels in Book 3 of *Paradise Lost*. Yet heaven is not only a region of glory, it also has its pastoral beauty with rivers and fountains and greenery. In this wondrous region, the angels stand "thick as stars" (3.61) around God, indistinguishable from each other. The fiery Abdiel, who finds himself in the group of rebel angels and has the courage to defy them, is the only one with a well-defined character. Otherwise, angels display individual characteristics only when they find themselves in the cosmos. In heaven they form a collective admiring group. Milton's depiction of heaven draws upon biblical, mythological, and classical sources rather than the controversial areas of knowledge he utilizes for the creation of chaos and the cosmos. Heaven's design might invite comparison with the cosmos, yet it is essentially a virtual world with the angels an idealized group.

Milton's cosmos is much more dynamic and interactive. In the construction of his cosmos, Milton draws upon materials from traditional cosmology and the new science, as well as magic and alchemy. The process of defining this cosmos is largely dependent on the perspectives of the angels, Satan, and Adam and Eve and their understanding of the cosmos in turn defines their character. In this intricately interwoven fabric, the traditional binaries of character and background dissolve into one interactive, tightly enmeshed structure. Space within the cosmos is constructed through angelic eyesight, the immense spaces revealed to Raphael and Satan as they look into the depths of the cosmos, and through their configuring of the stars as worlds. The immensity of the cosmos is further reinforced through Adam's anxiety about the "spaces incomprehensible" (8.20) through which the stars and planets seem to roll with such "incorporeal speed" (8.37). Raphael's extension of space through his perception of the stars as worlds is part of the exceptional generosity that marks his personality and makes him extend Adam's range of knowledge much further than he had been commissioned to do. This is in sharp contrast to Satan's perception of the stars as worlds. When Satan sails past the stars, which "seemed other worlds" (3.566), he wonders "who dwelt happy there" (3.570) but "stayed not to inquire" (3.571). It is important to note that at this point Satan does not yet know which of the celestial bodies is "the happy seat / Of some new race called Man" (2.347–48), or, indeed, if man had a "fixed seat" (3.669) at all or could, instead, move between the shining orbs. Satan's examination of the stars as inhabited worlds has sinister overtones as at this point of time he is seeking the dwelling place of man. His configuring of the stars as worlds is thus fueled by a colonizing ambition and is, again, an index to character.

Paradise Lost is an intensely dramatic poem with just two human characters—Adam and Eve. Milton peoples the void with angels, devils, and two sets of personifications—Chaos and Night, and Sin and Death. This supporting cast throws light on the human pair at the center. Our understanding of Adam and Eve becomes significantly greater once we understand the contrasts and parallels Milton sets up with their help. Of these other characters, Satan is unique and in every way the antithesis of the human pair. The Satan of *Paradise Lost* appears in many forms. He is the embodiment of evil, the infernal serpent who brought death into the world and all our woe, the jealous opponent of the Son of God, and the seducer of Eve. Satan is monarchist ('better to reign in Hell" [1.263]), a false revolutionary ("Whom reason hath equaled, force hath made supreme / Above his equals" [1.248–49]), and a false people's prophet ("From this descent / Celestial virtues rising, will appear / More glorious" [2.14–16]). He is remarkably intelligent, he can outwit the angels Uriel and Gabriel, and his intellectual reach is enormous as evident from the ease with which he masters the astronomy of Milton's universe. He is capable of great passion, even if the passions are those of hatred and despair. He is an accomplished dissembler, who can mesmerize both crowds (his followers in Hell) and individuals (Eve). Jealousy, deceit, and evil intentions are fundamental to his nature, but these are absent in Adam and Eve.

Insights into the strengths as well as flaws in the human pair are provided by the actions of Milton's angels within the cosmos, and their interactions with Adam and Eve. Stephen Fallon feels that Adam and Eve "share with Milton a potentially transgressive curiosity."[6] If Eve, and then Adam, appear to display unwarranted curiosity about the cosmos, that curiosity is encouraged, rather than suppressed, by Raphael. "Dream not of other worlds" (8.175), the angel says, *after* placing before Adam cosmic possibilities Adam could never have imagined. For Raphael, it is important that Adam should know that at all times obedience to God is mandatory. With that ensured, doubts and questions are admissible, even recommended. This larger vision is absent in Uriel and Gabriel, the two archangels who reside within the cosmos but with whom Adam and Eve have no direct contact. These angels are fascinated with the mechanism of the cosmos, but their wonder does not translate into admiration alone as recommended by Raphael (8.75). After all, the precise workings of the cosmos are hidden from both man and angels—"the rest / From man or angel the great architect / Did wisely to conceal" (8.71–73). The attempts of Uriel and Gabriel to utilize their knowledge of the cosmos lead to irresponsible delays and exploitative conduct. Adam's doubts and questions about the cosmos are more closely aligned to admiration, the ideal proposed by Raphael. On the other hand, the language of Eve's questions about celestial motion reminds us of Uriel and Gabriel as she relates the mechanism of the universe to herself—in her understanding the moon and stars have no need to shine when the inhabitants of Paradise are asleep. And in place of

Adam's uneasiness of immeasurable space, Eve's comment on space immediately after her transgression is its relevance to herself: "And I perhaps am secret; heaven is high, / High and remote to see from thence distinct / Each thing on earth" (9.811–13). Uriel, Gabriel, and Eve look upon the cosmos in terms of their own needs. They lack the detachment that Raphael and Adam display. Set within the context of cosmic details, nuances in the character of Adam and Eve are explored through comparison and contrast with angelic behavior. Such interactive configuring of background and character is one of the factors behind the immense power of Milton's version of the familiar story of the Fall of man.

Paradise Lost ranges over a wide field of knowledge. Science is not "occasionally touched with occultism and frequently lagging behind the newest discoveries" in the epic as Schultz believed.[7] Occultism, in the form of hermetic and cabalistic magic, and alchemy are major resources Milton draws upon, together with new areas of science, the new astronomy, optics, and vitalism. If Milton's approach is what we would call interdisciplinary today, it was adopted at a time when rigid demarcations into subject fields did not exist. Yet the seventeenth century acknowledged critical differences between alchemy and medicine, astrology and astronomy, even as the same individuals, many of them well-known intellectuals, shared a genuine interest in these diverse fields. A vibrant culture of debate and controversy was a natural consequence. All of these subjects engage Milton's mind as he writes his great epic poem and he is unusually alert to the debates and speculations generated by these subjects. This vital intellectual ferment could lead to extreme and rigid positions, as in Alexander Ross in the Ross- Wilkins controversy. It could encourage sensationalism as in the almanacs of William Lilly. It could entice established scientists such as Harvey to speculate on extreme forms of vitalism. It could also result in the kind of hesitations that mark Swan's popular encyclopedia, the *Speculum Mundi*. And it could create an atmosphere in which alchemy became a living force for some of the greatest scientific minds of the age such as Boyle and Newton. Most of all, it was an age when one of the greatest scientists of the century, Galileo, could exult in the audacity and wonder of his telescopic discoveries and simultaneously acknowledge the possibility of illusion and uncertainty in scientific findings. These complex currents of thought energize Milton's epic. While Galileo is recognized as a significant contemporary whose presence can be identified not only in the three passages where he is directly mentioned, but elsewhere in the epic, too, there are other unexpected presences in the poem. They may not be mentioned by name, but their ideas and the debates that surrounded them are a powerful presence in the text, accessible to the contemporary reader, lost in the process of time. John Dee, Giordano Bruno and Robert Fludd, Kepler and Tycho Brahe, Thomas Digges, and Robert Boyle share space in *Paradise Lost* with figures less well remembered today—John Bainbridge, John Pell, William Lilly. These controversial figures of the early modern period need to be reinstated in a contextual reading of the poem.

NOTES

I INTRODUCTION

1. Harriot resided with Henry Percy, ninth Earl of Northumberland, at Sion House from 1606 until his death in 1621. Northumberland was Harriot's chief patron and also a lifelong friend of Sir Walter Raleigh. For further details about this enigmatic figure, see Frances A. Yates, *A Study of Love's Labour's Lost* (Cambridge: Cambridge University Press, 1936); and Robert Fox (ed.), *Thomas Harriot, An Elizabethan Man of Science* (Aldershot: Ashgate Publishing Ltd., 2000).

2. Frances A. Yates, *Giordano Bruno and the Hermetic Tradition* (London: Routledge and Kegan Paul, 1964), p. 398. However, scholars have since questioned the decisiveness of this event, believing the erosion of the authority of the *Hermetica* to have been much more gradual.

3. John Maynard Keynes, "Newton the Man," in *Newton Tercentenary Celebrations 15–19 July 1946*, published by The Royal Society (Cambridge: Cambridge University Press, 1947), p. 27.

4. See "Alchemy, Magic and Moralism in the Thought of Robert Boyle," in Michael Hunter, *Robert Boyle (1627–91): Scrupulosity and Science* (Woodbridge: The Boydell Press, 2000), pp. 93–118. See also Lawrence M. Principe, *The Aspiring Adept: Robert Boyle and His Alchemical Quest* (Princeton, N.J.: Princeton University Press, 1998).

5. William H. Sherman, *John Dee: The Politics of Reading and Writing in the Renaissance* (Amherst: University of Massachusetts Press, 1995), p. xi.

6. John Swan, *Speculum Mundi, Or, a Glasse Representing the Face of the World* (Printed by the Printers to the University of Cambridge, 1935).

7. Although Copernicus's *De Revolutionibus* had been published in 1543, till late into the seventeenth century, three astronomical systems were at the center of a debate for acceptance—the traditional Aristotelio-Ptolemaic model, the new Copernican system, and the Tychonic geoheliocentric compromise.

8. Swan, *Speculum Mundi*, p. 107.
9. Bernard Capp, *Astrology and the Popular Press: English Almanacs 1500–1800* (London and Boston: Faber and Faber, 1979), p. 292.
10. Ibid., p. 23.
11. See Don Cameron Allen, *The Star-Crossed Renaissance: The Quarrel about Astrology and its Influence in England* (Duke University Press, 1941; rpt New York: Octagon Books Inc., 1966).
12. Capp, *Astrology and the Popular Press*, p. 23.
13. William Lilly, *Englands Propheticall Merline, Foretelling to all Nations of Europe until 1663. The Actions Depending upon the Influences of the Conjunction of Saturn and Jupiter 1642/3* (1644), from "The Address to the Reader."
14. See William Lilly, *William Lilly's History of His Life and Times from the Year 1602 to 1681, Written by Himself* (2nd ed., 1715), ed. by K. M. Briggs under the title *The Last of the Astrologers* (Ilkley, Yorkshire: The Scolar Press, Ltd., 1794), p. 32; Capp, *Astrology and the Popular Press*, p. 210.
15. William Lilly, The Starry Messenger, or An Interpretation of that Strange Apparition of Three Suns Seene in London, 19 Novemb. 1644. Being the Birth Day of King Charles (1644).
16. Lilly, Englands Propheticall Merline, p. 39.
17. Ann Geneva, *Astrology and the Seventeenth Century Mind* (Manchester and New York: Manchester University Press, 1995), p. 21.
18. Ibid., p. 257.
19. Oxford Dictionary of National Biography, 2004, vol. 30, p. 575.
20. Mark H. Curtis, *Oxford and Cambridge in Transition 1558–1642* (Oxford: Oxford University Press, 1959), p. 227.
21. See *Oxford University Statutes* to 1843 trans. G. R. M. Ward (London, 1845), 2 vols, vol. I, pp. 272–74.
22. For a survey of the position of astronomical knowledge in Renaissance England, see F. R. Johnson, *Astronomical Thought in Renaissance England* (New York: Octagon Books Inc., 1968).
23. A. R. Hall, The Scientific Revolution 1500–1800: The Formation of the Modern Scientific Attitude (London, New York, Toronto: Longmans, Green & Co., 1954), p. 193, footnote.
24. Paul Arno Trout, *Magic and the Millennium: A Study of the Millenary Motifs in the Occult Milieu of Puritan England, 1640–1660* (PhD Dissertation of the University of British Columbia, Canada, 1975). See *Dissertation Abstracts International*, A—The Humanities and Social Sciences, January 1976, vol. 36, no. 7.
25. See David Mulder, *The Alchemy of Revolution: Gerard Winstanley's Occultism and Seventeenth-Century English Communism* (New York, Bern, Frankfurt, and Paris: Peter Lang, 1990).
26. See Charles Webster, *The Great Instauration: Science, Medicine and Reform 1626–60* (London: Duckworth, 1975); Michael Hunter,

Science and Society in Restoration England (Cambridge: Cambridge University Press, 1981), pp. 21–31; Charles Webster, "The College of Physicians: `Solomon's House' in Commonwealth England," *Bulletin of the History of Medicine*, 41 (1967), 393–412; and "New Light on the Invisible College: The Social Relations of English Science in the Mid-seventeenth Century," *Transactions of the Royal Historical Society*, fifth series 24 (1974), 19–42.

27. James Orchard Halliwell (ed.), *A Collection Of Letters Illustrative Of The Progress Of Science In England From The Reign Of Queen Elizabeth To That Of Charles The Second* (London, 1841), p. 80. See also S. J. Rigaud (ed.), *Correspondence of Scientific Men of The Seventeenth Century* (Oxford: Oxford University Press, 1841), 2 vols.

John Pell (1611–58) was admitted to Trinity College, Cambridge, at the age of 13. He received his BA in 1628 and his MA in 1630 *before proceeding to Oxford in 1631.*

"Pye-bottoms" probably refer to sheets containing calculations to determine the assigning of Saints' days in the calendar. One of the meanings of "pie" or pye" in the OED is "a collection of rules adopted in the pre-Reformation Church, to show how to deal (under each of the 35 possible variations in the date of Easter) with the concurrence of more than one office on the same day, accurately indicating the manner of commemorating, or of putting off till another time, the Saints' days, etc., occurring in the ever-changing times of Lent, Easter, Whitsuntide and the Octave of the Trinity." This would account for the ironical tone of the passage, which suggests that the same set of numbers and signs could be both a device for conjuring spirits and an aid to Christian worship.

There may also be a reference here to the fact that in April 1643 Parliament decreed that it would hold as spy anyone who wrote in unknown characters or ciphers. See Geneva, *Astrology and the Seventeenth Century Mind*, p. 21.

28. See chapter six in this volume.

29. See J. L. E. Dreyer, *A History of Astronomy from Thales to Kepler*, 2nd ed. (New York: Dover Publications, 1953), pp. 374 and 405.

30. Harris Francis Fletcher, *The Intellectual Development of John Milton* (Urbana: University of Illinois Press, 1956), vol.1, pp. 301–302.

31. For an account of Bruno's Oxford debates, see Frances A. Yates, *Giordano Bruno and the Hermetic Tradition* (London: Routledge and Kegan Paul, 1964), pp. 166–68; and R. McNulty, "Bruno at Oxford," *Renaissance News* XIII (1960), 300–305.

32. The suggestion of Arthur and Alberta Turner, CPW1, 322, endorsed by Barbara Lewalski, *The Life of John Milton* (Oxford: Blackwell Publishers, 2000), p. 64. See also William Riley Parker, *Milton: A Biography*, 2nd ed., 2 vols, vol. I, *The Life*, revised

version ed. by Gordon Campbell (Oxford: Clarendon Press, 1996), p. 143.

33. Gordon Campbell and Thomas N. Corns, *John Milton, Life, Work, and Thought* (Oxford: Oxford University Press, 2008), pp. 85, 403.

34. Lewalski, *The Life of John Milton*, pp. 172–73.

35. See Urszula Szulakowska, *The Alchemy of Light: Geometry and Optics in Late Renaissance Alchemical Illustration* (Leiden, Boston, Koln: Brill, 2000), pp. 175–77.

36. J. H. Hanford, "Dr. Paget's Library," *Bulletin of the Medical Library Association* XXXVI (1945).

37. See ibid.; and Christopher Hill, *Milton and the English Revolution* (London: Faber and Faber, 1977), pp. 492–95.

38. William Poole, "Milton and Science: A Caveat," in *Milton Quarterly* vol. 38, no. 1 (March 2004), 18–34. See also George F. Butler, "Milton's Meeting with Galileo: A Reconsideration," in *Milton Quarterly*, vol. 39, no. 3 (October 2005).

39. Donald Friedman, "Galileo and the Art of Seeing," in *Milton in Italy: Contexts, Images, Contradictions*, ed. Mario A. Di Cesare (Binghamton, New York: Medieval & Renaissance Texts & Studies, 1991), pp. 159–74.

40. Julia M. Walker, "Milton and Galileo: The Art of Intellectual Canonization," in *Milton Studies*, ed. James D. Simmonds, vol. XXV (1989) (Pittsburgh: Pittsburgh University Press, 1990), pp. 109–23.

41. For earlier work on Milton and the new astronomy, see A. H. Gilbert, "Milton and Galileo," *SP* 19 (1922), 152–85; "The Outside Shell of Milton's World," *SP* 20 (1923), 444–47; Grant McColley, "The Theory of a Plurality of Worlds as a Factor in Milton's Attitude toward the Copernican Hypothesis," *MLN* 47 (1932), 319–25; "The Astronomy of *Paradise Lost*," *SP* 34 (1937), 209–47; "The Seventeenth-Century Doctrine of a Plurality of Worlds," *Annals of Science* 1 (1936), 385–430; "Milton's Dialogue on Astronomy: The Principal Immediate Sources," *PMLA* vol. LII, no. 3 (1937), 728–62; Marjorie Hope Nicolson, *The Breaking of the Circle: Studies in the Effect of the "New Science" upon Seventeenth Century Poetry* (Evanston, Ill: Northwestern University Press, 1950); "Milton and the Telescope," *ELH* (1935), 1–32; Kester Svendsen, *Milton and Science* (Cambridge: Harvard University Press, 1956).

For earlier work on Milton and magic and alchemy, see Marjorie Hope Nicolson, "Milton and the *Conjectura cabbalistica*," *PQ* 6 (1927), 1–18; R. J. Zwi Werblowsky, "Milton and the *Conjectura Cabbalistica*," *Journal of the Warburg and Courtauld Institutes* 18 (1955), 90–113; Denis Saurat, *Milton: Man and Thinker*, 2nd ed. (London: Dent, 1944).

42. Lawrence Babb, *The Moral Cosmos of Paradise Lost* (East Lansing: Michigan State University Press, 1970). See the chapter on "The New Astronomy."

43. Harinder Singh Marjara, *Contemplation of Created Things: Science in Paradise Lost* (Toronto, Buffalo, London: University of Toronto Press, 1992).

44. Angelica Duran, *The Age of Milton and the Scientific Revolution* (Pittsburgh, Pennsylvania: Duquesne University Press, 2007).

45. Joad Raymond, *Milton's Angels, The Early-Modern Imagination* (Oxford: Oxford University Press, 2010), p. 9.

46. Mary Ann Radzinowicz, *Toward "Samson Agonistes": The Growth of Milton's Mind* (Princeton: Princeton University Press, 1978), p. 351; emphasis in the original.

47. Columbia Milton, vol. XVII, p. 151; and *Life of Peter Ramus* in Don M. Wolfe et al. eds., *Complete Prose Works of John Milton*, 8 vols (New Haven, Conn.: Yale University Press, 1953–82), vol. II.

48. See Frances A. Yates, *The Occult Philosophy in the Elizabethan Age* (London: Routledge and Kegan Paul, 1979).

49. Christopher Hill, *Milton and the English Revolution* (London: Faber and Faber, 1977), pp. 379, 106.

50. Michael Lieb, "Encoding the Occult: Milton and the Traditions of *Merkabah* Speculation in the Renaissance." in *Milton Studies*, ed. by Albert C. Labriola, vol. XXXVII (Pittsburgh: Pittsburgh University Press, 1999), pp. 42–88. See also Michael Lieb, *The Dialectics of Creation: Patterns of Birth and Regeneration in Paradise Lost* (Boston: University of Massachusetts Press, 1970).

51. Lyndy Abraham, *Marvell and Alchemy* (Aldershot: Scolar Press, 1990).

52. Alastair Fowler (ed.), *Milton, Paradise Lost* (Harlow: Addison Wesley Longman Limited, 2nd ed., 1998). All quotations from *Paradise Lost* are from this edition.

53. John Rogers, The Matter of Revolution: Science, Poetry, and Politics in the Age of Milton (Ithaca and London: Cornell University Press, 1996).

54. Christopher Hill, *The Experience of Defeat: Milton and Some Contemporaries* (London: Faber and Faber Ltd., 1984).

55. Karen Silvia de Leon-Jones, *Giordano Bruno and the Kabbalah: Prophets, Magicians, and Rabbis* (New Haven and London: Yale University Press, 1997), p. 1.

56. Don M. Wolfe, *Complete Prose Works*, vol. II, p. 538.

2 Invocations: Milton as Moses

1. For an account of early modern chemical philosophy, see Allen G. Debus, *Man and Nature in the Renaissance* (Cambridge: Cambridge University Press, 1978), pp. 116–30.

2. See Brian P. Copenhaver, "Natural Magic, Hermetism, and Occultism in Early Modern Science," in *Reappraisals of the Scientific Revolution*, ed. David C. Lindberg and Robert S. Westman (Cambridge: Cambridge University Press, 1990), pp. 262–63.

3. See, e.g., Allen G. Debus, *Man and Nature in the Renaissance* (Cambridge: Cambridge University Press, 1978); and Lindberg and Westman, *Reappraisals of the Scientific Revolution*.

4. See Stephen M. Fallon, *Milton's Peculiar Grace, Self-Representation and Authority* (Ithaca and London: Cornell University Press, 2007). In particular, see chapter 8 "'If All Be Mine': Confidence and Anxiety in *Paradise Lost*," pp. 203–36.

5. J. Martin Evans, "The Birth of the Author: Milton's Poetic Self-Construction," in *Milton Studies*, vol. XXXVIII, ed. Albert C. Labriola and Michael Lieb (Pittsburgh: University of Pittsburgh Press, 2000), pp. 47–65, at p. 59.

6. Ibid., p. 60.

7. Michel Foucault, "What is an Author," in *Textual Strategies: Perspectives in Post-Structuralist Criticism*, ed. Josue V. Harari (Ithaca: Cornell University Press, 1979), pp. 141–60.

8. See Brian P. Copenhaver and Charles B. Schmitt, *Renaissance Philosophy* (Oxford: Oxford University Press, 1992). See also Richard Kieckhefer, *Magic in the Middle Ages* (Cambridge: Cambridge University Press, 1989, 2000). For Milton and cabalism, see Marjorie H. Nicolson, "Milton and the *Conjectura Cabbalistica*," *Philological Quarterly* 6 (1927), 1–18; Denis Saurat, *Milton, Man and Thinker* (London: J.M. Dent & Sons Ltd., 1946); R. J. Zwi Werblowsky, "Milton and the *Conjectura Cabbalistica*," *Journal of the Warburg and Courtauld Institutes* 18 (1955), 90–113; and Rosa Flotats, "Milton: *Paradise Lost* and the Question of Kabbalah," http://sederi.org/docs/yearbooks/06/6_6_Flotats.pdf.

9. Nicolson, "Milton and the *Conjectura Cabbalistica*," 1–2.

10. See Frances A Yates, *The Occult Philosophy in the Elizabethan Age* (London: ARK Paperbacks, 1983), pp. 21–22.

11. Karen Silvia de Leon-Jones, *Giordano Bruno and the Kabbalah: Prophets, Magicians and Rabbis* (New Haven and London: Yale University Press, 1997).

12. Ibid., p. 10.

13. Ibid., p. 137.

14. Giordano Bruno, *On Magic*, in Giordano Bruno, *Cause, Principle and Unity and Essays on Magic*, trans. and ed. Richard J. Blackwell and Robert de Lucca (Cambridge: Cambridge University Press, 1998), p. 107.

15. See Frances A. Yates, *Giordano Bruno and the Hermetic Tradition* (London: Routledge and Kegan Paul, 1964); Hilary Gatti,

The Renaissance Drama of Knowledge (London and New York: Routledge, 1989).

16. Christopher Hill, *Milton and the English Revolution* (London: Faber and Faber, 1977), pp. 34 and 107.
17. Ibid., pp. 56 and 76.
18. Hilary Gatti, *Giordano Bruno and Renaissance Science* (Ithaca and London: Cornell University Press, 1999); Hilary Gatti (ed.), *Giordano Bruno, Philosopher of the Renaissance* (Aldershot: Ashgate Publishing, 2002).
19. Yates, *Occult Philosophy.*
20. See Congreve's *The Way of the World,* Act I, scene 1, "last night was one of their cabal-nights."
21. Howard Dobin, *Merlin's Disciples: Prophecy, Poetry, and Power in Renaissance England* (Stanford, California: Stanford, University Press, 1990). See also Peter French, *John Dee: The World of an Elizabethan Magus* (New York: Routledge and Kegan Paul, 1972).
22. Dobin, *Merlin's Disciples,* p. 8.
23. Ibid., p. 209.
24. James Holly Hanford, "'That Shepherd Who First Taught the Chosen Seed,' A Note on Milton's Mosaic Inspiration," *University of Toronto Quarterly* 8 (1939), 403–19; Don Cameron Allen, *The Harmonious Vision: Studies in Milton's Poetry* (Baltimore: Johns Hopkins University Press, 1970); Jason P. Rosenblatt, *Torah and Law in Paradise Lost* (Princeton, N.J.: Princeton University Press, 1994).
25. Fowler, in his annotations, corrects Bentley's proposed emendation of *secret* to *sacred* pointing out that the top is *secret* anyway as being set apart and concealed by storm clouds. But *secret* here has more than a factual connotation.
26. William B. Hunter and Stevie Davies, "Milton's Urania: 'The Meaning, Not the Name I Call,'" *The Descent of Urania, Studies in Milton, 1946–1988* by William B. Hunter (Lewisburg: Bucknell University Press, London and Toronto: Associated University Presses, 1989), pp. 31–45, rpt from *Studies in English Literature* vol. 28 (1988), 95–111.
27. Ibid., p. 33.
28. Robert Fludd, *Philosophia Moysaica* (Gouda: Peter Rammazen, 1638); *Mosaicall Philosophy: Grounded upon the Essentiall Truth, or Eternal Sapience. Written first in Latin, and afterwards thus rendered into English...* (London: Humphrey Moseley, 1659). See also Stanton J. Linden (ed.), *The Alchemy Reader, From Hermes Trismegistus to Isaac Newton* (Cambridge: Cambridge University Press, 2003), p. 191.
29. Linden, *The Alchemy Reader,* p. 192.

30. Joscelyn Godwin, *Robert Fludd, Hermetic Philosopher and Surveyor of Two Worlds* (London, Thames and Hudson Ltd., 1979), p. 24.
31. Ibid., p. 90.
32. Ibid., p.17. From Fludd, *Philosophia Moysaica*, p. 304.
33. While the immediate source of this passage appears to be the "candle of the Lord" of the Cambridge Platonists, the Cambridge Platonists—Benjamin Whichcote, Nathanael Culverwel, John Smith, and others—were themselves well-versed in the Cabala.
34. Leon-Jones, *Giordano Bruno and the Kabbalah*, p. 45.
35. Mindele Anne Treip, "'Celestial Patronage': Allegorical Ceiling Cycles of the 1630s and the Iconography of Milton's Muse," in *Milton in Italy: Contexts, Images, Contradictions*, ed. by Mario A. Di Cesare (Binghamton, New York: Medieval & Renaissance Texts & Studies, 1991), pp. 237–77.
36. See John Rogers, *The Matter of Revolution: Science, Poetry, and Politics in the Age of Milton* (Ithaca and London: Cornell University Press, 1996).
37. Ibid., p. 10.
38. Ibid., p. 9.
39. Michael Lieb, "Encoding the Occult: Milton and the Traditions of *Merkabah* Speculation in the Renaissance," in *Milton Studies*, ed. by Albert C. Labriola, vol. XXXVII (Pittsburgh: University of Pittsburgh Press, 1999), pp. 42–88.
40. Ibid., pp. 75–77.
41. Jonathan Goldberg and Stephen Orgel (eds.), *John Milton, A Selection of his Finest Poems* (Oxford: Oxford University Press, 1994), p. xi.

3 "Unoriginal Night" and Milton's Chaos

1. John Leonard, "Milton, Lucretius, and 'the Void Profound of Unessential Night,'" in *Living Texts: Interpreting Milton*, ed. Kristin A. Pruitt and Charles W. Durham (Selingrove: Susquehanna University Press, 2000), p. 199.
2. Ibid., p. 202.
3. Edgar H. Duncan, "Robert Fludd," in William B. Hunter, Jr., *A Milton Encyclopedia* (Lewisburg: Bucknell University Press, 1978), vol. 3, pp. 109–10.
4. Leonard, "Milton, Lucretius, and 'the Void Profound of Unessential Night,'" p. 208.
5. Robert M. Adams, "A Little Look into Chaos," in *Illustrious Evidence: Approaches to English Literature of the Early Seventeenth Century*, ed. Earl Miner (Berkeley: University of California Press, 1975), p. 76.

6. A. S. P. Woodhouse, "Notes on Milton's Views on the Creation: The Initial Phase," *Philological Quarterly* 28 (1949), 229.

7. Kristin A. Pruitt and Charles W. Durham (eds.), *Living Texts: Interpreting Milton* (Selingrove: Susquehanna University Press, 2000), p. 220. See also John Rumrich, *Milton Unbound* (Cambridge: Cambridge University Press, 1996).

8. John Rumrich, "Milton's God and the Matter of Chaos," *PMLA* 110 (1995), 1043.

9. Leonard, "Milton, Lucretius, and 'the Void Profound of Unessential Night,'" pp. 204–206.

10. Juliet Lucy Cummins, "Milton's Gods and the Matter of Creation," *Milton Studies* XL (Pittsburgh: University of Pittsburgh Press, 2002), p. 96.

11. Ibid., p. 86.

12. Regina M. Schwartz, *Remembering and Repeating: Biblical Creation in Paradise Lost* (Cambridge: Cambridge University Press, 1988), p. 11.

13. Ibid., p. 35.

14. A. B. Chambers, "Chaos in *Paradise Lost*," *Journal of the History of Ideas* vol. xxiv (1963): 55–84.

15. Michael Lieb, "Further Thoughts on Satan's Journey through Chaos," *Milton Quarterly* 12 (Ohio, 1978), pp. 126–33.

16. The *OED*, giving the meaning of "unoriginal" as "having no origin" or "uncreated," cites this passage.

17. Denis Saurat, *Milton: Man and Thinker*, 2nd ed. (London: J. M. Dent, 1944), section 3, chapter 1.

18. Chambers, "Chaos in *Paradise Lost*," p. 55.

19. Cummins, "Milton's Gods and the Matter of Creation," p. 85.

20. See Joscelyn Godwin, *Robert Fludd: Hermetic Philosopher and Surveyor of Two Worlds* (London: Thames and Hudson, 1979), p. 24.

21. Ibid.

22. Ibid., p. 25.

23. Shirley Sharon-Zisser, "Silence and Darkness in *Paradise Lost*," in *Milton Studies* ed. by James D. Simmonds, vol. 25 (Pittsburgh: University of Pittsburgh Press, 1989), pp. 191–211.

24. Alastair Fowler (ed.), *Milton, Paradise Lost* (Harlow: Addison Wesley Longman Limited, 2nd ed., 1998), points out in his gloss on the lines that the Latin *aborior* means to set or disappear as applied to heavenly bodies.

25. Mary F. Norton, "'The Rising World of Waters Dark and Deep': Chaos Theory and *Paradise Lost*," *Milton Studies* XXXII (Pittsburgh: University of Pittsburgh Press, 1995), pp. 91–110.

26. Cummins, "Milton's Gods and the Matter of Creation," p. 85.

27. Ibid., p. 89.

28. Leonard, "Milton, Lucretius, and 'the Void Profound of Unessential Night,'" p. 206.
29. Ibid., p. 207.
30. John Rumrich, "Of Chaos and Nightingales," in Pruitt and Durham *Living Texts*, pp. 224–26.
31. Rumrich, *Milton Unbound*, p. 119.
32. Leonard, "Milton, Lucretius, and 'the Void Profound of Unessential Night,'" p. 207.
33. Rumrich, "Of Chaos and Nightingales," p. 219.
34. Marilyn R. Farwell, "Eve, the Separation Scene, and the Renaissance Idea of Androgyny," *Milton Studies* XVI (Pittsburgh: University of Pittsburgh Press, 1982), p. 5.
35. Helene Cixous, "Sorties," reprinted in David Lodge (ed.), *Modern Criticism and Theory* (London and New York: Longman, 1988), pp. 287–93.
36. Thomas Digges, *A Perfit Description of the Caelestiall Orbes* in *A Prognostication Everlasting* pub. by Leonard Digges, corrected and augmented by Thomas Digges, 1576 (Amsterdam and Norwood, N.J.: Theatrum Orbis Terrarum Ltd. & Walter J. Johnson, Inc., 1975).

4 "THIS PENDENT WORLD": THE
   COSMOS OF *PARADISE LOST*

1. Edmund Burke, *A Philosophical Enquiry into the Origin of Our Ideas of the Sublime and the Beautiful*, ed. J. T. Boulton (Oxford: Oxford University Press, 1958, rpt 1990), p. 59.
2. John Leonard, "Milton, Lucretius, and 'the Void Profound of Unessential Night,'" in *Living Texts: Interpreting Milton*, ed. Kristin A. Pruitt and Charles W. Durham (Selingrove: Susquehanna University Press, 2000).
3. Implicit in the Copernican system was the suggestion of infinite space, later emphasized by Digges, Bruno, and others, while the Danish astronomer, Tycho Brahe, was the first to dispense with the notion of solid orbs.
4. For an account of these early developments, see J. L. E. Dreyer, *A History of Astronomy from Thales to Kepler* (New York: Dover Books, 1953).
5. On the etymology, see Alastair Fowler, *Milton, Paradise Lost* (Harlow: Longman, Ltd. 2nd ed., 1998), p. 267.
6. Ibid., p. 201.
7. Harinder Singh Marjara, *Contemplation of Created Things: Science in Paradise Lost* (Toronto, Buffalo, London: University of Toronto Press, 1992), p. 190.
8. See chapter five.

9. Compass points have a critical role to play in William Blake's *Vala, or the Four Zoas*. Remembering that Milton was, for Blake, the most important poet, it is possible to suggest that Blake had a clearer understanding of Milton's epic than Romanticists assume.
10. See *Genesis*, ii 8.
11. See Fowler, *Milton, Paradise Lost*, p. 229.
12. See, e.g., Peter Heylyn, *Cosmography* (London, 1652).
13. Fowler, *Milton, Paradise Lost*, p. 35.
14. Marjara, *Contemplation of Created Things*, p. 207.
15. John Rogers, *The Matter of Revolution: Science, Poetry and Politics in the Age of Milton* (Ithaca and London: Cornell University Press, 1996).
16. James H. Hanford, "Dr. Paget's Library," in *Bulletin of the Medical Library Association* 33.1 (1945), 90–99.
17. Rogers, *The Matter of Revolution*, p. 107.
18. Ibid., p. 119.
19. Christopher Kendrick, *Milton: A Study in Ideology and Form* (New York: Methuen, 1986), p. 180.
20. See Walter Pagel, *Joan Baptista Van Helmont: Reformer of Science and Medicine* (Cambridge: Cambridge University Press, 1982), pp. 79–86.
21. See David Mulder, *The Alchemy of Revolution: Gerrard Winstanley's Occultism and Seventeenth-Century English Communism* (New York: Lang, 1990).
22. See chapter seven.

5   "THE VISIBLE DIURNAL SPHERE":
SPACE AND TIME

1. Maura Brady, "Space and the Persistance of Place in *Paradise Lost*," *Milton Quarterly* vol. 41, no. 3 (October 2007), 167–82.
2. For the relevance of alchemy in Milton's depiction of the cosmos, see chapter nine.
3. Brian P. Copenhaver, "Jewish Theologies of Space in the Scientific Revolution: Henry More, Joseph Raphson, Isaac Newton and their Predecessors," *Annals of Science* 37 (1980), 489–548.
4. See Joscelyn Godwin, *Robert Fludd, Hermetic Philosopher and Surveyor of Two Worlds* (London: Thames and Hudson Ltd., 1979), pp. 21–23.
5. See Deborah E. Harkness, *John Dee's Conversations with Angels: Cabala, Alchemy, and the End of Nature* (Cambridge: Cambridge University Press, 1999), pp. 73–77.
6. Stephen Hawking, *On the Shoulders of Giants: The Great Works of Physics and Astronomy* (Cambridge: Running Press, Perseus Books L.L.C, 2003), p. 632.

7. See Rolf Willach, "The Development of Telescope Optics in the Middle of the Seventeenth Century," *Annals of Science*, vol. 58, no. 4 (October 2001), 381–98.

8. Angelica Durran, *The Age of Milton and the Scientific Revolution* (Pittsburgh, Penn: Duquesne University Press, 2007), p. 281.

9. Johnson F. R. Johnson, *Astronomical Thought in Renaissance England* (Baltimore: The Johns Hopkins Press, 1937; rpt New York: Octagon Books, 1968), p. 27.

10. Harinder Singh Marjara, *Contemplation of Created Things: Science in Paradise Lost* (Toronto: University of Toronto Press, 1992), p. 78.

11. Hilary Gatti, *Giordano Bruno and Renaissance Science* (Ithaca and London: Cornell University Press, 1999), p. 128.

12. Ibid., p. 134.

13. Thomas Digges, *A Perfit Description of the Caelestiall Orbes*, in *A Prognostication Everlasting*, pub. by Leonard Digges, corrected and augmented by Thomas Digges, 1576 (Amsterdam and Norwood, N.J.: Theatrum Orbis Terrarum Ltd. & Walter J. Johnson, Inc., 1975).

14. See Bernard Capp, *Astrology and the Popular Press: English Almanacs 1500–1800* (London and Boston: Faber and Faber, 1979).

15. Johnson, *Astronomical Thought*, pp. 168–69, believes that Bruno may have been influenced by Digges's diagram.

16. Hawking, *On the Shoulders of Giants*, pp. 4–5.

17. Hilary Gatti, *The Renaissance Drama of Knowledge: Giordano Bruno in England* (London and New York: Routledge, 1989); Frances A. Yates, *Giordano Bruno and the Hermetic Tradition* (London: Routledge Kegan Paul, 1964).

18. On the multiple meanings of "worlds" in *Paradise Lost*, see Lara Dodds, "Milton's Other Worlds," in *Uncircumscribed Milton, Reading Milton Deeply*, ed. Charles W. Durham and Kristin A. Pruitt (Cranbury, N.J.: Associated University Presses, 2008), pp. 164–82.

19. William Empson, "Donne the Space Man," *The Kenyon Review* 19 (1957), 338.

20. A. J. Smith, ed., *John Donne: The Complete English Poems* (Harmondsworth: Penguin Books Ltd., 1971), p. 60.

21. Helen Gardner, *A Reading of "Paradise Lost"* (Oxford: Oxford University Press, 1965), p. 41.

22. Joad Raymond, *Milton's Angels: The Early Modern Imagination* (Oxford: Oxford University Press, 2010), p. 297.

23. Plato, *Timaeus*, section 7, p. 51.

24. See Dominic J. O'Meara, *Plotinus: An Introduction to the Enneads* (Oxford: Clarendon Press, 1993). See also Marjara, *Contemplation of Created Things*, pp. 52–54.

25. *De civitate Dei*, XI, 6.

26. R. D. Bedford, "Time, Freedom, and Foreknowledge in *Paradise Lost*," in *Milton Studies*, XVI, ed. James D. Simmonds (Pittsburgh: University of Pittsburgh Press, 1982), pp. 61–76.
27. Ibid., p. 71.
28. Hawking, *On the Shoulders of Giants*, chapter 2.
29. In *Ignatius his Conclave*, published in 1611, Donne shows his knowledge of the 1610 *Sidereus Nuncius*.
30. Michael S. Mahoney, "Infinitesimals and Transcendent Relations: The Mathematics of Motion in the Seventeenth Century," in *Reappraisals of the Scientific Revolution*, ed. David C. Lindberg and Robert S. Westman (Cambridge: Cambridge University Press, 1990), p. 461.
31. William Empson, *Some Versions of Pastoral: A Study of Pastoral Forms in Literature* (Harmondsworth: Penguin, 1966), p. 158; emphasis in the original.
32. Alastair Fowler, *Milton, Paradise Lost* (Harlow: Longman, Ltd. 2nd ed., 1998), p. 267.
33. See Malabika Sarkar, "Satan's Astronomical Journey, *Paradise Lost* IX, 63–66," in *Notes and Queries*, October 1979.
34. Amy Boesky, "*Paradise Lost* and the Multiplicity of Time," in *A Companion to Milton*, ed. Thomas N. Corns (Oxford: Blackwell Publishers Ltd., 2001), pp. 380–92.
35. Elizabeth Story Donno, *Andrew Marvell, the Complete Poems* (Harmondsworth: Penguin Books, 1972), p. 102.
36. The clock now at Strasbourg Cathedral is a replacement dated 1842.
37. "Stephen Powle to Mr. West. The copy of my letter to Mr. West wherein is the tower and fabricke of the horologe in Strasbourg described," in J. O. Halliwell (ed.), *A Collection Of Letters Illustrative Of The Progress Of Science* (London, 1841), pp. 21–29. See also Virginia P. Stern, *Sir Stephen Powle of Court and Country: Memorabilia of a Government Agent for Queen Elizabeth I, Chancery Official, and English Country Gentleman* (Cranbury, N.J. and London: Associated University Presses Inc., 1982).
38. "Tempus est mensura motus rerum mobilium"—time is the measure of movement. Aristotle, *De Caelo*.

6 SATAN AND ASTRONOMICAL SIGNS

A previous version of this chapter originally appeared in Malabika Sarkar, "Astronomical Signs in *Paradise Lost*: Milton, Ophiucus and the millennial debate," pp 82–95 in Juliet Cummins (Ed) *Milton and the Ends of Time* © Cambridge University Press 2003.

1. Citations of Donne's poems are from A. J. Smith (ed.), *John Donne: The Complete English Poems* (Harmondsworth: Penguin Books Ltd., 1971).

2. Stella P. Revard, "Milton and Millenarianism: From the Nativity Ode to *Paradise Regained*," in *Milton and the Ends of Time*, ed. Juliet Cummins (Cambridge: Cambridge University Press, 2003), pp. 82–95.

3. For the extent to which Aristotelio-Ptolemaic cosmology continued to dominate astronomical thought in the sixteenth century and even in the seventeenth, see Francis R. Johnson, *Astronomical Thought in Renaissance England* (Baltimore: The Johns Hopkins Press, 1937; rpt New York: Octagon Books Inc., 1968).

4. Cited in Deborah E. Harkness, *John Dee's Conversations with Angels* (Cambridge: Cambridge University Press, 1999), p. 32.

5. Bernard Capp, *Astrology and the Popular Press, English Almanacs 1500–1800* (London and Boston: Faber and Faber, 1979), pp. 149–50.

6. Johnson, *Astronomical Thought*, p. 156.

7. Tycho "d. 156.Hopkins Press, 1937; reers.tsBrahe, *De Nova Stella*, rpt in H. Shapley and H. E. Howarth, *A Source Book in Astronomy* (New York and London, 1929), p. 19. Tycho gave a detailed analysis of all books written about the new star in Cassiopeia in his *Astronomiae Instauratae Progymnasmata* (Prague, 1602). A partial translation of *De Nova Stella* appeared in London in 1632 as *Learned Tico Brahae his Astronomicall Coniectur of the new and much Admired Starre*.

8. *De Nova Stella*, p. 13..

9. Tycho Brahe, Astronomicall Coniectur, p. 14.

10. Ibid., p. 15.

11. Ibid.

12. Ibid., pp. 16–17.

13. "The Translatovr To The Reader," in ibid.

14. See B. S. Capp, *Astrology and the Popular Press* (London, 1979), p. 168.

15. Alexander Gil, The New Starr of the North, Shining Upon the Victorious King of Sweden (London, 1632).

16. Ibid., pp. 21, 22.

17. Ibid., pp. 8–9.

18. Johannes Kepler, A Thorough Description Of An Extraordinary New Star Which First Appeared In October Of This Year, 1604, trans. Judith V. Field and Anton Pestl, in Vistas in Astronomy (Oxford, 1977), vol. XX, p. 333..

19. Ibid., pp. 336–39.

20. John Swan, *Speculum Mundi* (London, 1635), pp. 114, 107.

21. Ibid., p. 115.

22. John Bainbridge, An Astronomicall Description of the Late Comet from the 18 of November 1618 to 16 of December following (London, 1619).

23. Ibid., p. 28.
24. Ibid., pp. 30–32.
25. Stephen M. Buhler, "Marsilio Ficino's *De Stella Magorum* and Renaissance Views of the Magi," *Renaissance Quarterly* 43 (1990), 348–71.
26. For the seventeenth-century debate on whether the Fall was catastrophic, affecting both microcosm and macrocosm at once, or whether it initiated a gradual decline, see William Poole, *Milton and the Idea of the Fall* (Cambridge: Cambridge University Press, 2005).
27. The phrase "car of night" is discussed in my note on "Satan's Astronomical Journey, *Paradise Lost* IX 63–66," *Notes & Queries*, New Series, 26 (1979), 417–22.
28. Ken Simpson examines the millennial implications of comets and falling stars in *Paradise Regained* in "The Apocalypse in *Paradise Regained*," in Cummins, *Milton and the Ends of Time*, pp. 202–23.
29. Helen Gardner, "Milton's Satan and the Theme of Damnation in Elizabethan Tragedy," in *A Reading of Paradise Lost*, ed. Helen Gardner (Oxford: Oxford University Press, 1965), pp. 99–120.

7   MILTON'S ANGELS AND CELESTIAL MOTION

1. Joad Raymond, *Milton's Angels, The Early-Modern Imagination* (Oxford: Oxford University Press, 2010), p. 257.
2. Angelica Duran, *The Age of Milton and the Scientific Revolution* (Pittsburgh, Pennsylvania: Duquesne University Press, 2007), pp. 71–110, 179–207.
3. Ibid., p. 71.
4. See John Rogers, *The Matter of Revolution: Science, Poetry, & Politics in the Age of Milton* (Ithaca and London: Cornell University Press, 1996). See also the discussion in chapter four.
5. Deborah E. Harkness, *John Dee's Conversations with Angel: Cabala, Alchemy, and the End of Nature* (Cambridge: Cambridge University Press, 1999), p. 72.
6. William Empson, "Donne the Space Man," *The Kenyon Review* 19 (1957).
7. Alastair Fowler (ed.), *Milton, Paradise Lost* (Harlow: Longman, 2nd ed., 1998), pp. 472–73. See also Harinder Singh Marjara, *Contemplation of Created Things: Science in Paradise Lost* (Toronto: University of Toronto Press, 1992), p. 267.
8. Duran, *The Age of Milton*, p. 91. Duran's acknowledgment of the limited roles of Uriel and Gabriel are, of course, set within her reading of angelic activity as pedagogical collaboration.

9. For further details, see Malabika Sarkar, "Satan's Astronomical Journey, *Paradise Lost* IX, 63–66," in *Notes and Queries*, October 1979.
10. Fowler, Milton, Paradise Lost, pp. 194–95.
11. Gabor Ittzes, "Satan's Journey through Darkness: *Paradise Lost* 9.53–86," *Milton Quarterly* vol. 41, no. 1 (20070, 12–21.
12. See Lynn Thorndike, *The Sphere of Sacrobosco and its Commentators* (Chicago: University of Chicago Press, 1949), p. 126.
13. Sherry Lutz Zivley, "Satan in Orbit: *Paradise Lost*: IX: 48–86," *Milton Quarterly* vol. 31, no. 4 (1997), 130–36.
14. Kent R. Lehnhof, "Uncertainty and 'the Sociable Spirit': Raphael's Role in *Paradise Lost*," in *Milton's Legacy*, ed. Kristin A. Pruitt and Charles W. Durham (Selinsgrove: Susquehanna University Press, 2005), pp. 33–49.
15. Ibid., p. 33.
16. Karen Edwards, "Inspiration and Melancholy in *Samson Agonistes*," in *Milton and the Ends of Time*, ed. Juliet Cummins (Cambridge: Cambridge University Press, 2003), pp. 224–40.
17. Grant McColley, "Milton's Dialogue on Astronomy: The Principal Immediate Sources," *PMLA*, vol. LII, no. 3 (1937), 728–62.
18. John Wilkins, *Discovery of a World in the Moone* (1638); Alexander Ross, *The New Planet No Planet or the Earth no Wandering Star* (London, 1646).
19. Marjara, *Contemplation of Created Things*.
20. Ibid., pp. 124–25.
21. On the ideal pedagogical role played by Raphael, see also Margaret Olofson Thickstun, "Raphael and the Challenge of Evangelical Education," *Milton Quarterly* vol. 35, no. 4 (2001), 245–57.
22. John Donne, "To the Countess of Bedford" ("To have written then…") in A. J. Smith (ed.), *John Donne: The Complete English Poems* (Harmondsworth: Penguin Books Ltd., 1971), p. 228.
23. Marjara, *Contemplation of Created Things*, p. 128.
24. Eileen Reeves, *Painting the Heavens, Art and Science in the Age of Galileo* (Princeton: Princeton University Press, 1997), p. 8.
25. Ibid., p. 9.
26. Robert Burton, *The Anatomy of Melancholy* (New York: De Capo Press, 1971), II, ii, 3.
27. Marjara, *Contemplation of Created Things*, p. 159.
28. Robert H. West, *Milton and the Angels* (Athens: University of Georgia Press, 1955), p. 180.
29. Raymond, *Milton's Angels*.
30. Anna K. Nardo, "The Education of Milton's Good Angels," in *Arenas of Conflict, Milton and the Unfettered Mind*, ed. Kristin Pruitt McColgan and Charles W. Durham (London: Associated University Presses, 1997), pp. 193–211.
31. Ibid., p. 208.

8 THE GALILEO QUESTION

1. Rolf Willach, "The Development of Telescope Optics in the Middle of the Seventeenth Century," *Annals of Science* vol. 58, no. 4 (2001), 381–98.
2. John Carey (ed.), *Milton, Complete Shorter Poems*, 2nd ed. (Harlow: Addison Wesley Longman Ltd., 1997), p. 81. All citations from the shorter poems, *Paradise Regained*, and *Samson Agonistes* are from this edition.
3. Lubomir Konecny, "Young Milton and the Telescope," *JWI* vol. 37 (1974), 368–73.
4. Julia M. Walker, "Milton and Galileo: The Art of Intellectual Canonization," in *Milton Studies*, ed. James D. Simmonds, vol. xxv (Pittsburgh: University of Pittsburgh Press, 1990), pp. 109–23. See also Michael Lieb, "Brotherhood of the Illuminati: Milton, Galileo, and the Poetics of Conspiracy," *Milton Studies*, vol. xlvii (Pittsburgh: University of Pittsburgh Press, 2008), pp. 54–95.
5. Doubts have been raised, though, about Milton's knowledge of Galileo's blindness. See Derek N. C. Wood, "Milton and Galileo," *Milton Quarterly* vol. 35, no. 1 (2001), 50–52.
6. On this point, apart from material in standard biographies of Milton, see S. B. Liljegren, *Studies in Milton* (New York: Haskell House, 1967); Wood, "Milton and Galileo"; and George F. Butler, "Milton's Meeting with Galileo: A Reconsideration," *Milton Quarterly* vol. 39, no. 3 (2005), 132–39.
7. Milton, *Areopagetica*, *CPW*, II, 538; emphasis in the original.
8. Frank B. Young, "Milton and Galileo," in *A Milton Encyclopedia* ed. William B. Hunter, Jr., vol. 3 (London: Associated University Presses, 1978), pp. 120–21.
9. See ibid.; and Barbara Lewalski, *The Life of John Milton* (Oxford: Blackwell Publishing, 2000, 2003), pp. 93–94.
10. For early discussions of this, see Allan H. Gilbert, "Milton and Galileo," *Studies in Philology* xix (1922), 152–85; Francis R. Johnson, *Astronomical Thought in Renaissance England* (Baltimore: The Johns Hopkins Press, 1937; rpt New York: Octagon Books Inc, 1968), pp. 286–87.
11. For details, see *Discoveries and Opinions of Galileo*, trans. Stillman Drake (New York: Doubleday Anchor Books, 1957), pp. 80–81.
12. "The Starry Messenger," in ibid., p. 112.
13. Ibid., p. 28.
14. Peter Heylyn, *Cosmographie in Four Bookes*, 1652.
15. Elizabeth Story Donno, *Andrew Marvell, The Complete Poems* (Harmondsworth: Penguin Books Ltd., 1972; rpt 1976), p. 89.
16. "The Starry Messenger," pp. 27–28.
17. Ibid., p. 27.
18. Ibid., p. 58.

19. Ibid., p. 34.
20. Donno, *Andrew Marvell, The Complete Poems*, p. 182.
21. J. E. Weiss and N. O. Weiss, "Marvell's Spotted Sun," *Notes and Queries* vol. CCXXV (August 1980), 339–41.
22. See Lyndy Abraham, *Marvell and Alchemy* (Aldershot: Scolar Press, 1990).
23. Lyndy Abraham, *A Dictionary of Alchemical Imagery* (Cambridge: Cambridge University Press, 1998), p. 189.
24. Amy Boesky, "Milton, Galileo and Sunspots: Optics and Certainty in *Paradise Lost*," in *Milton Studies*, vol. xxxiv (Pittsburgh: University of Pittsburgh Press, 1996), pp. 23–43.
25. Lara Dodds, "Milton's Other Worlds," in *Uncircumscribed Milton, Reading Milton Deeply*, ed. Charles W. Durham and Kristin A. Pruitt (Cranbury, N.J.: Associated University Presses, 2008), p. 166.
26. Walker, "Milton and Galileo: The Art of Intellectual Canonization," suggests Milton uses the term "Tuscan artist" to mean "scientist" or "intellectual" since neither word, as noun, was in use in his time.
27. "The Starry Messenger," pp. 38–39.
28. Ibid., pp. 123–24.
29. Donald Friedman, "Galileo and the Art of Seeing," in *Milton in Italy: Contexts, Images, Contradictions*, ed. Mario A. Di Cesare (Binghamton, New York: Medieval & Renaissance Texts and Studies, 1991), p. 169.
30. Ibid., p. 26.
31. Boesky, "Milton, Galileo and Sunspots," p. 40.
32. Angelica Durran, *The Age of Milton and the Scientific Revolution* (Pittsburgh, Pennsylvania: Duquesne University Press, 2007), pp. 64–65.
33. Judith Herz, "'For whom this glorious sight?': Dante, Milton, and the Galileo Question," in Di Cesare, *Milton in Italy*, pp. 147–57.
34. Maura Brady, "Galileo in Action: The 'Telescope' in *Paradise Lost*," in *Milton Studies*, ed. Albert C. Labriola (Pittsburgh: University of Pittsburgh Press, 2005), vol. xliv, pp. 129–52.

9 ADAM, EVE, AND THE "VIRTUOUS TOUCH" OF ALCHEMY

1. Elias Ashmole, *Theatrum Chemicum Britannicum* (London, 1652).
2. See Frances Yates, *The Rosicrucian Enlightenment* (London, New York: Routledge, 1972).
3. Allen G. Debus (ed.), *Robert Fludd and His Philosophicall Key being a Transcription of the manuscript at Trinity College, Cambridge* (New York: Science History Publications, a division of Neale Watson Academic Publications Inc., 1979), introduction, p. 6.

4. Ibid., p. 20.
5. See Lawrence M. Principe, *The Aspiring Adept: Robert Boyle and His Alchemical Quest* (Princeton, N.J.: Princeton University Press, 1998).
6. See Betty Jo Teeter Dobbs, *Alchemical Death and Resurrection: The Significance of Alchemy in the Age of Newton* (Washington, D.C.: Smithsonian Institute Libraries, 1990); and *The Janus Face of Genius: The Role of Alchemy in Newton's Thought* (Cambridge: Cambridge University Press, 1991).
7. For the history of alchemy, see specially Allen G. Debus, *Man and Nature in the Renaissance* (Cambridge: Cambridge University Press, 1978); and *Chemistry, Alchemy and the New Philosophy, 1550–1700* (London: Variorum Reprints, 1987). See also Stanton J. Linden, *The Alchemy Reader: From Hermes Trismegistus to Isaac Newton* (Cambridge: Cambridge University Press, 2003).
8. William Eamon, "From the Secrets of Nature to Public Knowledge," in *Reappraisals of the Scientific Revolution*, ed. David C. Lindberg and Robert S. Westman (Cambridge: Cambridge University Press, 1990), p. 352. See also Charles Webster, "New Light on the Invisible College: The Social Relations of English Science in the Mid-Seventeenth Century," in *Transactions of the Royal Historical Society*, ser.5, 24 (1974), 19–42.
9. Eluned Crawshaw, "Thomas Vaughan and 'That Slidyng Science,' Alchemy," in *The Anglo-Welsh Review* 19 (1969), 146–55.
10. Lyndy Abraham, *Marvell & Alchemy* (Aldershot: Scolar Press, 1990), p. 11.
11. See Lyndy Abraham, *A Dictionary of Alchemical Imagery* (Cambridge: Cambridge University Press, 1998; paperback rpt 2001), p. 55.
12. Abraham, *Marvell*, pp. 5–7.
13. James Kinsley (ed.), *The Poems of John Dryden* (Oxford: Clarendon Press, 1958), 4 vols, I, p. 231.
14. P. M. Rattansi, "Paracelsus and the Puritan Revolution," *Ambix* vol. XI, no. 1 (February 1963), 24–32.
15. Ibid., p. 29.
16. David Mulder, The Alchemy of Revolution: Gerrard Winstanley's Occultism and Seventeenth-Century English Communism (New York, Bern, Frankfurt am Main, Paris: P. Lang, 1990).
17. John Rogers, The Matter of Revolution: Science, Poetry and Politics in the Age of Milton (Ithaca and London: Cornell University Press, 1996), p. 47.
18. Mulder, *The Alchemy of Revolution*, pp. 53–54. The citations from Winstanley are also from Mulder.
19. See ibid., p. 60; and Christopher Hill, *Milton and the English Revolution* (London: Faber and Faber, 1977), p. 332. "Tincture" is an alchemical term signifying the philosopher's stone or elixir,

which tinges base metal into gold. See Abraham, *Alchemical Imagery*, p. 200.

20. Abraham, *Alchemical Imagery*, p. 83.

21. See Jackson I. Cope, *The Metaphoric Structure of Paradise Lost* (Baltimore: Johns Hopkins Press, 1962).

22. D. C. Allen, "Milton and the Descent to Light," *Journal of English and Germanic Philology*, Vol. LX, 1961, pp.614–630; p.618; p.626.

23. See J. H. Hanford, "Dr. Paget's Library," *Bulletin of the Medical Library Association* vol. XXXVI (1945); Hill, *Milton and the English Revolution*, pp. 492–95.

24. See Bryan Aubrey, *Watchmen of Eternity: Blake's Debt to Jacob Boehme* (Lanham, New York, London: University Press of America, 1986).

25. George Ward and Thomas Langcake (eds.), *The Works of Jacob Behmen* (3 vols), vol. 1 Aur.19:10–12; emphasis in the original. Cited also in Aubrey, *Watchmen*, p. 15.

26. Alexander Roob, *The Hermetic Museum: Alchemy and Mysticism* (Koln: TASCHEN GmbH, 2001), p. 104.

27. See ibid., p. 60; and Joscelyn Godwin, *Robert Fludd: Hermetic Philosopher and Surveyor of Two Worlds* (London: Thames and Hudson, 1979), p. 55.

28. Urszula Szulakowska, The Alchemy of Light: Geometry and Optics in Late Renaissance Alchemical Illustration (Leiden, Boston, Koln: Brill, 2000), pp. 175–77.

29. Godwin, *Robert Fludd*, p. 32.

30. See Aubrey, *Watchmen*, p. 18 ff.

31. Godwin, *Robert Fludd*, p. 34.

32. Szulakowska, *The Alchemy of Light*, p. 178.

33. Alastair Fowler, *Milton, Paradise Lost*, p. 205.

34. See ibid., 7.72n, p. 393 and 11.367n, p. 616.

35. Gareth Roberts, The Mirror of Alchemy: Alchemical Ideas and Images in Manuscripts and Books from Antiquity to the Seventeenth Century (London: The British Library, 1994), p. 78.

36. Johannes Fabricius, *Alchemy: The Medieval Alchemists and their Royal Art* (London: The Antiquarian Press, 1976).

37. Deborah E. Harkness, *John Dee's Conversations with Angels: Cabala, Alchemy, and the End of Nature* (Cambridge: Cambridge University Press, 1999), p. 201

38. Ibid., p. 201.

39. Gordon Campbell and Thomas N. Corns, *John Milton, Life, Work, and Thought* (Oxford: Oxford University Press, 2008), p. 339.

10 CONCLUSION

1. Peter C. Herman, Destabilizing Milton: "Paradise Lost" and the Poetics of Incertitude (Basingstoke: Palgrave Macmillan, 2005).

2. Ibid., p. 21.
3. Ibid.
4. Lara Dodds, "Milton's Other Worlds," in *Uncircumscribed Minds: Reading Milton Deeply*, ed. Charles W. Durham and Kristin A. Pruitt (Selingrove: Susquehanna University Press, 2008), p. 176.
5. *Revelations*, Chapter 21, verses 18–21.
6. Stephen M. Fallon, *Milton's Peculiar Grace, Self-Representation and Authority* (Ithaca and London: Cornell University Press, 2007), p. 206.
7. Howard Schultz, *Milton and Forbidden Knowledge* (New York: Modern Language Association of America, 1955), p. 179.

INDEX